# The Baby Chase

## Also by Leslie Morgan Steiner

*Crazy Love: A Memoir*

*Mommy Wars: Stay-at-Home and Career Moms Face Off
on Their Choices, Their Lives, Their Families*

# The Baby Chase

## How Surrogacy Is Transforming the American Family

# Leslie Morgan Steiner

St. Martin's Press ➤ New York

# Author's Note

Some names and identifying characteristics of individuals in this book have been changed. In a few instances, composites were used to illustrate common situations. This book is intended to raise awareness about surrogacy and infertility and should not be relied upon as recommending any course of action. Due to rapid changes in medicine and law, some information in this book may have changed before, or after, you read it. Also, the fact that an organization or Web site is referred to as a citation and/or a potential source of further information does not mean that the author or the publisher endorses the organization or Web site or the information it may provide.

THE BABY CHASE: HOW SURROGACY IS TRANSFORMING THE AMERICAN FAMILY. Copyright © 2013 by Leslie Morgan Steiner. All rights reserved. Printed in the United States of America. For information, address St. Martin's Press, 175 Fifth Avenue, New York, N.Y. 10010.

www.stmartins.com

Photograph on title page of Wile siblings © Stevy Fletcher. Reprinted with permission from Stevy Fletcher.

All other photographs courtesy of the Wile family unless otherwise indicated.

Photographs on pages 274–276 by Cara Roth, 210 Photography, and courtesy of the Wile family.

The Library of Congress Cataloging-in-Publication Data is available upon request.

ISBN 978-1-250-00294-5 (hardcover)
ISBN 978-1-4668-3468-2 (e-book)

First Edition: November 2013

10  9  8  7  6  5  4  3  2  1

For Blaze, Dylan, and Jett

# Contents

# Part 1

---

## What's the Big Deal About Not Having Babies, Anyway?

Mother's Day, 2011. In the golden twilight of her cactus-studded front yard in Mesa, Arizona, forty-year-old Rhonda Wile looked nothing like a woman who had endured six harsh years of failed fertility treatments. One surprise vasectomy. One heartbreaking miscarriage. A painful divorce. One suicide attempt.

Most of all, Rhonda looked absolutely nothing like a woman who, after years of despair, was finally expecting twins in August.

Instead, sipping iced tea in the auburn shimmer of the sun setting on the desert, Rhonda Wile looked like a stunningly attractive-yet-approachable young wife posing for a Cialis or Viagra commercial. She wore a red cotton V-neck shirt and crisp white shorts that accentuated her trim, hourglass waist. Her long blond hair was glossy and thick. She appeared surprisingly well rested for a nurse who had just come off a twelve-hour shift. Over five feet seven inches tall, with a striking, curvaceous figure and a friendly grin, she smiled with the warmth of a woman not overly aware of her charm.

Despite the fact that she'd spent Mother's Day working her usual 8 A.M. to 8 P.M. schedule, Rhonda radiated optimism like a halo. Rhonda had spent most of a decade mired in fear that she'd never join her sister, mother, and childhood friends in that most exclusive club: motherhood. These days, she mainlined hope like a drug—even when she shopped at Target, changed an IV drip at work, or slept at night next to her husband of eleven years.

This Mother's Day, for the first time since being a child, hope felt like an emotion Rhonda could count on.

As a nurse, Rhonda knew, objectively at least, that her mad, burning desire to have children sprang from the universe's most powerful biological craving: to create life. Perpetuation of our species is the instinct behind our sex drive, the logic behind sexual attraction. Nature wants us to give in to both urges, the sexual impulse and the deep craving to have children.

That intellectual understanding did not make Rhonda long for children one iota less.

Gerry Wile, Rhonda's husband of more than a decade, had stayed home on Sunday while Rhonda worked. A Maricopa County firefighter, Gerry was a six-foot-tall, broad-shouldered, heavily muscled, former military man with a buzz cut. He, too, looked straight out of central casting, the type of handsome, rugged man who revs a Dodge Ram pickup truck through a muddy ravine, smiling reassuringly as dirt spews out from the mammoth back tires.

Gerry was barefoot and shirtless in the dry Arizona heat, watering the cacti and walking with the light feet of a quarterback. His body was accustomed to jumping out of airplanes and carrying 110-pound, five-inch-diameter hoses from his fire truck directly into the wildfires that raced through the desert brush. Laugh lines were etched into his sunburned cheeks. He was a guy who, while hauling you safely out of a burning building, would crack a joke to make it seem like you'd come through a memorable adventure, not a near-death experience.

The fading Arizona sun showed off the butterfly tattoo on Gerry's ripped right calf. On his left rib cage, there was another design, large and intricate enough to rival Lisbeth Salander's famous dragon tattoo. The ink depicted a huge elephant head. It was an elaborate representation of Ganesh, the Indian god devoted to removing obstacles. The elephant head was overlaid with two tiny baby footprints, the type you see stamped onto a hospital birth certificate.

Strange ink for a forty-four-year-old fireman and military veteran.

As a firefighter, Gerry knew that the desire to nurture and protect children was nearly as powerful as the urge to create them. Nothing generates more adrenaline in firemen than children's toys scattered on the porch of a burning home with a family trapped inside. This is also a biological imperative of our species, because as any firefighter knows, human infants are among the most helpless offspring in the animal kingdom.

For most parents, as for most firefighters, the instinct to protect children outweighs even our instinct for self-preservation. Even though we sometimes cannot stand our own kids. Even though no one, not even Rhonda or Gerry, *wants* to sit next to a crying baby on an airplane, few parents would hesitate to run into traffic—or a burning building—to save a child.

All just as nature intended.

Rhonda and Gerry knew the U.S. Department of Justice statistic that every year in the United States over 100,000 children are abducted. A distinctly unnatural desire: to steal someone else's child. Imagine what you would do if your child were kidnapped, if a force outside your family, someone with no interest in how deeply you love your child, had the ability to destroy your family, your biological link to eternity.

How much would you pay to rescue that child?

How far would you travel?

Would you ever abandon the search?

Rhonda, sitting on her brown living room sofa with Frankie, her white shepherd-Catahoula pooch, often watched *America's*

*Most Wanted* on television alone during the long evenings when Gerry worked overnight shifts at the firehouse. From the show, she had learned the comforting data that, fortunately, the vast majority of abducted children are found within hours. Only roughly one hundred kidnappings a year result in the death of a child. It consoled Rhonda to know that few parents understand this misery firsthand.

However, Rhonda and Gerry understood all too well an anguish nearly identical to the trauma of losing a child. Failure to conceive or give birth to a baby is a kidnapping of a different variety. Over the course of their eleven years together, Rhonda and Gerry's dreams had been stolen. It didn't matter that their lost children were never born.

Every year in the United States, an astonishing number of children—more than one million babies—are lost to infertility and miscarriage. These losses don't make national headlines. At times, even best friends and close family members never learn of them.

Yearning for a child—and not being able to have one—represents an ache that is complicated to capture or measure, even for sufferers and fertility doctors. For some, to die without creating life adds up to two deaths: one's own, and the opportunity a child represents to defy mortality.

"It feels like constant starvation," says Rhonda Wile, speaking slowly, searching the cobalt desert horizon outside her home like a crime victim trying to recall an assailant's features for the precinct sketch artist. "You're hungry all the time, even when you're sleeping. You gradually understand that you are going to be starving, starving for a child, for the rest of your life."

How far would you go to have a child?

Would you harvest your eggs or sperm at age twenty-two, your fertile peak?

How many rounds of long subcutaneous needles, hormones

flooding your body, and invasive, expensive surgeries would you endure?

Where could you find the money? Would you sell your car, your house? Ask your parents to hock their retirement condo?

What would you do to help someone *else* have a child? Write a character recommendation for an adoption agency? Lend a friend money? Donate an embryo? Carry a stranger's baby in your uterus?

Picture that you'd spent your life savings on in vitro fertilization (IVF) and other fertility treatments, and you still didn't have a baby. Could you make one final reckless gamble? Would you be able to find the nearly $100,000 needed to finance the most desperate solution: paying another woman to create and carry a baby in her uterus for you?

At forty, nearing the end of her fertility road, Rhonda knew the answer. She and Gerry, after trying to get pregnant dozens of times, dozens of different ways, had found a radical new solution.

Rhonda and Gerry had spent nearly $50,000 trying to have children together, more than they spent on their house down payment and the purchase of their two cars. Rhonda and Gerry's baby chase had led them thousands of miles from home, to a perplexing, entrancing country with over 11 million unwanted infants and one of the highest female illiteracy rates in the world. They'd ventured to a faraway land they had never once dreamed of visiting, all in search of a baby they could afford on a nurse and firefighter's income.

The reason Rhonda looked so svelte was simple.

Although she and Gerry were expecting twins, Rhonda was not pregnant.

The unborn twins were Rhonda and Gerry's babies, but they were not growing inside Rhonda's body. Another woman was pregnant with Rhonda and Gerry's twins. Her name was Gauri.

A dozen times a day, while Gauri went about her chores, when she heated water for breakfast tea for her husband, or scrubbed her children's dark blue school uniforms, the thought jerked Gauri like a truck horn suddenly blaring in the night: she was pregnant from a twenty-minute medical procedure, without having had sex with the baby's father. The babies she had carried for five months had been created from another woman's egg and a stranger's sperm; she had no genetic connection to them. And she was going to become rich beyond her wildest dreams in exchange for growing these babies for two people she had never met.

Her body. Their babies.

The Wiles knew Gauri's height and weight, the ages of her son and daughter, her husband's income, what she ate for breakfast, and the results of her latest blood draw. But they had not met the woman carrying their babies. In fact, they had never even talked to her. Gauri didn't speak English. Plus she had no telephone. Finally, the woman bearing the Wile twins lived twelve time zones and 8,847 miles away in a small temporary apartment in the Bhandup West neighborhood of Mumbai, India.

"Which made it kind of hard for the three of us to catch up," says Rhonda today, with a rueful smile.

Having a baby is natural, right?

Also as natural—and as ancient—as the human species itself is difficulty conceiving and carrying babies. Long before words were written on papyrus, or horses painted on Paleolithic cave walls, long before doctors understood what causes infertility, and centuries before birth control and women's rights advocacy enabled women to delay childbearing, infertility afflicted humans at a steady rate of 10 to 12 percent.

Surprising, then, that studies have shown that almost all

women wildly overestimate our ability to get pregnant, at every age, and to have as many children as we want in our lifetime. Infertility is one affliction no one talks about, or assumes will happen to them, until it actually happens to them.

Throughout time and in every culture, women like Rhonda Wile have erroneously borne the burden of blame. The inaccurate historical assumption has long been that infertility was strictly a women's issue. In the Old Testament, written sometime in the fifth or sixth centuries BC, Abraham's wife Sarah was barren until a miracle son, Isaac, was born long past her childbearing years. In Genesis, the Lord closed Rachel's womb until she cried out to Jacob, "Give me children or else I die." Michal, the daughter of King Saul; Hannah; Elisha; Samson's mother; even the Virgin Mary's mother, Anna, and her cousin Elisabeth, all were labeled "barren" women who could not bear children.

The Bible never refers to any men as barren. U.S. history books rarely note that the father of our country, George Washington, was not an actual father. He created no offspring, despite marrying a demonstrably fertile young widow, Martha Dandridge Custis, who had given birth to four children with her first husband by the time she turned twenty-five. Today's infertility specialists suspect that Washington suffered from Klinefelter's syndrome, an affliction with symptoms including bad teeth (Washington lost his by his early twenties), unusual height (he was six foot three), and sterility.

Human understanding of male infertility came only with twentieth-century medical technology. The reality is that for 30 percent of cases, experts don't know what causes the inability to conceive. In couples where doctors can pinpoint the origin, 50 percent of problems lie with the man.

Bias lingers nevertheless. Many cultures continue to shun women when a couple experiences sterility. Many women, in the United States and other countries, blame themselves if they have difficulty getting, or staying, pregnant. An accepted solution in many cultures, cited over twenty times in the Old Testament, was for men to turn to other, potentially more fertile, women to try again, sometimes with legal and societal sanction. An ancient, respected form of surrogacy.

Hiring a surrogate is now, in certain circles, a badge of hipness. Trendsetters today make magazine covers with their surrogate babies. Nicole Kidman. Elton John. Sofia Vergara. Angela Bassett. Neil Patrick Harris. Sarah Jessica Parker. They all have beloved babies born from other women's wombs. Among the less famous, an amazing 2,000 to 4,000 babies are born each year to surrogate mothers to whom they have no biological connection.

In short, infertility has been a reality for the human race, disproportionately affecting women, for centuries. And surrogacy has always been one of the solutions.

*What's wrong with not being able to have babies, anyway?*
*You could save a lot of money on birth control and diapers.*
*With seven billion people, who needs more children in the world?*
*Maybe infertility is God's way of controlling the population.*
*Why don't you just adopt?*

Try telling that to anyone who wants a baby.

Few parents would limit how much they would sacrifice for their children. To anyone with a child, this seems indisputably true. Children are priceless.

Especially to people who cannot have them.

Unless you've experienced infertility firsthand, it seems an uncommon affliction. It's definitely not a "disease." When infertility strikes a friend or a celebrity on the pages of *People* magazine, the inability to conceive is easy to brush off as fate. God's brusque message that, *Sorry, kids are not in the cards for you*. Few beyond the infertile know the causes of sterility or its commonality. Infertility remains a hidden, taboo disease, with corrosive psychological effects on individuals, couples, and families.

Yet people seeking treatment spend $10 billion a year globally in search of a positive pregnancy test. In the United States alone, $5 billion is spent every year by sufferers willing to pay almost any amount to create a child.

If you have been touched by infertility, your understanding deepens immediately. Dr. Robert J. Stillman from the Shady Grove Fertility Center outside Washington, D.C., has spent most of his sixty-four years immersed in the agonies of infertility and the joys of treating it successfully. He is one of thousands of doctors today who dedicate their entire careers to assisted reproductive technology.

"Are children a gift?" Robert Stillman asks rhetorically, looking around his office crowded with medical charts, pictures of the Grand Tetons and Utah's Anasazi Indian cliff dwellings, and a large, powerful Dell computer, as he struggles to explain the desire to have children. In a way, this same drive—to help infertile couples—has gotten him out of bed, and in front of a classroom or a patient, each morning for over forty years.

"No. Not just a gift. Are children a human right? No. Not just a 'right.' Children are a biological *necessity*. Making babies is why we human beings are here on earth. Procreating is the number one biological imperative for our species. Infertility is a disease, like cancer. Treating infertility helps the human race survive. Helping someone have a baby does not hurt anyone— you are not taking a baby away from anyone else. Asking people who want to have children not to have children is cruel, inhumane, and against the natural, Darwinian survival of ourselves. In the most fundamental way, treating infertility is as pro-life as you can get."

Today's range of fertility treatments has transformed what a diagnosis of infertility means. What's different now: infertility is treatable. Medical and societal innovations expand the baby chase every day. Determination and outrageously expensive, sophisticated treatments have taken the place of quiet, lifelong anguish, despair, and disappointment.

Even so, some couples facing infertility give up their dream of having a baby. The loss can embitter their lives until the end, a grief too great to be borne gracefully. Others accept and embrace childlessness, finding that a child-free life offers its own peace and reconciliation.

Once the infertility highway narrows to what feels like a dead end, some people who still really, really want a baby start contemplating two ideas they may have hoped they'd never be forced to consider.

One is accepting that adoption, despite the competitiveness of modern adoptive procedures, and costs that can exceed $60,000, may be the right way to build a family.

The other, increasingly popular response is to hire a woman to create and carry a baby for you.

This radical solution—surrogate pregnancy—to some seems the domain of science fiction, conjuring Margaret Atwood's 1985 dystopian novel *The Handmaid's Tale*, where young, fertile women are forced to gestate babies for older women. However, fundamental advances in medically assisted reproductive technologies, particularly in vitro fertilization, have made surrogacy simultaneously easier, and more complex, than at any time in history.

Today, nearly anyone—single, married, gay, straight, sexually active, a virgin, or a nun—can have a baby. Anyone. One way or another or another.

Assuming, of course, that they can afford it. Because hiring a surrogate can run north of $100,000. In the United States, at least.

Every child *is* precious. That doesn't mean that everyone can afford one.

In 2011, Rhonda and Gerry Wile were finally building their family, utilizing methods unavailable to their own parents merely a generation before. However, it certainly felt unusual, to say the least, to have their babies growing in another woman's body two continents and eight thousand miles away. Their siblings, cousins, and best friends all had their babies at the local hospital. Still, Gerry and Rhonda counted themselves lucky.

Years before they first boarded a plane to India in search of a baby, though, they had had to learn more than what 99 percent of parents on the planet know about surrogacy, sex, and conception.

"It wasn't easy," explains Rhonda today.

First, the Wiles learned, mostly through hours of Rhonda's late-night online research, that surrogacy is legal only in some countries and certain states. Unpaid "compassionate" or "altruistic" surrogacy, often involving a friend or family member who carries a baby when someone she loves cannot, is possible, but rare. More common and quickly growing in popularity is paid, or "commercial" surrogacy.

Surrogacy—once the Wiles absorbed the audacity of it, the legal, medical, and insurance risks, the peculiar queries and emotional reactions from family and friends—offered the exhilarating possibility that Rhonda and Gerry could have a baby, a baby that felt like theirs from the moment of conception.

No home visits by adoption social workers. No grueling,

invasive applications. No birth mother who might change her mind quixotically at any moment.

No questions from their child, at six or sixteen or sixty, about why her "real" parents didn't want her. A baby that would be theirs, forever, from the instant Rhonda and Gerry heard its heartbeat on the six-week sonogram. A baby no one could take away.

"Our baby," says Rhonda, making the two words sound priceless.

What the Wiles found equally breathtaking—and heartbreaking—about surrogacy was its cost.

Rhonda drew in a harsh breath the night she totaled the amounts on her computer calculator. Several articles and blog entries quoted a fee of $25,000, paid directly to the surrogate. Plus the surrogate's medical and living expenses for one year. Plus the hospital delivery costs.

Plus lawyers' fees to draw up a surrogate contract and adoption papers for the Wiles to legally adopt their own baby once he or she was born. Plus additional travel costs, since as far as Rhonda could tell, most American surrogates lived in Pennsylvania, Colorado, Maryland, and California, all states that were very supportive of assisted reproductive technology (ART).

Then Gerry reminded Rhonda: she needed to factor in hormone injections and egg retrieval and embryo transfer costs for herself and the surrogate.

She came up with a conservative estimate: $80,000 to $100,000. If nothing went wrong. If the surrogate did not deliver early. If no one—not the surrogate, not the state, not the hospital—disputed the surrogacy arrangement.

One hundred thousand dollars to have a baby?

"So, for me and Gerry, the question wasn't ever, 'How much is a baby worth?'" Rhonda says now, years later, still trying not to tear up. "The question was actually, unfortunately, so much more crass. The real question was 'How much could we afford to pay for a baby?'"

This is a question no one should ever be forced to answer.

Rhonda would have paid $1 million for a baby. She would have sacrificed anything. But this nurse and firefighter were never going to come up with $100,000.

On a blue-sky afternoon in early November, a few days after Halloween, yellow leaves and a few Reese's candy wrappers littered the cobblestone sidewalks ringing the Maryland State House. The circa-1772 redbrick, white-columned Annapolis landmark is the oldest American edifice still in legislative use. Our infertile founding father George Washington resigned his military commission here in 1783. Three years later, patriots rallied in the State House to call the thirteen American colonies to assemble for the Constitutional Convention. Another 225 years later, red, white, and blue American flags, as well as Maryland's black, gold, and red ones, fluttered at every window.

On the third floor of a small, anonymous office building directly across the street, Sherrie Smith sits behind her desk. She works only a few blocks from the Annapolis wharf, with its rustic "shoppes," historic landmark buildings, pretty white sailboats, and blue-glass water. Close-shaved cadets in black uniforms walk to town from the nearby United States Naval Academy.

Sherrie is always too busy to see much of the historic scenery outside her office. She's buried in her e-mail queue, conducting interviews via Skype, and answering the phone. Her job is educating, listening to, and holding the hands of anxious, usually very wealthy, prospective parents from around the globe. She is the program administrator for the Center for Surrogate Parenting (CSP), one of the oldest, most respected surrogacy agencies in the world.

"The biggest misconception about American surrogates?" she clarifies in the beige-on-beige CSP conference room where she spends much of her days. Today, Sherrie wears a deep purple silk suit that sets off her white-blond hair. "That they do it for the money. Having a baby for someone else is as far from easy money as you can get."

Sherrie Smith has run the East Coast office of the Center for Surrogate Parenting since 1998. She's now in her sixties. Although she chose not to have kids of her own, she and CSP have helped nearly 1,700 surrogate babies come into this world. CSP's most famous babies include two sets of twins for *Good Morning America* host Joan Lunden, and Zachary Jackson Levon Furnish-John, the baby boy born on Christmas Day 2010 for pop rocker Elton John and his husband, David Furnish.

Sherrie's company was founded in Los Angeles, California, in 1980. Gerry Wile was fourteen. His future wife, Rhonda, only ten. Sherrie's boss—a Los Angeles lawyer by the name of William Wolf Handel—wrote a third-party reproduction agreement, now called a "surrogacy contract," as a random, one-off request for a client. Word quickly spread among infertile clients desperate to hire surrogates to have babies. The phone at Handel's Los Angeles law office started ringing off the hook.

Bill Handel and his staff—all women except the boss—at first struggled to craft a workable set of guidelines in the brave new world of contractual baby making. They knew they'd stumbled upon a promising business opportunity—but a risky one. *What if the surrogate changed her mind?* many desperate prospective parents asked. A reasonable question, without a clear-cut answer; no legal precedents had been established. So Bill Handel's female-centric firm came up with an innovative business philosophy: the surrogate herself would have equal standing among the team of doctors, wealthy clients, and lawyers. With a democratic approach, Handel figured that they had a good chance of solving any problems that arose.

"It was impossible to write a contract—or create a company—that was unfair to women when all my employees and partners were women," Handel explains today. Other women in Handel's life added their two cents. In addition to his estrogen-rich office, the female clients who hire him, and the surrogates his company hires, insert one wife and two daughters. Women surround Bill Handel twenty-four hours a day.

"I live in a world where the toilet seat is *never* left up," Handel laughs.

Lucky for him, the approach proved wildly successful. Almost by accident, the Jewish, Brazilian-born Bill Handel became a pioneer in California surrogacy law. Over the years, his advocacy—plus a plethora of wealthy, high-profile celebrities who publicly embraced surrogacy—helped make California arguably the most surrogacy-friendly environment in the United States. It also made CSP one of the finest, and most expensive, providers of surrogates in the world.

The first surrogate Sherrie Smith encountered had been hired by someone she loved so much, Sherrie would have supported her adoption of a Pet Rock: her sister Fay. After years of negative pregnancy tests and myriad infertility diagnoses, her sister became one of the earliest American women to go public about hiring a paid surrogate. Sherrie's niece and nephew were both born via surrogate in California, in 1990 and then 1994.

During the years since, Sherrie has learned a great deal about the American surrogates who carry babies for infertile clients from around the world.

The clients are usually older, richer, and better educated than the surrogate mothers they hire. They are also more likely to come from large urban cities like New York, Los Angeles, Paris, and Tokyo, and are far better traveled. Intended parents (IPs) come from an astonishing range of more than fifty countries, from Denmark to Papua New Guinea to Taiwan.

17

The majority of intended parents are heterosexual couples. Some are infertile due to biological abnormalities. Others face fertility challenges wrought by hysterectomies, car accidents, paralysis, or other medical problems. More and more are gay male couples. (Lesbian couples rarely hire surrogates, given the inexpensive, thoroughly screened sperm on the market and the statistical improbability of two female partners both being infertile.) Increasingly, there are more single women and single men who are consciously and openly choosing to become solo parents. CSP originally worked only with couples, but in 2009 the company changed its guidelines to welcome single parents.

The surrogates are obviously all female, and they're noticeably younger—the average age is about twenty-eight. The typical profile runs like this: married, Christian, middle-class, with two to three biological children, working a part-time job, living in a small town or suburb rather than a big city, with a degree of college education but usually without a college degree. Women who shop at Walmart and Costco, not Whole Foods and Neiman Marcus.

In the United States, statistics show that surrogates fall into the average household income category of under $60,000. About 15 to 20 percent are military wives.[1] Some are single women. Those who are married have husbands who support paid surrogacy; surrogacy is obviously not something you can hide, or withstand with a spouse who is not on board emotionally. They have health insurance. They get paid well—the surrogacy fee paid directly to surrogate mothers who work for CSP runs from $20,000 to $30,000 per pregnancy, tax-free. Surrogates who have already carried babies for clients often command higher fees; as in any position, experience counts. Of the women who serve as surrogates for CSP, roughly 35 percent repeat the experience; in the United States there is no limit to the number of times a surrogate can carry for-profit babies.

CSP is not alone in its strict criterion for surrogates.

Ethical surrogacy agencies and lawyers don't accept two specific categories of potential surrogates. First, they reject women below the poverty level who may be at greater risk for health concerns and coercion, and who probably do not have medical insurance. Second, they reject women who don't have children. Women who are already mothers have proven they are fertile, and have a more comprehensive grasp of what it will mean to surrender a baby to its legal parents.

Although the money makes a difference, no surrogate signs up just for the money.

"It would be easier to get a job at McDonald's," Sherrie insists. "The money doesn't begin to compensate them for what they do. A surrogate pregnancy means working twenty-four hours a day, seven days a week, without a break, for nine months. Pregnancy is risky; pregnancy taxes your body tremendously. Our surrogates come to us because they love children, they want to help people who cannot have them, and they like the feeling of creating a family for other people."

Yet undeniably, you've got "have" and "have not" differentials at play in the surrogate–intended parent relationship. The surrogates already have what the IPs desperately want—the ability to create babies. What the IPs have is money; they are usually better educated, and far more economically secure. They must be, in order to afford the surrogate's fee, agency and legal fees, and surrogacy's medical expenses.

The IPs are consumed by desperation. As a result, their surrogate becomes, at least for nine months, the superwoman in their lives, the embodiment of their most fervent hopes and dreams. Working at McDonald's or temping as a law firm receptionist can't compare to being Nicole Kidman and Keith Urban's savior. Sometimes these economic and fertility dynamics create subtle tensions; many times the enthusiasm of the surrogate and the gratitude of the intended parents smooth over any jagged feelings.

There are some quirks about surrogates. There are very few Jewish surrogates—and almost zero Jewish egg donors. Black surrogates carry babies for white families and vice versa. Surrogates do not pay taxes on the payments from clients, which legally are for pain and suffering incurred, not for carrying a baby. Daughters of surrogates frequently decide to be surrogates themselves; surrogacy can become a family tradition. Gay men, like Puerto Rican pop star Ricky Martin, are the favorite clients of many surrogate moms; one emotional complication is removed from the tricky relationship, because the gay intended parents don't suffer the understandable jealousy/ inferiority issues that can plague infertile intended mothers.

CSP selects only twenty of the four hundred women who apply each month to be surrogates. The most common reasons for rejection? The surrogate lives in a state where commercial surrogacy is not legal. She has health issues such as high blood pressure or obesity. Her motivation is too heavily focused on money. She lives too far away from a level-two neonatal intensive care unit (NICU). She has not yet had a child.

What takes up most of Sherrie's time is interviewing and managing the clients who retain CSP to oversee the complex surrogacy process. Step one is completion of an online form, available from CSP's Web site, followed by a phone call with Sherrie. Step two is a half-day interview, conducted in person in Sherrie's conference room or via Skype (particularly useful for international clients, who account for close to 50 percent of CSP's parents). The interview includes a forty-five-minute preliminary psychological consultation with one of the independent counselors who work with CSP. Then clients must meet with an attorney familiar with state-by-state surrogacy laws and contracts, as well as international citizenship regulations if the client is from another country.

The first phase in surrogacy has nothing to do with babies, and everything to do with meetings.

During these lengthy consultations, everything about the process—the risks, unknowns, legal paradoxes, and costs—is laid out. Sherrie is a skilled communicator; the most important part of her job is talking and listening. She goes through the minutiae of health insurance clauses that exclude coverage for surrogate pregnancies. She diplomatically broaches whether a surrogate or a client would be amenable to reducing a multiple pregnancy, or terminating a pregnancy if the fetus has birth defects, both important issues to clear up long before they become realities, especially because forcing a surrogate to have an abortion is legally, and ethically, problematic.[2]

Sherrie Smith *wants* to see glassy eyes on her prospective clients' faces, even if they belong to Elton John or Elizabeth Banks.

"The only surprise we want clients to have," Sherrie makes clear, "is whether they're having a boy or a girl."

*Far away from* Rhonda and Gerry Wile, across the Atlantic Ocean and the Arabian Sea, the young mother named Gauri spent long days caring for her extended family in an enormous Mumbai slum crowded with shacks made of tin walls covered with bright blue plastic sheeting. Like many Indian girls, Gauri was paired as a teenager with a man her parents picked in an arranged marriage. Before she was twenty she had two children. She lived with her husband's family in one of the large, crowded Mumbai slums which house over 55 percent of the city's residents.

Her primary responsibilities were caring for her young son and daughter, her husband, and his parents—cooking, cleaning, collecting water from the communal slum pump, shopping daily for food, and hand-washing their laundry. She had never in her life received payment for work. There were few places where an impoverished and uneducated Indian woman with almost no skills and limited literacy could find paid employment. Most of the slum jobs—toiling on a makeshift assembly line in one of the illegal slum factories, driving a rickshaw— were jobs only for men.

This lack of opportunity for herself, and the inherent sexism facing Indian women, did not trouble Gauri. The immediate, and far more serious, problem in Gauri's life was her husband's difficulty finding regular work himself. Her husband, a quiet, whip-thin, hard-working Indian man in his early twenties, was unable, like nearly one in three male Indian slum residents, to secure steady employment. On many days there was not a single rupee in their tiny tin shack, and Gauri had to beg a few handfuls of her neighbors' rice to feed her children.

So when Gauri heard that a Mumbai medical clinic, run by a female doctor—a strange and surprising concept itself— had paid a slum friend thousands of rupees to have a baby for someone else, she was astonished. The friend had gone to live at the clinic during the pregnancy and to recuperate after the birth. She'd spent her days in an apartment with a maid and a cook; she'd been given good food and vitamins and seen a doctor more often than during the rest of her life in total. She had given birth in the private yellow sandstone hospital near the slum, a place only wealthy Indians and Westerners had the money to afford, a six-story building Gauri passed every day but had never seen from the inside. The amount of money for nine months of this "work" was enough that her friend was able to buy a home on the slum outskirts that was large enough for her extended household, transforming herself from a seen-but-not-heard wife, daughter-in-law, and mother into the neighborhood hero.

The friend explained, with a stern look, that she had not had sexual intercourse with the baby's father. The doctor had put the baby in her body during an operation. It wasn't her baby. She just grew it. And was paid a huge sum of money

22

when the baby was born. Her friend excitedly explained she even got extra money because the baby had to be delivered via Cesarean section—she made a slash across her lower abdomen with her fist, as if holding a knife.

Gauri thought of all the rice and lentils that money could buy for her children.

The woman said she would make enough with a second surrogate pregnancy to send her daughter to college. Gauri shook her head at the audacity of a slum mother thinking her child could ever attend university, practically unheard of throughout the Mumbai slum world. Just as Gauri did not know any women who earned money by working, she did not know any girls who had gone to college. And anyway, Gauri would be happy just to have enough rupees to feed her son and daughter, without worrying about sending them to university a decade in the future.

All this was legal under Indian law? Her friend assured her it was. And she offered, quietly, to take a very nervous, but also secretly hopeful, Gauri to the clinic if she ever wanted to see it for herself.

*Further complicating the* dilemmas confronting Rhonda, Gerry, Gauri, and everyone else involved in surrogacy, are the different physical types of surrogacy. Medically and biologically, there are two forms of surrogate conception. Rhonda learned—and explained to Gerry late at night when their grueling shifts coincided—that "traditional surrogacy" is when a surrogate uses her own egg to conceive and carry a baby whom another parent, or parents, will raise. The resulting child is created from the surrogate's egg, fertilized by sperm from a donor via artificial insemination. The woman carrying the baby is the genetic and biological mother, also known as the "bio mom." Although he never publicly labeled his path to

parenthood as traditional surrogacy and many conception details remain unclear, this is presumably what deceased pop
rocker Michael Jackson did through his relationship with
nurse Debbie Rowe. Rowe bore two children for Jackson, in
1996 and 1998, and after the couple divorced in 1999, Rowe
terminated her parental rights and received $8 million from
Jackson.

Traditional surrogacy, like many medical treatments, involves risks and side effects, although at heart they are emotional
perils, as Debbie Rowe eventually discovered. Biologically, a traditional surrogate is giving up her own child. Some traditional
surrogates suffer grief and doubt during the pregnancy, and long
after relinquishing the child—a deep regret and guilt akin to the
sorrow felt by mothers who give up babies for adoption. Debbie
Rowe twice attempted to regain her parental rights, with mixed
results. Perhaps, if a traditional surrogate like Rowe is lucky,
this grief and guilt are combined with the sense that she has
given another person, or couple, the gift of a child.

What also disturbed Rhonda was the risk that she—known
formally as the "intended" mother—might experience inchoate,
crippling feelings of insecurity as a parent.

"My most haunting fear was that someone in my family, or
a friend or acquaintance, and maybe one day even my child,
would decide I was not the 'real' mother. Just because of the
lack of biological connection," Rhonda explained as she explored the strange and worrisome idea of traditional surrogacy. "What if I didn't feel like my baby's true mother?"

For some intended mothers, as with some percentage of
adoptive parents, this pain also lasts a lifetime. It can warp the
experience of motherhood. During conception, pregnancy, and
the rest of the child's life—Rhonda learned from blog confes-
sions and magazine articles—some intended mothers suffer an
intense and debilitating conviction that they risk losing their
child, emotionally or physically. Although in many states tra-

ditional surrogates are not legally allowed to change their minds after they've signed a surrogacy contract, the intended mother sometimes worries that the bio mother is out there, perhaps merely a town or two away, potentially able to reclaim her child, physically or psychologically.

"Also, any traditional surrogate we hired," Rhonda clarified, shaking her head, "could have other children, biological half siblings to my child, any time. My child's surrogate could produce a half sibling for one of my neighbors, someone from work, a family from their school, complete strangers. One day, my child might share a surrogate, siblings, their blood, their genetics with other families. Most moms I know can't bear to share a babysitter."

Rhonda thought this was a terrible price to pay for the privilege of being a mother. She had already been through years of dashed hopes and painful, expensive surgeries; she didn't know how much strength she had left. Rhonda could see—and feel—that traditional surrogacy was haunted by short-term and lifelong risks and penalties. For Rhonda, traditional surrogacy was a far from ideal solution to infertility.

But then she discovered gestational surrogacy (GS), made possible by in vitro fertilization. It made so much better sense to her, it seemed too good to be true. GS differs fundamentally from traditional surrogacy. Embryos are created in a medical lab by combining sperm and an egg unrelated to the surrogate. The resulting embryo, or embryos, can then be implanted in the surrogate's uterus. The woman carrying the baby has no genetic link to the child. She is providing—some people sardonically call it "renting out"—a healthy uterus on a temporary basis.

"I liked this kind of surrogacy much, much better," says Rhonda now.

However, not everyone does. This mind-boggling change in conception and gestation shakes the human race's centuries-old definition of pregnancy and traditional motherhood. Today, a mother of a child, the real mother, the legal mother, does not have to be pregnant or give birth. Sex is not part of conception; nothing even vaguely resembling sexual intercourse is required. One woman, with or without a male partner, can control her destiny by arranging for a baby, her baby, to be created purposefully and intentionally via another woman.

Likewise, one man can buy another woman's egg and hire a surrogate, to become a parent without a female partner. Surrogacy nullifies the biological imperative for sexual attraction, arousal, and intercourse that have preceded parenthood since the beginning of the human race. The only requirement is intent to be a parent, and, at least at this moment in America, an enormous amount of money to pay a surrogate, a lawyer, and an IVF doctor.

This transmogrification of pregnancy and parenthood diverges fundamentally—and radically—from natural conception. It also differs distinctly from traditional surrogacy, which requires uncomplicated artificial insemination of the egg already inside a woman's body; not drastically different, in terms of mechanics, from natural conception. Gestational surrogacy also differs profoundly from a child naturally conceived and later adopted by genetically unrelated parents.

For the first time in human history, it has become conceptually and medically possible to intentionally separate and outsource the three fundamental building blocks needed to create human life.

Sperm from one source. An egg from another. A womb wholly separate from both.

This is gestational surrogacy, the new bridge bypassing infertility.

"Wow" was all Gerry could say when Rhonda explained it to him.

For Rhonda and Gerry, GS was an exhilarating concept. From the view of surrogates, intended parents, and lawyers, gestational surrogacy amends many of traditional surrogacy's inescapable flaws. The critical difference: the surrogate is not biologically related to the baby she gestates. She does not have legal or ethical or genetic claims to parenthood—or any of the guilt that goes along with giving away or selling her baby. Psychologically and practically, the baby is never hers. This makes it far easier for her to be a surrogate, whether she is doing so as an altruistic good deed, or for financial compensation, or a bit of both.

Without a surrogate's genetic link to the child, there are fewer legal and emotional complications for intended parents like the Wiles, and any resulting children, as well. Separating the egg donor, the sperm donor, and the person who gestates the baby jettisons many of the potentially heartbreaking and complex aspects of assisted baby making.

The baby would always be Rhonda and Gerry's—long before it was born.

And forever after as well. There would be no "real" mother in the shadows, haunting Rhonda with any claim to the child, now or in the future. Often the gestational surrogate lives in another state or another country. After the birth, if she wants, the surrogate can vanish like chalk erased from a blackboard. For many parents, an *advantage* of gestational surrogacy is that their children will never meet the woman who gestated them. This may sound coldly self-centered or psychologically immature, but a critical component of any parent-child bond, no matter how the child was conceived or gestated, is the hue of mutual belonging: we are a family, *you* are my mother, you are *my* child. No one else's.

Gestational surrogacy also has the potential, perhaps, to make traditional male-female parenting obsolete, as well as to reduce much of the incentive to create and sustain traditional marriages. The separation of sperm, egg, and uterus, and the lack of reliance upon heterosexual sex to create life, disassembles the biological imperative that has long driven individuals to pair off in order to start a family.

Gestational surrogacy's only undisputed disadvantage versus traditional surrogacy is that GS requires IVF, increasing its cost and complexity. However, today there are hundreds, if not thousands, of doctors in the United States and other countries who can perform IVF.

It's the future. And it's already here.

A *few facts* about Gauri's country:

Over 1.2 billion people live there. By the time you've read this sentence, it could be 1.3 billion.

India is the world's largest democracy, with a population nearly four times that of the United States and over twice Europe's.[3]

India is as ancient as infertility. One of the world's earliest civilizations, it can be traced to the Indus Valley between approximately 3100 and 1700 BC, over four thousand years before the United States became the United States.[4] Thousands of years before Jesus Christ was born, India maintained one of civilization's most advanced systems of town planning, burials of the dead, sanitation, and drainage. India produced some of history's earliest, and greatest, astronomers and mathematicians between AD 100 and 900.

There are twenty-nine states in India. Many have origins dating back 2,600 years. The largest state, Uttar Pradesh, is home to over 165 million people. If Uttar Pradesh were a separate country instead of a state, it would be the world's fifth most populous nation, smaller only than the United States, Indonesia, China—and of course, India itself.

Large and small are different in India. There are fifty Indian cities with populations greater than Dallas, Texas.[5] An isolated rural outpost in India—for instance, one like Hubli, situated between Mumbai and Bangalore, which as recently as twenty years ago was connected to other parts of the country only by train—has 900,000 residents. More people than San Francisco. Nearly twice the entire population of Wyoming.

A small town, India style.

India has eighteen official languages including Hindi, Marathi, Gujarati, Kannada, Tamil, and Malayalam.[6] Approximately 65 percent of the population speaks English, a result of the long reign of the British Raj. However, roughly 45 percent of the country's population is illiterate, unable to read any language.[7]

There are dozens of religions practiced in India, from Parsi to Judaism to Jainism. The majority of people, roughly 85 percent, practice Hinduism. The second-largest religion is Islam, with 150 million practicing Muslims; Islam has been present in India since the eighth and ninth centuries AD[8] and today India has the world's third-largest community of Muslims. Buddhism originated in India in the sixth century BC — Buddha himself was Indian—and the religion is still practiced there by a small minority. Christianity is also somewhat common at 2.3 percent of the population, again with ancient origins in India dating back to the first century AD.[9]

By most measures, India is a diverse, loosely knit democracy of multifarious people, languages, and religions, all coexisting, albeit at times uneasily.

An exception to India's societal tolerance is the country's 3,500-year-old caste stratification. This ancient system of graded inequality was based on one's birth family. For much of India's history, it was impossible to change castes.

Male Brahmins, or the priest caste, ruled at the top of the human hierarchy of castes or "varnas." The Brahmin outlook placed women at the bottom of all hierarchies. Yet ironically, the term *Brahmin* originated with Lord Brahma and Goddess Brahmani. Millions of female goddesses from the ancient

Vedic religion of early Hinduism are still worshipped throughout India today.

Until the 1950s, despite the abundance of female deities, only male Brahmins were granted access to political power, property ownership, wealth accumulation, and education. Only men had access to medical and scientific knowledge, including yogic and ayurvedic teachings. For centuries, only Brahmin men could practice sun salutations, read books, own property, and make laws.

The Kshatriya, or warriors and landowners, came next below the Brahmins. The Vaishya, or merchants, ranked below the Kshatriya. They were followed by Shudra, or servants. At the very bottom—not even technically on the varna hierarchy— were the Dalits, or Untouchables, Gauri's caste.

Untouchables like Gauri's ancestors were historically responsible for disposal of human waste, sweeping, cleaning, and removal of dead animals. They were not allowed to touch members of other castes—elaborate purification ceremonies had to be performed if contact occurred. Untouchables, or Dalits, were not supposed to make eye contact with or even look at Brahmins.

Although Dalits practiced the Hindu religion, they were banned from their own Hindu temples. They were prohibited from drinking from common wells or eating where non-Dalits ate. Their children were barred from schools. All Dalits were forbidden to share clothing, utensils, or transportation with other Indians.

Untouchables were required to carry small terra-cotta pots to collect their spit, so their saliva would not pollute the ground. They had to wear brooms attached to their backsides to sweep away their footprints. Wherever they went, Untouchables had to announce their impending arrival via small tinkling bells or a prescribed chanted warning. In all practices, Dalits were treated worse than wild dogs; dogs, after all, were permitted to drink from human wells and to walk without cleaning up after themselves.

The Indian constitution officially outlawed the caste system in 1950. However, much of the informal societal preferences, privileges, and prejudices remain, especially when it comes to education, job opportunities, and intermarriage between castes. The majority of residents of India's infamous slums are Untouchables. Dharavi—arguably Mumbai's most examined slum as the focus of a case study by Harvard Business School and the movie *Slumdog Millionaire*—has one million residents living in a space two-thirds the size of New York City's Central Park. Yet the people of Dharavi are remarkably skilled and industrious, producing nearly $1 billion of annual income through makeshift garment and leather-goods factories.[10]

The Indian government is the largest employer in the world. The Indian Ministry of Railways alone employs 1.5 million people, nearly three times the entire population of Washington, D.C.[11] After decades of bureaucratic restrictions, economic stagnation, and widespread corruption, starting in 1991 the Indian government adopted an economic policy of liberalization, privatization, and globalization.

As a result, India's economy today is emerging, with some bumps along the way, as one of the fastest growing in the world.

One of India's most robust nascent industries is gestational surrogacy, legal since 2002. There are over five hundred surrogacy clinics in India. India's surrogacy industry is thriving because of the country's world-class private hospitals, abundance of English-speaking doctors, plethora of poor but healthy women of childbearing ages, and government regulations that promote surrogacy. A World Bank report projects that India's commercial surrogacy industry will reach $2.5 billion by 2020. India has become the largest provider of gestational surrogates to the Western world's infertile couples, outside of the United States. Ironic for a country that already suffers from too many children born every day.

India is full of similar contradictions. Indira Gandhi, prime minister between 1966 and 1984, is recognized as one of the most powerful female leaders of the twentieth century. Indian religious iconography is rampant with female deities such as Lakshmi, the goddess of wealth, and Bhavani, the bestower of life. Yet women's status overall in India is woeful.

Roughly 50 percent of India's women are illiterate. India is estimated to have the lowest average age of marriage in the world. Fifteen percent of India's poorest girls are married at or below age ten. Female genocide of fetuses and infant girls is rampant, with estimates of 15 percent of females in some states being killed before birth or within the first few weeks of life.

From 2001 to 2011 in the state of Maharashtra, which includes India's largest city, Mumbai, only 888 girls were born for every one thousand boys.[12] Despite population growth rates of 20 percent, there were only 914 girls for every one thousand boys under the age of six in India overall in 2011, according to Indian census figures. Due to abortions and infant suffocations, today's ratio is the highest gender imbalance since the country won independence in 1947.

"There are entire villages with no girls under [age] five," said Rohini Prabha Pande, an independent demographer who analyzes gender issues in India.[13]

In India, being a woman means belonging to a separate caste all its own.

Strikingly absent from India's entrenched prejudices, contradictions, inventions, accomplishments, spiritual teachings, and astronomically high population figures is the most breathtaking number in humanity's comprehension: the concept of zero.[14] Despite inventing the binary system—the basis of modern mathematics—the country's ancient, brilliant mathematicians, scientists, and astronomers failed to grasp, or utilize, the powerful idea of nothing.

Zero? It doesn't exist in India.

Which may explain why the idea of zero children is not comprehensible in India, either.

*Web sites and* travel books promoting India usually tout the Taj Mahal temple, the elephant rides in Jaipur, the beautiful shrines, the delicious spicy foods, and the spiritual and religious wonders of a country with 330 million deities.

A fact that doesn't usually make the tourism brochures: India has an outstanding health-care system, for those who can afford to pay for medical care. The wealthiest Indians have access to private treatments, operations, and hospitalizations that rival any country in the world. Particularly in large urban areas like Mumbai, where over 35 percent of the population lives, there are top-notch private hospitals and treatment centers, as well as several good government hospitals.

However, the weakness in India's health-care system—and it is a grave and fatal flaw—is that there are not enough doctors or medical facilities to serve the vast and impoverished Indian population. Not nearly enough. As a result, many of Indian's poorest citizens get little to no health care over the course of their entire lives. As a Band-Aid solution, all 700,000 of India's doctors are required to spend one year practicing medicine in a poor, rural area, where the medical infrastructure, particularly for women, is weakest.

Indian surrogates for wealthy international clients, though, enjoy far more generous health benefits than many pregnant women in the United States. As standard preventive care, Indian surrogacy clinics provide extensive prenatal testing and solicitous support. Pregnant surrogates often move into the clinics for much of the pregnancy to avoid the stress and debilitation of cooking, cleaning, shopping, or working. If the surrogate suddenly goes into preterm labor or needs emergency medical care, she is close to medical staff and world-class hospitals. The surrogates remain in the hospital for several days following delivery, and often recuperate at the clinic for an additional week or longer.

In the United States, the average hospital stay for a woman who has just given birth is 1.9 days.[15]

*Back at the* Center for Surrogate Parenting, if, after Sherrie's marathon interviews, an infertile couple (or individual) decides to proceed, they next sign three separate retainers and cough up three different financial deposits. One is for CSP. The next contract is between the client and a separate psychological counseling agency, required by CSP. Unlike many agencies, CSP does not have clients browse through an online catalog of surrogate profiles. Instead, CSP's counseling team reviews key factors like geographic proximity, preferences in terms of race, religion, and age, and health insurance logistics, and then proposes a liaison between like-minded surrogates and intended parents.

The third retainer is for the attorney who will oversee the contract, birth certificate/passport logistics, and parental rights paperwork. A lawyer experienced in surrogacy and adoption is critical to ensure that clients take their baby home from the hospital as *their* baby. With their names on the birth certificate.

In some states, when a child is born to a surrogate, a court petition must be filed to amend the birth certificate to include both intended parents as the baby's legal parents (even when they are the genetic parents). Other states allow the intended parents' names to be listed on the original birth certificate. A few states will grant gay dads two birth certificates, one with each father's name listed.

Some states, such as Louisiana, Michigan, and New York, outlaw paid surrogacy. These states do not recognize surrogate births or surrogacy contracts. The disparity in state laws can wreak havoc on IPs' dreams, such as in 2012 when Michigan sheltered a Connecticut gestational surrogate who refused to abort a client's fetus with severe birth defects. Some jurisdictions, such as Nebraska, New Mexico, and Minnesota, require a formal stepparent adoption of a surrogate baby. Some countries, such as Canada, ban surrogacy outright, which, for the Wiles, meant Rhonda's family couldn't help her.

Of course, if you are the citizen of another country coming to the United States to have a baby via surrogate, you need to make sure your homeland will recognize the baby legally as yours, and as a rightful citizen as well.

The country-by-country, state-by-state logistics and laws can bedevil any rational person. Maryland and California, where CSP's offices are located, are among the states most friendly to surrogate pregnancy. Prebirth orders designating IPs as the unborn child's legal parents are routine. Such an order puts the IPs' names on the child's birth certificate, and terminates any rights of the gestational carrier. California, where the Center for Surrogate Parenting was founded, is the state that pioneered *intent to become a parent* as the decisive factor in parental legality—not biological connection. In certain cases, California does not require a mother's name on a birth certificate at all.

At the other end of the spectrum, states such as Virginia require extensive home study of the intended parents, before the issue of a prebirth order. Washington, D.C., sandwiched between Virginia and Maryland, each with different laws, bars all forms of surrogacy. And even in Maryland, traditional commercial surrogacy, in which the surrogate mother has a genetic link to the child she carries, can be interpreted as a violation of Maryland's anti-baby-selling law.[16] Only gestational surrogacy is allowed when payment is involved.

When CSP began, most surrogacies were traditional—not gestational—with the surrogate providing the egg herself. Now, given widespread access to IVF, almost all of the hundred-plus babies CSP helps create each year are borne by gestational surrogates who have no genetic link to the fetus.

"Most surrogates don't want the biological connection," says Sherrie Smith. "Lawyers don't either."

Thus the second leg in gestational surrogacy is all about contracts, signatures, and money.

Then, finally, the process turns to baby making. Compared to the meetings, the lawyers, the detailed contracts, and the decoding of state regulations, the medical procedures are relatively simple. For each couple, the process is different. Some use their own egg and sperm. Some need eggs, others need sperm. The fertilization takes place in a petri dish, and the resulting embryo or embryos are implanted in the chosen surrogate.

CSP stays extremely involved, like a case manager or general contractor on a very complex and expensive custom-home construction job. Whether the clients are actors Sarah Jessica Parker and Matthew Broderick, who had twin girls via surrogate in 2009 after six years of trying to have a second baby following the natural conception of their son, James Wilkie, or anonymous private citizens, the process remains the same from CSP's view. Every baby is precious. Every surrogate is assigned a dedicated liaison. The intended parents get their own personal Web site that tracks all medical results, along with a timeline, and other information related to their surrogate's pregnancy. Helping gestational surrogates and intended parents make a baby is client-centric craftsmanship, not a high-volume mass market business. CSP is there for every milestone.

It is not as if the clients—whether they are celebrities or your next-door neighbors—pay a huge sum so that *poof!* nine months later they may magically walk out of a hospital with a baby. The surrogate calls her IPs when she takes that first pregnancy test (often she asks CSP or the fertility doctor to call if the result comes back negative). The intended parents talk or Skype with the surrogate about once a week, discussing medical updates, doctor's appointments, and the pregnancy overall. The intended parents and the surrogate arrange regular face-to-face meetings.

All parties, including the surrogate's husband, are usually in the hospital delivery room (CSP does not sanction home births or midwife births). And the parents are asked by CSP not to leave the area with the baby or babies until the surrogate leaves the hospital. No one wants the surrogate to feel like *wham-bam, thank you, ma'am, we've got our baby and we're gone.* The new parents are encouraged to visit her at her home, if she wants, to show her family the baby, before returning to their home.

"We don't want the surrogate, the parents, or the children to look back and feel used or disappointed by overenthusiastic promises made during the pregnancy," Smith explains.

This meticulous, communication-intensive process makes for a very personal, private, and collaborative pregnancy and birth experience. For celebrities like Sarah Jessica Parker, Sofia Vergara, and Ricky Martin, this discretion is obviously useful. Their surrogates, unfortunately, were stalked and targeted by the media. As a result, in support group meetings run by CSP counselors, surrogates are never allowed to use their intended parents' names.

But respect means just as much to everyday parents. Pregnancy and parenting are confidential, personal life experiences. CSP tries to keep the experience emotionally safe for everyone involved.

The third trimester of a surrogate pregnancy—like any

pregnancy—is all about prepping for the baby's arrival. Most important are the legal issues relating to parental custody; the client's lawyers get very busy in the last three months. Intended parents are encouraged to get a hotel room with a kitchenette within a few miles of the hospital, and to book a minimum ten-day stay. They are issued hospital name tags to get them admission to the maternity ward and delivery room. CSP cautions them to be prepared for premature delivery, unexpected hospital costs, time lost at work—exactly as if they were the gestational parents.

Clients who live close to their surrogate's hospital are warned that they are most likely to miss their babies' birth. Because they are nearby, many underestimate the time it takes to get to the hospital and check in. Despite the years, dollars, and heartbreak it took them to have this baby, local IPs are, refreshingly, just like other expectant parents who live a little *too* close to their hospital.

*Even Gauri, despite* her meager education, knew the name Gandhi. And not just because the Mahatma's spectacled face smiled at her on paper rupee bills, when Gauri was lucky enough to have a few rupees. Under Gandhi and his nonviolent compatriot Nehru, India won its independence, or "home rule," from Britain in 1947, after two centuries of British colonialism and dominance.

Or so history books report.

The reality is that half the population won independence in 1947.

Not Gauri's half. The male half of India won independence in 1947. At least, as much freedom as one can experience in a vastly overpopulated, impoverished country bound by centuries of tradition and caste dictates.

For most Indian women, life did not change significantly

after 1947. Women's oppressors—Indian men, British men, and centuries-old mandates from both cultures—dominated nearly every aspect of women's daily lives.

In 1947, many people around the world believed women were inferior to men, or at the very least, quite different from men. Not just in India.

Halfway through the twentieth century, many countries were struggling, to varying degrees, with granting women rights equal to men. American women had been voting for fewer than three decades. Women had been graduating from the two oldest universities in the world—Oxford and Cambridge—for a mere twenty-seven years. Chinese girls were still having their toes and foot arches broken for the crippling yet desirable "lotus feet," which prevented them from running—or even walking— away from men and their families.

However, the reality even now, despite advances in women's equality, is that over 500 million Indian women and girls today, including Gauri, lead bleak daily lives without the right to pick whom they marry, to learn to read, to work for pay, to inherit money, or to own property. Additionally, because laws designed to protect women are rarely enforced, Indian women do not have the right to prosecute a rapist, to divorce a physically abusive husband, or to seek justice if abducted and forced into prostitution.

India has allowed certain women—to be fair, several thousand—to benefit from the same educational and legal opportunities offered Indian men. Many of us in North America have female Indian professors, female Indian doctors, Indian college classmates, and Indian colleagues who buck the stereotype of illiterate Indian women with scant education and dismal earning potential. A country of over 500 million women will, invariably, produce a few strikingly tough, brilliant, stereotype-defiant women with the luck, enlightened fathers, and intelligence required to burst through India's glass crawl space.

The most obvious is India's powerful, iconic leader, Nehru's daughter Indira Gandhi. (Despite their shared last name, neither Indira Gandhi, her husband, nor any of their descendants are related to the famous male Gandhi; Indira's maiden name was Nehru.) Indira Gandhi ruled India for fifteen nonconsecutive years during the 1960s, 1970s, and 1980s, until her assassination in 1984.

Indira Gandhi has been India's only female prime minister. Let's just say, not everyone loved her. She was considered excessively authoritarian and corrupt by her enemies. She implemented India's nuclear power program in 1967. She instituted cruel and discriminatory actions against India's poorest citizens under cover of her 1975 to 1977 "state of emergency," bulldozing slums that provided shelter to millions of India's lowest-caste citizens.

In 1984, she mobilized the Indian military against the Sikh population in the Punjab region, entering and destroying the Golden Temple of Amritsar, a sacred Sikh sanctuary that extremists were using for shelter. Her aggression triggered her assassination later that year. Her own trusted bodyguards, Beant Singh and Satwant Singh, fired over thirty shots into Indira Gandhi's body on a bright, lovely autumn morning on the grounds of the prime minister's residence at One Safdarjung Road in New Delhi, until she was dead two or three times over.

But despite these failings, Indira Gandhi was, without dispute, a powerful, undeniably successful Indian woman.

There are many others.

Dr. Muthulakshmi Reddy's life spanned two very different Indian centuries, from 1886 to 1968. She was the first—and one of the most respected—female Indian doctors. She was the first female student to be admitted into an all-male college; the first woman surgeon in the Government Maternity and Ophthalmic Hospital; the first woman legislator in British India; the first chairperson of the State Social Welfare Advisory.

Hands down, a great woman and leader.

Another name that springs to mind is Agnes Gonxha Bojaxhiu. Although she was born in Skopje, Macedonia, her Catholic ministry was based in Calcutta. She was an Indian citizen. She became known throughout India, and the world, as Mother Teresa.

Five of the top one hundred richest women in the world are Indian. Including billionaires Savitri Jindal of Jindal Steel and Anu Aga of Thermax energy. Biocon's Kiran Mazumdar-Shaw is ranked seventy-fifth on *Forbes* list of the world's richest women, with a net worth of $900 million.

And let's not forget the dozens of famous female Bollywood actresses, including Katrina Kaif, Juhl Chawla, Shilpa Shetty, Kashmira Shah, Madhuri Dixit, Kareena Kapoor, Tanuja, Rekha, and Kajol, to name a few.

However, here's the truth about India, despite these exceptions: the best you can say is that the country neglects a valuable resource, its average female citizens. The ones not destined to lead a country, become a beautiful Bollywood star, or get into Stanford Medical School.

Another, perhaps more blunt, characterization is that India conducts war against most of its women throughout their lives: through gender-based abortions, female infanticide, child labor, child prostitution, forced marriage, slavery, dowry murders, gang rapes, and wife burning.

Can a country judge itself only by its most spectacular citizens? What about people born without any advantage or privilege? One of the most astonishing truths about this remarkably astonishing, ancient, and prescient country is that much of India's customs and traditions treat girls as if they simply do not count as human beings.

In India, as in most societies, women conceive, gestate, nurse, feed, discipline, nag, nurture, and raise their country's children. On a daily basis, women promulgate the country's future in ways inconceivable to most men. India would not exist without its women. Paradoxically, the most ancient and most popular Indian deity is female: the Great Mother goddess Devi, whose cult dates back more than three thousand years, and whose powers include intense feminine sexuality, warfare and weaponry, and death.[17]

Yet nearly every family in India values men and boys more than girls.

Despite Indira Gandhi, Mother Teresa, and the many brilliant Indian women many of us know personally, most girls eat last in Indian families. Historically, girls are educated last, in inferior schools, if they are educated at all. Girls are raised to be servants; millions work as unpaid cooks, housekeepers, and nursemaids every day of their lives.

Every day in India, seven thousand girls are killed before they are born, according to research presented by Walter Astrada in his 2009 Alexia Foundation documentary, *Undesired.*[18] Conducting an ultrasound to determine a fetus's gender, and selective abortion based on gender, are both illegal—for parents and doctors—in India. Ditto for cheap fetal DNA blood tests that determine a baby's sex, with more than 95 percent accuracy, at only seven weeks of pregnancy. Yet widespread bribery and cultural bias against girls makes gender-based ultrasound and abortion of female fetuses almost routine among middle- and upper-middle-class Indian families.

Impoverished families cannot afford the technology of ultrasound, blood tests, or abortion. Instead, girls born into poverty are frequently "put to sleep"—smothered by their mothers in infancy.[19] The *Hindustan Times* and the UK's *Telegraph* have both also reported stories of Indian doctors who perform sex-change operations on infant girls, resulting in neutered genitalia, apparently convincing enough to persuade relatives, and to justify the mutilation.

Poor girls and women like Gauri can be bought and sold in

India. Forced by their fathers to marry when they do not want to. Discarded by their husband's families if they do not serve obediently or produce male offspring. *The New York Times*'s Nicholas Kristof estimates that India has more modern female slaves, imprisoned in brothels as young girls, than any other country on earth.[20] Rigid estate laws dictate that only the eldest boy may inherit unless there is a legal will explicitly designating female heirs. If a man dies without a will, his female children have no recourse—although there is a rumor whispered around Mumbai about a female heir to millions who voluntarily underwent a genital sex change operation as an adult in order to legally inherit her family's estate.

Without sons or husbands, women become largely invisible and disposable. The practices of abandoning, beating, burning, and divorcing women who do not produce sons is tolerated by much of India's culture and government, despite official laws against these practices. As recently as 1987, widows committed sati, or self-immolation on their husbands' funeral pyres, despite the practice having been outlawed in 1829.[21] Bride burnings in retaliation for insufficient dowries were reported as recently as 2010.

Much of the prejudice against women and girls in India is based upon the outdated but stubborn societal construct that boys grow up to earn and inherit money, while girls devour resources with no return on investment. Girls are expensive to raise, the logic goes. They cannot legally inherit family wealth, and they cost families great sums of dowry money when they become marriageable. Men, hypothetically at least, are obligated to support their parents, wives, and children financially; this agreement is not always honored, particularly if their wives do not produce male children.

When a daughter marries, her primary obligation is to serve her husband's family. Like Gauri, women are obligated to spend their lives cooking, cleaning, bearing and raising children, caring for aging in-laws. Their natural families come second, if at all, making grown daughters nearly useless to their families of origin.

It seems to make scant difference that this cultural imperative was long ago made irrelevant by education, birth control, changes to inheritance laws, and employment opportunities for women as India's economy has become increasingly globalized.

Today's reality is that in most cases, it is far cheaper to educate a girl than to pay a dowry. The Indian government offers financial incentives to educate girls. Yet the practice of devaluing women and the work they do for their families continues.

An estimated 20 million female Indian infants were killed before birth, or born healthy but killed by their parents, from 1985 to 2005.[22] Those girls lucky enough to be born and to survive infancy are regularly abandoned to the streets or to homes for unwanted girls. These girls grow up to be beggars, most commonly, earning roughly one rupee a day. One rupee is equivalent to about two American pennies.

A day.

*Today surrogacy is* becoming common, increasingly unremarkable, throughout the United States and around the world. Infertile celebrities and famous gay men smile on magazine covers, holding cherubic babies created via U.S. surrogacy agencies. Hope has been granted the ordinary infertile, too.

All because of a breakthrough that occurred on July 25, 1978.

The place was Oldham, England, 208 miles from London. The ancient Anglo-Saxon town of roughly 100,000 people lies in Lancashire. Surrounded by windswept moorland, heath and bracken, the town sits eleven miles from the stadium where the famous Manchester United soccer team plays its home matches today.

Oldham literally means "old town." Flint arrowheads suggest humans inhabited Oldham as long as ten thousand years ago. More recently, Oldham was a boomtown during the Industrial Revolution of the late 1800s, spinning more cotton than France and Germany combined. But by the 1970s, Oldham was a declining, depressed, boarded-up town without significant industry.

Except for two highly focused, very motivated scientists.

The first was a brilliant gynecological surgeon named Patrick Christopher Steptoe. Dr. Steptoe was quiet and cerebral looking, with black bushy eyebrows and a small, pursed mouth. The expression on his face combined intelligence, concentration, and determination. He perennially seemed to gaze off into the distance, to a point beyond the horizon. People looking at him got the sense that his mind always grappled with hard-to-solve problems.

His partner was Professor Robert Geoffrey Edwards, a visionary British researcher specializing in the study of human embryos, tiny little organisms no bigger than a freckle. Bob Edwards was more relaxed, an outgoing, rugged outdoorsman with bottle-glass spectacles and a kindly face. He had a wide, easy smile and a hearty laugh.

Conception the old-fashioned way involves one man and one woman. Various simultaneously erotic and precise biological factors must take place inside the woman's body at the right time, under the right circumstances, in the correct order. The health of both sperm and egg, as well as the timing of their release and meeting, must be impeccable for a baby to be created.

By contrast, in Oldham in the 1970s, these two men were obsessed by what went *wrong* inside a woman's body during conception. They sought to correct nature's mistakes through a science fiction recipe for procreation. Steptoe and Edwards were working toward a single goal: to replicate human reproduction by extracting a woman's egg, fertilizing it with sperm in a test tube, and implanting the resulting embryo back in the woman's uterus to create a baby. They called the process, as yet unproven, in vitro fertilization. They were determined to create pregnancies in a glass tube for couples who could not conceive by themselves the old-fashioned way.

Why did they want to do such a thing? Were they mad scientists? Misguided do-gooders with a God complex? Biotech businessmen looking to create a multibillion-dollar industry?

Not exactly.

The two men shared a revolutionary, humanitarian ideal: that everyone who wanted a baby should have a baby. They did not believe that nature, or human biological quirks in men's or women's bodies, should discriminate against people who craved babies. Instead, they fervently agreed that the inability to have babies should be treated as a disease that could be cured. That doctors could, and should, use their knowledge and skills to help fix nature's reproductive mistakes.

"Eye hoop they all have babies!" Professor Edwards told *Washington Post* reporter Liza Mundy in 2005 in his Yorkshire brogue. "What coood be better than a baby?"

Although surrogacy and ART represent recent, revolutionary, extremely expensive medical developments, human eggs have been fertilized outside a woman's body since the 1940s. An American doctor, John Rock, and his research assistant Miriam Friedman Menkin, first successfully fertilized eggs with sperm in a test tube in a lab in Boston in 1944—the very year the American Society for Reproductive Medicine was founded by a tiny group of fertility experts in Chicago.

Dr. John Rock was a Harvard-educated ob-gyn, father of five, and eventual grandfather of nineteen. He married the granddaughter of Civil War hero William Tecumseh Sherman, Anna "Nan" Thorndike, in 1924. He then went on to get credit for inventing the birth control pill in 1960 despite being a devout Roman Catholic. Now that's a fact the church doesn't publicize—that a Catholic doctor oversaw the clinical trials that resulted in Enovid, the first FDA-approved birth control pill. Rock's brainy assistant, Menkin, was a Cornell-educated divorcée. Together, they were the first medical team to fertilize live ova with live sperm outside the human body.

However, Rock and Menkin never attempted to transplant the fertilized eggs back inside a woman's uterus. They let all their fertilized embryos die in the lab. Test tube fertilization was accomplishment enough.

For John and Miriam, at least.

But not for infertile women desperate for babies.

In the 1940s and 1950s, after the results of his experiments were published, women deluged Dr. Rock with written inquiries and desperate phone calls about how their eggs could be fertilized. The next phase of IVF research proved both exciting and controversial. During the 1960s and 1970s, many doctors and scientists attempted to transplant fertilized embryos back into women's bodies. Infertile women urgently wanted and needed medical help.

Yet federal regulations restricting IVF experimentation curbed the race to create the first test tube baby. In 1973, a New York doctor at Columbia-Presbyterian Hospital attempted IVF. His boss stopped the experiment, removed the fertilizing egg from an incubator, and exposed the embryo to room temperature. This halted the cell division necessary for maturation.

The IVF movement was at a crossroads, in the United States, at least. The technology was almost there. American society wasn't.

In 1962, back across the pond in England, Professor Edwards and Dr. Steptoe continued experimenting with in vitro fertilization, focusing on the critical step of getting a fertilized embryo back into a woman's uterus. Steptoe had developed an innovation in abdominal surgery called laparoscopy. The procedure allowed the easy retrieval of mature human eggs—a critical advancement in the science of IVF.

Doctors Steptoe and Edwards spent nearly two decades experimenting with the multiple steps of IVF. They completed over 750 experiments. They attempted over eighty embryo transplants with anesthetized women desperate for babies naked on their examining table.

Each and every transplant failed to produce a pregnancy.

Then came the very first Big Fat Positive.

In 1977, a thirty-year-old British woman, Lesley Brown, and her husband, a truck driver named John she had met when she was only sixteen, had been trying for nine years to conceive a baby. Lesley Brown produced healthy eggs, but her fallopian tubes were blocked by disease. The scarring prevented her eggs from making it to her uterus to meet up with John's sperm during ovulation. For thousands of years, women like Lesley Brown spent their entire fertility life span trying to conceive a child, without a single pregnancy, and without ever understanding why their bodies could not make a baby.

Steptoe and Edwards were still experimenting. Critics of their research predicted their treatment would lead to terrible abnormalities and birth defects. Every one of the doctors' attempts at in vitro had failed.

But Lesley Brown was willing to try anything in order to get pregnant. She agreed to let the doctors try to fertilize one of her eggs, using her husband's sperm, in a test tube outside her body.

One cold November day in 1977, Steptoe successfully extracted a single newly ovulated egg from one very anesthetized Lesley Brown. In a room nearby, John Brown provided fresh semen—20 million sperm, give or take a few. Edwards doused the single mature egg extracted from Lesley's ovaries with her husband's fresh sperm. The resulting fertilized embryo grew in a petri dish for two days, dividing and subdividing. Then, once the fertilized embryo had matured and stabilized, Edwards transferred it back into Lesley's uterus. In December, Lesley Brown was officially pregnant. The resulting baby— Louise Joy Brown—was born in 1978, shattering centuries of infertility.

For good.

A breakthrough had been achieved in the old town of Oldham. The first successful in vitro fertilization was quickly replicated around the globe. Five thousand miles away in Calcutta, India, physician Subash Mukhopadyay had been performing experiments on his own with primitive instruments and a household refrigerator. His tinkering resulted in a test tube baby, later named "Durga" (alias Kanupriya Agarwal), who was born on October 3, 1978, three months after Baby Brown's arrival.[23]

Within four years, Louise Brown had a younger sister, Natalie, also born via IVF under Steptoe and Edwards's tutelage. Natalie Brown was the world's fortieth test tube baby; soon after, people stopped counting. The process of retrieving eggs from a woman's ovaries via laparoscopy became routine in Europe and the United States, requiring ten minutes in an outpatient doctor's office. Almost every subsequent fertility innovation—the injection of hormones to trigger ovulation, intracytoplasmic sperm injection, gamete intrafallopian transfer, embryo cryopreservation, egg donation, and even gestational surrogates—has built upon Steptoe and Edwards's bedrock IVF methodology.

Because of Steptoe and Edwards, these days, in vitro fertilization is a procedure that you and I refer to conversationally. Like everyone else on the planet, we throw the internationally known acronym IVF around casually.

As in, "My sister did IVF and now she has twins."

Or, "My boss didn't get married until she was forty-two, did IVF once, and now she has a three-year-old."

Or, "Who cares if that numbnut broke up with you on your thirty-ninth birthday? You can just freeze your eggs and do IVF when you're fifty."

However, what Edwards and Steptoe accomplished was anything but blasé. Their focus led to what many believe to be the single most impactful technologic invention affecting women's reproductive lives and their ability to have babies today. In 2010, in Stockholm, Sweden, their medical audacity won the Nobel Prize.[24]

Edwards and Steptoe tackled a terrible affliction that ironically was never a big problem for the human race. Not on a macro level. Look around: there are over 7 billion of us, after all.

What made their determination so compelling, compassionate, and unique is that infertility is a problem *only* for the person who's got it. Then infertility can become an insurmountable, intensely personal, crushing, soul-sucking, lifelong affliction. Steptoe and Edwards's 1978 success did not banish infertility—or its heartbreak—from the face of the earth. But what the good doctors created, along with their amazing medical innovations, was hope.

Gerry and Rhonda Wile first traveled to India thirty years after Steptoe and Edwards's first test tube baby was born. They left from Arizona for Mumbai on Friday, April 4, 2008. Rhonda had never before ventured outside North America. Gerry's military service had taken him to Europe and the Middle East, but this was his first trip to Asia in civilian clothes. Although they'd been married for eight years, in many ways, this trip resembled the honeymoon the Wiles had never had the time, or the money, to take.

If Gerry and Rhonda Wile had been born in Mumbai, they would never have met, dated, or married. Separation of the sexes and arranged marriage are still commonplace in India. A national poll conducted in 2006 showed that 72 percent of Indian respondents believed that parents—fathers in particular—should have the final say in their children's choice of marriage partners.[25] Although in a curious way, Rhonda's parents, especially her father, did play a key role in their marriage.

When the Wiles landed at Chhatrapati Shivaji International Airport, Rhonda, in her wrinkled travel clothes, was first struck by the heat and humidity, as powerful as a blast from an oven. And then the smells—of women sweating in silk saris, men in the khaki pants introduced by the British during their long reign, the spices, the diesel exhaust fumes. And the bright colors of the children's school uniforms, the chocolate eyes of their taxi driver, the colorful billboards lining the road from the airport to their hotel.

Until a few years ago, several of the floors at the international airport were unpaved dirt. Most of the running water is not safe to drink—in the few places that have indoor plumbing. Electricity is scarce as well, and current surges and blackouts, even in hotels, hospitals, and the airports, are common occurrences

Over 20 million people live on the cluster of seven islands collectively known as Mumbai, the world's most populated metropolis. Mumbai is located on the west coast of the country, and is the capital of Maharashtra, India's second-largest state. The city's name was officially changed from Bombay to Mumbai in 1995, reflecting its ancient patron goddess Mumbadevi. But the former name is often still used.

The city sprawls along a deep natural harbor in the Arabian Sea, which long ago attracted the traders who established Mumbai as India's commercial capital. Once a Portuguese princess's wedding gift, later a paean to neo-Gothic British architecture and culture, Mumbai today is an enigma of slums, world-class hospitals, film production companies, and expensive skyscrapers clinging to pieces of the globe's priciest real estate. Like Manhattan and Hong Kong, Mumbai epitomizes a beggar's dream—and an urban planner's nightmare.

The sound of Mumbai today, at any hour of any day of the week, is a never-ending cacophony of honks and whistles coming from the cars, bicycles, rickshaws, motorcycles, and motorized carts that clog every road, and most sidewalks, throughout the city. Despite the malarial mosquitoes and less-than-pure water sources, the most dangerous act in Mumbai is simply crossing the street.

Rhonda and Gerry celebrated their eighth wedding anniversary on April 14, 2008, at Lilavati Hospital in the heart of Mumbai.

"There was no more romantic or exciting place in the world, for both of us at that moment, than that hospital in India, eight thousand miles from home, making a baby," says Gerry now. "It was a miracle, what we were doing together."

It was also miraculous, in an entirely different way, that two people had to travel so far, and spend so much money, to make a baby together.

The Wiles found the city's roads and walkways muddy and wet, as they often are leading up to Mumbai's monsoon rains. The air is hot and humid and polluted much of the year. Packs of small, skinny wild dogs and 2,000-pound humpbacked Brahman cows with long, dark brown horns roam the streets freely, sleeping undisturbed in front of ATMs and gelaterias. Over 55 percent of Mumbai's people live on dirt floors in makeshift metal shacks in the city's enormous slums. Most slums have inadequate toilet and washing facilities; on the way to the hospital one day, Gerry and Rhonda saw a child squat and lift her pink ruffled skirt to defecate on a crowded roadside as their taxi whizzed by.

Not the ideal place that anyone, particularly Americans who routinely carry hand sanitizer in our purses, sterilize our vegetables with spray cleaners, and refuse to sit on a public toilet without an untouched, crinkle-free paper seat liner, would envision to have a baby.

"To our surprise," Rhonda says with a laugh now, in her American kitchen two continents away from Mumbai, "we both felt right at home."

# Part 2

---

## Baby Making Becomes
## Big Business

*Modern surrogacy blew* a milestone on a misty Kentucky morning in 1980, when Rhonda and Gerry Wile were still tweens.

At 10:42 A.M. on November 9, 1980, in the maternity ward of Audubon Hospital in Louisville, Kentucky, an empathetic but troubled thirty-seven-year-old Illinois mother of three delivered an eight-pound ten-ounce baby. A healthy boy. The baby was conceived using the woman's egg, fertilized via artificial insemination with the sperm of a man whose wife was infertile. In a precedent-setting legal arrangement, the woman, who called herself Elizabeth Kane to protect her family's identity, agreed via contract to relinquish all rights to the baby at birth in exchange for $10,000.

Elizabeth Kane was the first recorded traditional commercial surrogate—a woman who was paid to use one of her eggs to create and carry a baby for someone else—in the United States.

"It's the father's child," she acknowledged in a 1980 interview with *People* magazine, countering accusations that she'd sold her baby.[1] "I'm simply growing it for him."

The contracted birth occurred less than three years after the first IVF baby was born in England, an early indicator of how quickly fertility innovations would spread as the end of the twentieth century approached. However, IVF's medical advances actually had no bearing on Elizabeth Kane's pregnancy. Kane became pregnant via artificial insemination, not IVF. Hypothetically, any fertile woman could have been a commercial, traditional surrogate like Elizabeth Kane years, or decades, or centuries before.

Louise Joy Brown's scientific creation marked a profound medical innovation. But an equally significant breakthrough occurred in people's *minds*. The amount of global media coverage the first IVF birth received made it possible—conceivable, acceptable—for other new forms of assisted reproduction to flourish in the United States and around the world.

An invisible barrier had been shattered. Following the first test tube baby, infertile couples and their doctors began experimenting with the creation of babies using surrogate mothers like Kane. People opened their minds to the idea of *paying* other women to conceive and carry babies for them.

Elizabeth Kane's 1980 commercial endeavor also revealed the mix of emotions many surrogates feel, and the moral and societal complications that accompany traditional surrogacy.

"I had empathized with relatives and friends who were childless," Kane explained, with stilted emotional detachment, in *People* magazine.

"I often wondered why I couldn't bear a child for one of them. I was naïve to think that this could be just another pregnancy, that I could keep from becoming attached to the child. I did not and do not want another child. I cannot handle another child financially or emotionally. But I did love this baby. I often lay awake in the darkness talking silently to him, waiting breathlessly for the next poke under the ribs or bump of his head against my pelvis."

Even after giving birth, Kane continued to insist the surrogacy had been positive. At least that's what she told *People* magazine at the time—although her statement reads today suspiciously like a scripted, hollow response:

"The baby was going home to his parents, and I was elated. I knew he belonged with his father and mother, who needed him and wanted him. The joy I had received from seeing him in their arms would last a lifetime. I went home with no regrets at all. I don't ever want his mother to feel that she has to share him with someone else. She is his mother. My part is over."

Unfortunately, unlike surrogates today, Elizabeth Kane was completely alone. She subsequently wrote a book about the experience that made it clear she had no idea what she was in for, psychologically, when she agreed to be a surrogate.[2] Unlike today's surrogates and infertility sufferers, back in the early 1980s, Elizabeth Kane received no support or counseling, and she had no peers to comfort her. Perhaps as a result, she experienced depression, financial troubles, and the end of her marriage. Ultimately, Kane turned against surrogacy and became an advocate for the National Coalition Against Surrogacy.

You may not recall Elizabeth Kane, but you probably know the name of the most famous traditional surrogate in the United States: Mary Beth Whitehead. Whitehead was a married New Jersey mother of two who signed a contract to be the traditional surrogate for a childless couple in the mid-1980s when IVF and surrogacy were still medically experimental, as well as socially, legally, and ethically controversial.

In 1984, Mary Beth Whitehead answered a newspaper ad for women willing to help infertile couples have children. She was hired by William and Betsy Stern, and signed a contract paying her $10,000 to carry a baby fertilized with William Stern's sperm via artificial insemination. She would be paid the full amount when the baby was born.

That baby—a girl, later known as "Baby M"—was born on March 27, 1986. Soon afterward, Mary Beth Whitehead, like many birth mothers, made the emotional, difficult decision that she could not give up the baby. It felt like her baby, no matter what contract she had signed. She refused the $10,000 surrogacy payment. She named the baby Sara Elizabeth Whitehead and her husband, Rick Whitehead, was listed on the birth certificate as the baby's father. (It was common practice in the United States at the time for the husband of a pregnant woman to be listed as the legal father, regardless of whether or not he was the biological one.)

Judge Harvey Sorkow made several decisions in favor of the intended parents, William and Betsy Stern—and in favor of surrogacy contracts. After the case was appealed to the New Jersey Supreme Court, the Sterns were given primary custody of Mary Beth Whitehead's baby. But even the state's highest court struggled with the ethics presented by surrogacy, granting Mary Beth Whitehead the right to visit her own child. A surrogacy precedent was established: the legal agreement Whitehead signed trumped the majority of rights stemming from her biological connection as the baby's mother.

The case grabbed national headlines because surrogacy was shocking at the time; plus any controversy involving motherhood and babies tends to sell newspapers. The Mary Beth Whitehead case forced the nation to examine, up close, the underbelly of traditional surrogacy: most people, women especially, recognize that the bond between mother and child can feel more binding than any legal contract. New Jersey appellate court outlawed surrogacy as a result of the case. Paid surrogacy is still illegal there today.

In 1978, the conception geniuses Steptoe and Edwards hardly envisioned a $10-billion market or a revolution in surrogate pregnancies around the world. They were thinking only of helping women conceive and carry babies with their own eggs in their own bodies. The doctors' decades of experiments in the 1960s and 1970s focused exclusively on using IVF to put a woman's own fertilized embryos back into her womb. There was no reason to think IVF would spark a worldwide revolution in surrogacy. After all, "traditional" surrogacy had always been an option, albeit not widely sanctioned, long before IVF, and it had never become a mainstream fertility treatment.

However, given how overwhelmingly powerful the procreation desire can be, as soon as Edwards and Steptoe discovered how to reinstall a fertilized embryo back inside a woman's uterus, it became inevitable that one day, somewhere, a desperate woman with faulty eggs or problems with her uterus would plead with her doctor to utilize IVF to create a baby from someone else's egg and put it into her uterus to make it *her* baby. Or to put her own healthy eggs into *another* woman's uterus to gestate that tiny, test tube embryo into her very own living, breathing, bawling infant. Some infertile couples—along with ambitious, entrepreneurial doctors—saw that IVF technologies opened up a bold new world of possibilities. The miracles of science, along with legal contracts and money, together meant that one day, anyone would be able to have a baby to call his or her own.

Thus the first test tube baby led, unintentionally, to the rapid rise of surrogate pregnancies in the United States and elsewhere. This seems obvious in hindsight. But, initially, no one envisioned the vast and sweeping changes the first IVF baby would bring to motherhood.

The next logical surrogacy milestone—a woman who gestated and gave birth to a baby genetically unrelated to her—took fewer than seven years. In 1985, the respected *New England Journal of Medicine* reported that Wulf Utian, a South African gynecologist and reproductive biologist, had created a baby using one woman's uterus, a man's sperm, and an unrelated woman's egg. The first gestational surrogate pregnancy.

Both traditional and gestational surrogacy caught on in the United States more quickly than in other countries, due to demand for babies, lack of organized cultural or religious opposition, and the wealth of couples able to afford IVF and surrogacy. The new surrogacy "agencies" found that whenever infertile couples were offered a choice between gestational or traditional surrogacy, far more couples chose gestational surrogates over traditional ones, despite the extra cost of IVF. GS paved the path for surrogacy to become a widespread solution to infertility.

The lure of commercial gestational surrogacy is that the baby, from conception, belongs to the intended parents. Although each of the three baby benefactors—egg donor, sperm donor, and uterus provider—plays a critical role, none can argue the baby is their baby. The IPs plan for the baby. They are legally and financially responsible for the baby. They control all decisions from preconception to birth.

The legal morass is simplified because it is easier to recognize the intended parents as the legitimate parents. In gestational surrogacy, *intent* to create a baby—not biology—becomes the factor determining a baby's "real" parents. There is no genetic connection between pregnant woman and baby; this mind-bending but very clear boundary makes the experience easier all around, for parents, surrogates, doctors, lawyers, and the babies they create together.

Parents must confront the full, intense weight of decades of parenthood condensed into a few sheets of legal paper before their child has been conceived. The IPs pick a surrogate, as well as egg and/or sperm donors, essentially selecting their baby's biology. Additional decisions that usually take months or years to make must be settled in days, and captured in binding legal agreements.

Commercial surrogacy contracts require parents to list who the guardians will be if both parents die, and how custody will be handled if the couple divorces before the baby is born. Whether it is Elton John or the neighbor next door, IPs must commit via contract whether to reduce a multiple pregnancy, or terminate a pregnancy if prenatal tests show certain birth defects. Financial penalties are assigned—miscarriage, still-birth, and hysterectomy are all given an economic value—in terms of how much the surrogate must be paid if they occur.

This level of control sickens some and frightens others. Is this genetic engineering? Outsourcing procreation? Maybe.

But control offers thrilling compensation, too. Your grand-mother was from Paris? There are lots of French egg donors. You've always had a thing for height, dark hair, and strong features? Pick those qualities for a sperm donor (just exactly as you did, or didn't, when searching for a husband or wife).

The unborn—unconceived—baby's life is in the IPs' hands. An intense responsibility. But one that is, in fact, very natural.

While the good doctors Steptoe and Edwards were feverishly trying (and failing) to create the first test tube baby, our Arizona firefighter with the baby tattoo—Gerald David Wile—was busy being born the old-fashioned way. He arrived on March 13, 1966, in New Brunswick, Canada. Gerry was the second of three children, squashed between an older brother and a younger sister. After his father completed military stints in Germany and a smattering of postings in the Canadian Air Force, the family settled back in their small Canadian home-town, New Germany.

New Germany was a *very* small hometown, population 464.

Gerry's father's nickname said a lot about the Wile family and Gerry's boyhood: people called Gerry's father "Moose." Gerry took after his father, even as a boy. Gerry was never a small child; he already resembled the six-foot-tall, handsome, muscular military man he would grow up to be. He was one of those children about whom mothers say, "He's all boy." Athletic, rough, easygoing.

As a child coming up in this tiny and isolated far northern

town, with strong military influences and a dad named Moose, his idea of gender roles never strayed from the strictly traditional, either.

"I just got the idea that a mom cooks and cleans, and a dad works," Gerry says now, looking around his cluttered kitchen in Mesa, far from the cold isolation of Canada's ocean playground. "I liked being around little kids and I figured I'd have a family, but I never thought for a minute much about how or when I'd ever have 'em."

Growing up in Nova Scotia, Gerry never knew a person who was not Caucasian, not Lutheran, and not Canadian. As a boy tooling around a town of fewer than five hundred people, he knew them all. One summer in high school Gerry worked on an eight-man highway construction crew. Two of the other hires were also named . . . Gerald Wile.

One autumn night when he was nineteen, Gerry leaned his motorcycle around a blind corner, only to discover a car double-parked in the middle of the road. The owner was checking his mailbox. To avoid the car, Gerry steered the bike off the road into the Canadian woods. His right foot, still in his boot, was twisted backward in the crash. His leg was badly shredded. He wasn't even twenty years old when his doctor told him he might never walk again.

To regain full usage of the right foot, ankle, and lower leg, he needed almost a year of intense physical therapy. Every day, Gerry worked through excruciating joint and muscle pain. The assistant to his physiotherapist was a pretty young woman. She comforted him after his agonizing sessions, listening to him as no other woman ever had.

A single mom, she needed someone. It felt good to be needed. Gerry married her later that year. He was twenty years old.

Gerry adopted her two-year-old daughter. Two years later the young couple had a daughter of their own. Like many twenty-two-year-old fathers, Gerry doesn't remember much of the girls' early childhood milestones. Asked twenty years later if he recalls how the girls were toilet trained, he shrugs and laughs as if considering how to program a rocket launch to Saturn.

A few years into the marriage, his wife had a brush with cancer. Worried from a magazine article about possible links between the Pill and cancer, she told Gerry she was convinced taking birth control pills caused it. As an act of support and practicality so his wife could abandon taking the Pill, Gerry had a vasectomy. The Canadian military, which Gerry had joined, performed the surgery at no cost.

Gerry was still in his twenties. It never occurred to him that one day he might want another child. Or two or three.

The marriage faltered. Gerry and his wife were too young. Gerry was gone on military deployments for stretches that lasted as long as a year, leaving his wife to care for the girls almost as a single mother. After one particularly lengthy absence, Gerry came home to an angry, disillusioned wife demanding a divorce.

Gerry and his ex-wife shared custody of the girls. Then his ex-wife wanted to move back to her hometown; Gerry gave in to keep the peace. The change meant he lost all daily contact with both of his daughters. No school plays. No soccer games. No parent-teacher conferences. It was as if Gerry wasn't a parent any longer.

Gerry had been gone for long periods. He had not been closely involved in his daughters' daily lives. Yet when he lost them, their absence cut deeply in ways he'd never anticipated. Two decades later, his younger girl is deeply involved in church missions to Ecuador, Africa, and India. His older daughter has four kids of her own. Gerry is now a grandfather.

Talking about the loss of contact with his young daughters can still bring Gerry Wile, a tough man who doesn't remember wanting to have children, to tears.

In 1978, there were zero surrogacy agencies in the United States.[3]

The first American baby created via IVF was born in 1981.

By 1987, the year Steptoe died, tragically before knowing his work had won the Nobel Prize, there were four hundred IVF clinics in the United States alone.[4]

Thirty years after the first test tube baby, in 2008 alone, 61,426 ART babies were born in the United States who otherwise would not have existed.

Every decade since 1978, the number of ART babies born in the United States has more than doubled.

The Centers for Disease Control estimates that 1 percent of American babies born each year are due to some form of ART.

The CDC also estimates there are 500,000 frozen embryos in the United States, awaiting thawing and possible implantation in someone's uterus.

Over four million children have been born around the world as a result of the spread of IVF, surrogacy, and other forms of assisted reproductive technology. Robert Edwards got his wish: millions of babies being born due to the technology he and Patrick Steptoe pioneered. Teenagers and young adults afflicted with cancer have been able to preserve their reproductive options, even if facing radiation, hysterectomy, and bilateral orchiectomy, the fancy term for removal of the testicles. Childless women have become mothers through eggs donated by younger, more fertile women. Gay men who always dreamed of being fathers now are fathers.

Ask anyone who has a child due to surrogacy and ART, and the news is all heartwarming and positive.

But of course, there are negatives.

Surrogacy and the ART practices that remedy infertility remain vexed by prickly financial, medical, religious, societal, ethical, legal, political, and feminist adjudications. An elitist marketplace has developed; if you are wealthy and infertile, you can have children.[5] If you are poor and infertile, chances are you cannot afford surrogacy, since conception, gestation, and birth of a surrogate baby can cost more than the lifetime expense of raising a child.[6] Inevitably, such a large market combined with such vermilion emotions will lead to a degree of fraud, waste, heartbreak, and corruption. Doctors and scientists excitedly—and sometimes predatorily—develop and market hope in the form of promising new treatments and solutions.

Ethicists untangle—or tangle—the moral implications of creating, and sometimes destroying, human life. Insurance companies grapple with what treatments to cover and how many repeat procedures to reimburse—and what to deny. Egg donor ads—*Apply online! Call 1-2-3-Donate! Earn $5,000!*—dominate morning drive-time radio shows trawling for young, highly fertile women in their mid-twenties. Doctors battle with couples to decide whether to "reduce" multiple pregnancies; at the extreme we have Nadya Suleman, the California mother who bore eight babies simultaneously and became known around the world as the infamous Octomom.

Advances in surrogacy force all of us to ask a new question: what does it mean to be a family?

Take rocker Melissa Etheridge. In the late 1990s, Etheridge and her partner, filmmaker Julie Cypher, wanted to become parents. Instead of using an anonymous sperm donor, the lesbian couple asked longtime friend and rock legend David Crosby, of Crosby, Stills & Nash fame, to be their sperm donor. Crosby agreed, and legally relinquished his parental rights. Cypher, using her own eggs, gave birth to the couple's daughter Bailey in 1997, followed by son Beckett in 1998. At first, Cypher and Etheridge didn't reveal Crosby's role in their family making. The children's parentage fueled an intense rumor mill that included everybody from Brad Pitt to Bruce

Springsteen. Then, in early 2000, Etheridge, Cypher, Beckett, Bailey, Crosby, and his wife Jan posed for the cover of *Rolling Stone*, revealing Crosby's paternity and details of their arrangement in "Melissa's Secret."[7]

But families that start out complicated can get even more complicated, especially when celebrities are involved. A few months after the splashy *Rolling Stone* cover appeared on newsstands, Cypher and Etheridge split. Cypher later married Matthew Hale and returned to relative anonymity in Los Angeles, working as a yoga therapist. Melissa Etheridge then married Tammy Lynn Michaels; the couple had twins, this time using an anonymous sperm donor and Tammy Lynn Michaels's eggs. And they later split as well.[8]

So, one family: a mom, Etheridge, who has no biological connection to any of the four children; two kids with Cypher as their biological mother, David Crosby as their bio dad, and Matthew Hale as their stepdad; Michaels's twins who are genetically related to their mother but no one else in the family; and let's not forget, one anonymous sperm donor.

Today, the family spectrum ranges from multiple parents to one parent: single mothers and fathers are two of the fastest-growing ART patient groups. Sometimes you can have three legal parents: in April 2007, a Pennsylvania appellate court ruled that two lesbian co-parents and their sperm donor friend were all legal parents of the children they had created.[9] You can also have one father and no mother: the same year, a Maryland man won a court case to have no mother listed on the birth certificate of twins he created using his sperm, a gestational surrogate, and donor eggs.[10]

More than anything, surrogacy has expanded—and continues to transform—what it means to be a mother, and how each of us defines our family. As the very idea of "family" changes, both fathers and mothers are becoming expendable in ways unfathomable prior to gestational surrogacy and assisted reproductive medicine. The societal changes and rapid acceleration of assisted pregnancy across formerly barren groups may interest ethicists, preachers, politicians, psychologists, and doctors.

However, the eight million people trying, and failing, to reproduce on their own, aren't asking these perplexing questions.

They just want babies.

A *pretty blond* baby girl, whose parents named her Rhonda, was born on June 17, 1970, in Niagara Falls, Canada, over one thousand miles southwest of where four-year-old Gerry Wile was tearing up his small Nova Scotia hometown. Doctors had warned Shirley Reycraft that the pregnancy might kill her, but she desperately wanted a fourth baby. Rhonda was the last girl in the perfectly patterned Reycraft family: boy, girl, boy, girl.

Her father had always loved the name Rhonda. He had, in fact, wanted to use the name for his *first* daughter. However, the inaugural Reycraft girl was born only sixteen months after the Reycraft's firstborn, Ron. Shirley Reycraft worried that strangers might assume "Ron" and "Rhonda" were twins. She made her husband wait a few more years, but he eventually got his Rhonda.

Rhonda grew up watching *Romper Room*, and later, *Happy Days*. She loved playing dress-up. Her favorite candy bar was called Eat-More, a chewy chocolate, toffee, and peanut confection that came in a green and yellow wrapper. She never had a favorite color—she was the kind of sunny girl who loved *every* color.

Rhonda's mom is a pretty, trim, five-foot-nine woman whose glossy hair is now yellow-silver. In person, she's outgoing and gregarious. Even in Rhonda's family photos, lining her Arizona living room shelves today, Shirley Reycraft looks straight at the camera, head back in laughter.

However, being pregnant four times did not rank as delights in Shirley Reycraft's life. She suffered debilitating morning sickness throughout her four pregnancies. Her doctor sternly cautioned the Reycrafts that each pregnancy and labor had the power to destroy her. Rhonda herself was born nearly dead, with her umbilical cord wrapped around her neck. Yet throughout Rhonda's childhood, her mom told and retold the story of her profound joy at each of her children's births, weaving a woman's pain and sacrifice during pregnancy with the blessing of a child's healthy birth.

Rhonda's mom was happy as a stay-at-home wife and mother in 1960s and 1970s Canada. Yet she stressed female independence to her children, insisting that her two perfectly spaced teenage daughters must have the practical ability to earn a living in case they needed to be self-sufficient in life. Rhonda's older sister became a Canadian mounted police officer at twenty-three. Rhonda got her three-year nursing diploma at twenty-four.

Rhonda's parents recently celebrated their fiftieth wedding anniversary. They still hold hands. Watching them makes you wonder whether a reality show crew lurks nearby. But, no, it's true love.

"It actually might have been easier for us kids if they occasionally fought or got angry with each other," Rhonda explains now, shrugging her shoulders. "We grew up with a *Leave It to Beaver* marriage as a model. We were all real naïve when it came to the realities of more typical relationships. We just assumed all marriages were like theirs."

Rhonda would find out soon enough that married life could be more *Jersey Shore* than June Cleaver.

Soon after she earned her nursing degree, Rhonda moved south to the United States, to Lake Charles, Louisiana. She married a Texas man she'd been engaged to for thirteen months. Her new husband often declared to Rhonda (and others) that she was the best thing to ever happen to him. He said that after working so hard to get his golden girl, he was never letting her go. Rhonda's own happily-ever-after married life had begun.

Yet there were trip wires. The young couple fought too often. Rhonda started to suspect her husband was an alcoholic. And a compulsive liar.

Rhonda began to feel dread creeping like a spider on her leg every day when she headed home from work. This relationship was nothing like her parents' fairy-tale marriage.

A year and a month after their wedding, one day Rhonda left as usual for her job as an assistant nursing director at a local rehab center. When she came home that evening, she found a small shrine on the flowered bedspread she'd smoothed so carefully that morning before going to work.

"The outfit I wore on our first date. Some Mardi Gras beads we'd worn together. His favorite picture of us together."

And a good-bye note.

Baffled, heartbroken, and feeling helpless, Rhonda became unnerved and depressed. She cried all day. She couldn't get dressed, eat, or make it to work. Her long-distance family intervened; even at twenty-seven, she was still the baby. Her brother, who was married and living in Canada, flew to Louisiana. Within three weeks of finding her husband's bizarre note, her brother helped Rhonda, who was still in a daze, quit her job and pack all her belongings into her SUV.

Her only consolation was one prized possession. A few months before, Rhonda had noticed a small black-and-white classified ad in the local Lake Charles *American Press*: MIXED CATAHOULA AUSTRALIAN SHEPHERD PUPPIES, $25.

Rhonda went to the breeder's home one night after work, still dressed in her nursing clothes. It was already dark out back where the two remaining puppies whined in a small wire pen with their Australian shepherd mother. A friendly dark brown puppy ran to Rhonda, standing up on the pen wire with his huge front paws and licking her face. Based on his paws, and the size of his Catahoula father, this outgoing boy was going to grow up to be a *huge* alpha male. Too huge for Rhonda's small, neatly kept home.

Rhonda looked in the back corner of the pen where another puppy sat quietly, as if waiting for her.

"It was love at first sight," says Rhonda.

The small, white female puppy had a left ear that looked like someone had dipped it in black ink. She was the spitting image of Nipper, the famous RCA icon poking her head into the brand's gramophone. She was eight weeks old. Rhonda had zero pet supplies at home—no kibble, no water dish, no dog bed.

"But I couldn't stand to leave without her," Rhonda explains.

The puppy rode home that night in a cardboard box on Rhonda's upholstered backseat. Rhonda stopped at Walmart to buy a few pet essentials. When Rhonda came back to the car, the little white puppy was standing with her black nose pressed against the driver's window, looking out the glass for her new owner.

Rhonda named her Frankie.

Now, with her husband suddenly and completely MIA, Rhonda drove to Florida with Frankie on the passenger seat next to her. Every few hours, she burst into tears, but she kept on driving. Following in another car were her sister-in-law and two nieces, who'd come to Louisiana to help her move, to make sure Rhonda left Lake Charles.

The short-term plan was for Rhonda and Frankie to resettle with her oldest brother's family in Florida. Her brother and his wife, who had three young children and a small one-story Florida home, rearranged their house so Rhonda could stay in their five-year-old son's room while the boy slept on his parents' bedroom floor. She could take the time she needed to recover from the devastating abandonment of a man she thought would be her mate for life, surrounded by her brother's noisy, loving, hopefully distracting, family.

A few weeks later, she received a letter saying her husband wanted a divorce. But it wasn't from *him*. The note was from his parents.

Should Rhonda believe the words on the page? Was her husband too cowardly to end the marriage directly? In her heart, Rhonda knew he still wanted to be married, and was succumbing to pressure from his parents, who had never cottoned to her. Maybe she could counter their influence if she could just talk to him. Every time she called his parents' Texas phone number, they claimed they had no idea where their son might be.

At the end of February, Rhonda shut down. She had ricocheted from fury one minute, to numbing depression the next, for over three months. Mornings were the worst. She woke each day already feeling drained of hope, cast aside like an empty tube of sunscreen on the beach. The bleak days stretched before her. Getting through each twenty-four-hour period felt nearly impossible, like clinging to the slippery edges of an old abandoned well.

One gray February morning after her sister-in-law and the kids had left the house, still in her pajamas, sitting on her nephew's twin bed holding Frankie, Rhonda emptied all her prescription bottles of antidepressant medicine onto the Batman comforter.

"I didn't want to bother my brother's family anymore," Rhonda says as she describes the troubled thought process now, fifteen years later. "I knew my parents would adopt Frankie. There was nothing about me that anyone was going to miss. My husband didn't love me. I had no kids that would be devastated by my being gone. No one would ever want me again. I felt worthless. Life was too much for me."

As a nurse, staring at the round white tablets littering the bedspread like leftover confetti, she knew there weren't enough pills.

"I swallowed them anyway," she explains.

Her brother, who was just about to leave for work, found her rummaging through his bathroom looking for more medicine. Although the antidepressant overdose had yet to take full effect, he knew from her shuffling gate and unfocused eyes what she'd done. He called their mother in Canada. After he hung up the phone, he drove his little sister to an emergency suicide intervention center.

Despite the fog of the overdose, Rhonda insisted that if she were to be hospitalized, her nursing license could be revoked. She was also in the process of applying for a green card from U.S. Immigration under spousal sponsorship. Her brother worried that the loss of hope for the future would destroy his fragile younger sister. The doctor examined the empty prescription containers and confirmed that Rhonda hadn't accumulated a lethal dose. So instead of admitting Rhonda to the hospital, her brother brought her home.

Rhonda never tried to hurt herself again.

Bizarrely, for the first time since walking out shortly before Thanksgiving, Rhonda's husband called her at her brother's home the night of the suicide attempt. Had one of her siblings called to tell him what she'd done? They all insisted they hadn't. Somehow, perhaps intuitively, her husband had known to call.

He cried guiltily when she admitted she'd tried to overdose. He said he loved her, that she was his world. He vowed to repair the marriage. He said he would never divorce her. He'd move to Florida, so that she could continue to have family support while they started over. Together.

Weeks passed. Rhonda was never able to contact him directly. His family maintained he was in jail and couldn't be reached. He never called her again.

Eventually, bitterly, Rhonda hired a private detective. Followed by a divorce lawyer. She mailed the divorce papers to her husband's parents in Houston, the only known address the detective could locate for him. The papers came back, signed on the dotted line. To this day, Rhonda is uncertain whether her husband, or one of his parents, signed the documents legalizing the end of her first marriage.

Without an American husband, Rhonda lost her spousal sponsorship immigration status. She had to halt her green card application; she would have to start the process over as an applicant sponsored by an employer, which could take years. Rhonda was twenty-eight. She had declared bankruptcy and relinquished the home in Louisiana she had shared during her thirteen months of marriage. She was depressed, ashamed about the inexplicable demise of her brief marriage, and financially dependent upon her parents—far from the independent woman her mother wanted her to be. She was a failure in the marriage arena which her parents made look so effortless. Her family feared another suicide attempt, no matter what Rhonda promised.

Her mother flew south. Together, they put Rhonda's few belongings in a U-Haul truck. The two women, plus Frankie, drove to Lake Charles to pack up Rhonda's remaining furniture and a few belongings from her married life. Then they drove home to Canada.

Rhonda sat in the passenger seat for the entire trip, 2,496 miles total. She was too listless to drive, and instead watched the miles slowly go by outside the window. Frankie insisted on sitting on the bench seat between them.

"For all three of us," Rhonda recalls grimly, "it felt like a very long trip."

Orlando, Florida, attracts over 51 million visitors every year—more than twice the number that visit Washington, D.C., annually. About 48 million are American. Close to four million travel from other countries.

Over eight in ten come to visit the area's world-class theme parks—SeaWorld, Universal Studios, Disney's Magic Kingdom, Blizzard Beach water park. And, of course, the 50,000-square-foot Disney Store where you can buy princess outfits, Mickey and Minnie salt shakers, Tinker Bell diamond jewelry, and underwear featuring your favorite Disney character.

Roughly 10 million slightly more serious visitors come to the nearby Orlando Convention Center for conferences and sales conventions. With 2.1 million square feet of space, the Center can accommodate a lot of friends. In October 2011, over ten thousand guests came to sunny Orlando for the American Society of Reproductive Medicine's sixty-seventh international convention.

The American Society for Reproductive Medicine, founded in 1944, now has seven thousand worldwide members. Every major city in the United States has a thriving fertility clinic. In Los Angeles, there are forty-eight separate infertility practices, most of which facilitate surrogate pregnancies. Fifty-four in Chicago. Forty-nine in Atlanta. Twenty-one in Iowa. Eleven in Phoenix. There are even two in Nova Scotia where Gerry Wile was born.

There were 8,500 registrants at the sixty-seventh annual gathering. Five days of panels and lectures. Over 1,000 exhibitors. The Merck booth alone measured 2,500 square feet, larger than many American homes.[11]

The ASRM gathering was, on the surface, like most sales conventions. Free cappuccinos. Squishy toy handouts. A booth with an indoor basketball hoop. Paradoxically overeager-yet-jaded salespeople ready to pounce on any registrants who slowed down in front of their booth.

What set ASRM apart: the products and technologies on display.

A ten-foot-long bulbous white sperm, the size of a beach

ball, rode an electric blue bicycle in front of the European Sperm Bank booth. A medical instruments video showed finely chiseled titanium scalpels trimming bloody fibroids inside a woman's uterus. The Centers for Disease Control Division of Reproductive Health offered decades of fertility clinic data on CD. The stress ball handed out by the Fertility Source was shaped like a human oocyte.

There were over a dozen companies specializing in egg donation. An equal number of sperm banks. International shipping firms that can pack and deliver cryogenically frozen fertilized human eggs. And three separate firms offering hundreds of international gestational surrogates to carry your baby.

Many of the exhibitors are household names—Abbott Labs, Pfizer, GE Healthcare. Others sound vaguely like names plucked from George Orwell's *1984*. California Cryobank (that's the booth with the basketball hoop). Norgenix. BabySentry. InVitroCare. Prodimed. Reprogenetics. Fertility Bridges. Vitrolife.

Clearblue Digital Pregnancy Tests? Well, naturally.

Infertility has become an enormous business. It's an industry, in fact—with $10 billion in annual revenue and millions of clients worldwide. This puts it on par with the U.S. textbook market, for instance, or the entire indoor heating and air-conditioning marketplace.

The clientele attending the industry's largest annual conference, all 8,500 of them, were unique, however. They were far more geographically diverse than most sales convention attendees. The infertility industry has gone completely global. The desire for babies—and doctors who can create them—is universal.

There was an Indian doctor wearing a baby-blue sari. Another dark-skinned woman in full brown burka. Several Israeli men wearing yarmulkes on their close-cropped heads. Mod Italians in faded blue jeans. Men and women speaking Korean, Spanish, Japanese, Hindi, and Swedish.

Most registrants had an intellectual, scholarly mien—and almost every one sported the no-nonsense glasses of heavy readers. They are the people who sat in the front row in elementary school, college, and eventually medical school. These are the foot soldiers of the global assisted reproduction community.

Finally, the oddest thing about the ASRM convention was that despite the thousands of square feet of synthetic hormones, ovulation drugs, medical devices, and innovative reproductive technologies proudly on display—representing decades, and billions of dollars, in research and development dedicated to creating babies for those who cannot do so themselves—there was not a baby in sight.

Although ART pioneers Steptoe and Edwards were all about babies, the assisted reproduction market they helped create has evolved to focus, fairly exclusively, on pregnancy. Achieving a pregnancy is the measure of success for infertility doctors, clinics, and patients. In fact, once you are pregnant, you are done with ART: both surrogates and traditional mothers get "referred out" of the clinic that helped them get pregnant, and turned over to a general practice ob-gyn. This explains the ironic reality that the ART industry pursues pregnancy as its primary quarry, with babies a distant, almost secondary, result.

However, the surrogacy subindustry is focused purely on babies. Creating a baby, not achieving pregnancy itself, is the ultimate goal for surrogates, their agencies, and the infertile clients who hire them. Conceiving and carrying a healthy baby to term is a comparative cakewalk for surrogates. Uncomplicated, drama-free pregnancies are what clients hire them for, and why they want to become surrogates in the first place. No one who hated being pregnant would want to be a surrogate mother. And you would never hire a woman who had trouble getting, or staying, pregnant to be yours.

Other complicated issues—financial, ethical, and medical questions—plague insurance adjusters, surrogates, doctors, sociologists, economists, spiritual advisers, and infertile intended parents, and they probably, one day, will perplex the babies that surrogates produce.

None of this bothers Jamie Williams.

Williams, an attractive, no-nonsense blonde with a throaty chuckle, had a two-year-old son when she first decided to become a surrogate in California in 1997, during the early days of surrogacy's societal acceptance. In 1997, confessing you were a surrogate, or had hired one, evoked shocked reactions—as if you had said you led your local Wiccan coven, or swapped husbands every Friday night.

Raised eyebrows, dropped jaws, awkward silences.

Jamie Williams had her tubes tied following her son's birth—she was one of those women who *definitely* did not want more children—so she couldn't be a traditional surrogate. Only gestational surrogacy, where she did not share a biological link with the fetus, was an option. Perhaps this explains why surrogacy came naturally to her, why she never felt conflicted about the babies she carried for other women.

When Jamie was pregnant during her first paid surrogacy in 1997, her young son grew adept at explaining the process to people in the grocery store.

"No, that's not going to be my mommy's baby. There is a nice lady whose tummy is broken. My mom is having this baby for her."

Jamie figured if a toddler could explain surrogacy to strangers, how complicated could it be?

Her Catholic mother-in-law felt differently. Surrogacy was wrong, she told Jamie. It was disgusting. Immoral. Unnatural. If God wanted those people to have babies, she said, he would have gotten them pregnant himself.

"Don't play the God card with me," Jamie says today. "I'm

a Christian and I can talk about God all day long. So if I get cancer, I shouldn't treat it? Because God *wants* me to die a horrible early death? I don't think so. Surrogacy is as old as the Bible. We're just helping other people have babies. It's a beautiful thing."

Williams has given birth to four surrogate children since 1997: one set of twins and two singletons. Along the way, she became California's mama bear of surrogates, a staunch and stubborn defender of the practice who suffers little ambivalence about its ethics. Williams has guided hundreds of traditional and gestational surrogates, and their babies' intended parents, for three different California-based agencies over the past fifteen years. She currently works as a spokesperson and advocate for the Surrogacy Source, a California-based agency that has helped over two thousand parents since 2003.

"From day one, surrogacy is not like being pregnant with your own baby," Williams explains. "When it's your baby, a hundred times a day you think about what baby name to pick, what clothes your baby will wear, what color crib sheets to buy.

"When you're pregnant with someone else's baby, one hundred times a day you think about *their* baby, how happy *they* are going to be when it's born, how delirious *they* will be to take *their* baby home from the hospital to *their* house. You're not abandoning your baby or giving her up or selling it. None of that. You're doing a beautiful thing and you know from the first second that it is never going to be your baby. It's all worthwhile because you are completing someone else's family. The birth is the final chapter for you—but it's the first chapter for them."

Despite Jamie's persuasive passion and three successful surrogacies, her mother-in-law never came around.

Based on her years of experience, Jamie Williams crafted a written outreach to potential surrogates for the Surrogacy Source, which is run and staffed largely by former surrogates themselves. (The Surrogacy Source chooses to facilitate only gestational surrogacies, largely to simplify its legal and public relationship positions, and because most clients today prefer gestational surrogacy over traditional.) Jamie's tone mixes businesslike, pragmatic information, reassurance, and heartfelt empathy for both surrogates and infertile families. It reveals the appeal of tackling such an emotionally fraught endeavor.

> If you become a surrogate mother you will be changing the lives of a very grateful infertile couple. You will choose, meet, and have a special relationship with your intended parents. You will be remembered and appreciated long after you become a surrogate mother. Every time that baby has a birthday, they will think of the special role you played in their lives, and how you carried their baby with grace. The benefits of becoming a surrogate mother are that you are actually changing the lives of another couple or individual forever.

Like Sherrie Smith at the Center for Surrogate Parenting, Jamie Williams insists on debunking the biggest myth about American surrogates: their primary motivation is *not* money. For women who are leading very ordinary, unremarkable, relatively anonymous lives as wives, mothers, and part-time employees, there's something even more seductive than cold hard tax-free cash: granting privileged, wealthy strangers an invaluable gift, and feeling unique and appreciated for the rest of your life because of it. In its way, surrogacy gives surrogate mothers a rich whiff of immortality.

Yet let's not get too sentimental here. Money—being money—has an admittedly concrete value itself, especially in our capitalist country. And the large payment surrogates receive reinforces the value of their "gift" as well as their significance to the intended parents.

Surrogacy enables you to stay home with your children. Reimbursement of living expenses starts at $27,000 for new surrogates to $37,500 for experienced surrogates, and you will meet others who have decided to become surrogate mothers also. Ultimately, becoming a surrogate allowed me to give "THE GIFT OF LIFE."

Think about it: five figures for nine months of work—and it's not even work, exactly. A sack full of cash sings its own siren song. Naturally, the large sums surrogates earn can turn a lot of people's heads.

But as with any high-paying job, only the most qualified need apply, Jamie explains in the online application:

The requirements for becoming a surrogate mother are first that you enjoy easy and uncomplicated pregnancy, live in California, Colorado, Illinois, Massachusetts, Maryland, or Texas, have at least one child that you are raising in your home, you are between the ages of 21 and 38, nonsmoker, living in a stable household, have reliable transportation, not be receiving state financial assistance (welfare), have not been arrested or been in a substance abuse program within the last 10 years. If you would like to become a surrogate mother, we will run a full criminal background check on you and your husband or partner. As well as a urine drug screen for STDs, HIV, hepatitis, and a full female medical exam, including an ultrasound to look at your uterus.

Then it's on to the nitty-gritty. At times, the instructions sound almost like this is a regular job interview. It's easy to forget we're talking about creating a baby here.

To become a surrogate mother, you will need to fill out our surrogate mothers application in full, schedule your in-home interview, and make an appointment for your psychological evaluation. We will be running your criminal background check at this time. Once all these clearances are received, you will be presented with profiles to select your intended parents, you will meet with our staff and intended parents to make sure that this is the right couple for you. You will then need to call and schedule your legal consultation to sign the surrogate agreement. Your medical screening with the IPs' fertility clinic will be scheduled during this time.

You will need to take all medications and injections according to your calendar, follow all Dr. orders and inform your IPs AND the Surrogacy Source when any and ALL appointments are scheduled. You will need to be able to get to all appointments on time . . . transportation cannot be an issue. You will need to make sure your monthly expense form is faxed into our office by the 15th of each month to receive your check on the first of the following month. You will be required to attend our monthly support group meeting for surrogate mothers.

Finally, call if and when you go into labor. This will be a very special day for you and your intended parents. The benefits of becoming a surrogate mother are that you are actually changing the lives of another couple or individual forever.

Becoming a surrogate mother will be a very rewarding experience for you; we will do everything possible to make sure you are happy with your intended parents and our staff here at the Surrogacy Source.

If you would like to apply to become a surrogate mother through the Surrogacy Source, begin our surrogate application or contact us with any questions. We are so grateful for our surrogate mothers and look forward to meeting you![12]

So . . . ready to sign up?

In July 1998, a few months after Rhonda and Frankie returned to Canada, one of Rhonda's closest friends from childhood called. Debbie lived three hours away in Belleville, a small city located at the mouth of the Moira River on the Bay of Quinte in southeastern Ontario, about three hours west of Syracuse, New York.

Debbie was single too. She knew Rhonda was discouraged and depressed. Rhonda had seen a Canadian psychiatrist who diagnosed her as chemically deficient in serotonin; the doctor said in all likelihood, Rhonda would need to take low-level antidepressants for the rest of her life to defang her negative emotions. Rhonda felt deeply grateful to know the biological cause for her depression, and to trust that medical treatment would alleviate her crippling emotional lethargy. But the medication had yet to take full effect.

"Want me to come down for the weekend and go on a booze cruise?" Debbie asked.

"I could use that," Rhonda answered, laughing for the first time in months.

Debbie drove to Niagara Falls. The girls went on the booze cruise. Somehow that weekend marked the end of Rhonda's depression.

In October, a few months after the Prozac-like cruise, Rhonda, wearing makeup and new clothes for the first time in nearly a year, went to Belleville for a two-week vacation with Debbie and Debbie's new boyfriend, Dan. Debbie had met Dan at a local park through their dogs, two large German shepherds. Dan had a good friend named Gerry, a handsome thirty-two-year-old who'd recently gotten divorced, left the Canadian military, and was casting about for the next phase of his life. All Gerry would say was that he was looking for a "nice girl."

Dan and Debbie planned a double date to introduce Gerry and Rhonda.

At the last minute, Gerry changed his mind. He told Dan and Debbie it was useless. He was never going to meet anyone nice. Why bother going on the date?

An hour later he changed his mind again. He drove to the mall where Dan, Debbie, and Rhonda were having dinner. He looked down at himself, realized his shirt was dirty, and quickly bought a new shirt at the mall and put it on. Rushing to the restaurant with the plastic shirt tags still attached, he was pushing through one revolving door when Rhonda, Debbie, and Dan came through the same door going in the opposite direction.

"I saw Rhonda, and I just knew," Gerry explains twelve years later. "I couldn't stop talking to her all night. I asked her out the next day, and the next. We spent the whole week together. She was the nicest girl I'd ever met."

Her name helped. Moose was Gerry's father's nickname, not his real name. His father had a traditional, if old-fashioned, Nova Scotia given name: Rhonddah, spelled in customary Nova Scotia style. The family had used it for Gerry's younger sister as well. Yes—Gerry had a sister and a dad named Rhonda.

Gerry felt he'd found his soul mate.

Rhonda was less impressed about the fateful nature of their meeting. Six feet tall, muscular from his years in the military, Gerry was too good-looking for her, she thought. All her relationships had developed slowly, from friendship into something more. She didn't trust the strong initial attraction she felt for Gerry. It was just lust, she thought. So she tried to keep her feelings practical, matter-of-fact, unemotional, detached.

The day she left for home, she sat Gerry down.

"I'm twenty-eight," she told him. "I've been around the block. I'm realistic. I know this week has just been a fun summer-camp-type fling. We like each other, but I'm going to go home and we'll probably never see each other again."

Gerry stared at Rhonda, unable to speak.

Then Rhonda left.

*In the 1980s* and early 1990s, despite the growth of surrogacy and infertility treatments, couples grappling with childlessness tended to keep their journeys private. The concept of infertility as a disease was still new. Treatments were considered experimental. Surrogacy made the cover of *People* not because celebrities were doing it, but because the practice was considered, by some, bizarre and morally reprehensible. Doctors who performed ART, their patients, and the surrogate mothers who carried others' babies, were practicing in the dark ages of ART.

The infertile couples themselves, especially women openly salivating for babies, were viewed as slightly . . . wacky, so desperate for a baby they would do *anything*. ART treatment was fodder for whispered gossip and wild speculation. Needles? Sperm insemination? Ovulation predictors? Hiring a surrogate *mother*?

American society experienced a collective schadenfreude, a morbid public curiosity coupled with deep gratitude that we were not quite that pathologically depraved, morally suspect, and crazed by baby lust. The lucky fertile, not understanding how randomly fortunate they were, exclaimed: *I'd never do that! My husband just looks at me and I'm pregnant!*

Although most infertility scientists and doctors around the world have been male, women like Lesley Brown and Rhonda Wile provided the desperation and the money that inspired doctors and researchers, driving ART from the 1940s until today.[13] Women's natural biological desire to have a child heightened the pressure on—and provided incentives for—doctors to develop technologies that made surrogacy and other treatments possible. Over time, even women who had conceived easily came to sympathize with infertile women's desperate desire to have a baby, even if that meant growing your baby in another woman's body.

For much of the 1980s and 1990s, women conducted an underground railroad of informal sympathy, assistance, and doctor recommendations about surrogacy. Information was shared via telephone and on the playground among infertile women, and their friends, sisters, colleagues, and acquaintances. As online technologies exploded in the early 2000s, this network became a vast, detailed, immensely personal superhighway of infertility and surrogacy blogs. The most popular, by far, was started by our Arizona friend Rhonda Wile, on April 1, 2008.

But that's getting ahead of this story.

*The weekend after* Gerry and Rhonda met, Gerry drove to Niagara Falls. To Rhonda's parents' house. Gerry had called to let Rhonda know he was coming, but he made good time and arrived early. The beautiful girl he came to see was at the gym. Gerry spent two hours chatting with Rhonda's mom until Rhonda came back.

In some essential way, after that day he never left.

Rhonda's parents—the ones who are still holding hands after fifty years together—sensed something profound and lasting about Gerry and the relationship, despite Rhonda's denials. A few weeks later, October was drawing to a close. Rhonda's dad asked if Gerry could help in his window-washing business. Did he want to move in with them?

Gerry did.

One day soon after, in Rhonda's car, some words slipped out of Gerry's mouth. Rhonda whirled around. She thought she'd heard Gerry say, "I love you."

"Did you just say what I think you said?" she asked, blushing.

Gerry turned red, too. Then he caught himself.

"I did. And I do. I love you. I'm not going to apologize for how I feel."

Around this time, a friend asked Rhonda who she was seeing who was so special. Rhonda asked why. The friend laughed. "Oh Rhonda, because it's written all over your face."

Still Rhonda couldn't admit she was in love with Gerry. Gerry proposed. Rhonda told him she didn't know if she ever wanted to get married again. Certainly not so soon. After her marriage's abrupt, inexplicable dissolution, it had taken her so long to put the pieces of herself back together. She was too afraid of being abandoned again.

It took a year and a half for Gerry to get Rhonda Reycraft to change her mind.

After the black grief hits when you accept that your body cannot make a baby, the promise of a gestational surrogate making a child for you—your baby, with no legal or emotional strings attached—is exhilarating, an adrenaline rush of hope and joy, karmic sunshine that feels that much warmer because of the cold desolation and betrayal that came before.

Until you see the price tag.

Now, if you are in the top wealthiest percent of American households, someone like actress Elizabeth Banks, the cost is largely irrelevant. The pretty blond actress who plays District 12 escort Effie Trinket in *The Hunger Games*, met her future husband, Max Handelman, on her first day of college in 1992 and married him in 2003. Banks struggled with infertility until she was thirty-seven, ironically playing a pregnant woman in *What to Expect When You Are Expecting* although she herself was never able to conceive. Banks and Handelman had two sons via surrogate, one in March 2011 and the second in November 2012. "It's essentially a test tube baby—it's just that the test tube is another woman," Banks told *Allure* readers in the June 2012 issue. "That you can grow a baby outside of yourself! It's just amazing!"[14]

Every surrogacy agency charges clients differently. But the norm is that clients must deposit several thousand dollars up front. The surrogate's medical expenses must be paid as they are incurred; the bulk of her fee, separate from medical costs, is billed monthly following a positive pregnancy test at six weeks. A typical, agency bill looks like this:

### What It Costs to Have a Surrogate Baby

**Agency fee:** $15,000 ($2,000 additional for international clients)

**Surrogate fee:** $20,000–$30,000 (depending upon the state she lives in, and how many times she has been a surrogate) paid over ten months

**Surrogate expenses:** $45,000–$65,000 This includes her attorney's fees, allowance for psychological counseling and support groups, maternity clothes, a life insurance premium, her travel expenses to meet with the intended parents and for doctors' visits, child care when she needs to leave her children at home, plus miscellaneous costs.

**Separate legal and medical costs:** These costs are for the attorney who executes the contract between clients, agency, and surrogate, as well as navigates all local, state, and county regulations regarding finalization of parental rights; the fertility clinic's charge for IVF/ embryo transfer; the egg donor's fees and medical costs, which can total close to $40,000; the insurance policy and deductibles, co-pays, and unreimbursed

medical expenses incurred by the surrogate and the
newborn baby or babies.

**Additional variable fees:** These fees include the surrogate's lost wages for six weeks after a vaginal delivery
and eight weeks after a C-section; lost wages for her
spouse; $3,000 if she needs to have a C-section; $5,000
per additional baby if she carries multiples; $1,000 if
she must undergo selective reduction of a fetus; $1,000
if she needs to have an abortion due to birth defects;
$1,000 if she miscarries; $3,000 if the pregnancy or
birth causes her to have a hysterectomy.

All this adds up to a simple, awful reality: almost no one
can afford to hire a gestational surrogate. All these line items
total a cool $100,000—if you are lucky and come in on the low
end of the expenses, premiums, deductibles, and fees. If you
need donor eggs, your surrogate has trouble getting health insurance, or your baby is born early or needs neonatal care, the
costs can easily—and quickly—add up to more than $200,000.
There are cases where the total expenses for a surrogate pregnancy and neonatal care have run north of $500,000.

None of the surrogacy fees or expenses are covered by
health insurance.

You can't get a bank loan to pay for surrogacy. Instead,
clients must cough up the cash up front. Millions of Americans
finance big-ticket items like a car or house, with plenty of
banks willing to lend them far more than $100,000, because
the car or house acts as collateral security in case of default.

A surrogate pregnancy offers no asset to pledge to a lender.
You can't turn your baby over to the bank if you miss a few
payments. Surrogacy is thus a cash-in-advance deal, making it
unrealistic even for the millions of Americans who qualify for
$1-million bank financing for suburban mansions or Cadillacs.

That's hardly the way nature designed baby making.

*Outside the gleaming* white Dade County Courthouse at 73 West Flagler Street in Miami, Florida, a dozen palm trees waved in the breeze. The courthouse was originally built in 1904 of white coquina rock, with an elegant red-domed top, a tribute to Miami's pride. It was rebuilt in 1928 to serve the civil and criminal needs of the fast-growing city. Until 1972, it was the tallest building in Miami.

Architecturally termed a "classic revival skyscraper," the courthouse in 2000 consisted of a large metal detector leading to a creaky old elevator and twenty-eight stories of offices, jail cells, reception halls, and courtrooms. The building looked like a skyscraper that had longed to be a plantation in its youth—shining white marble steps flanked by tall, proud white columns, dwarfed in turn by layers of windows and office floors.

Rhonda Reycraft and Gerry Wile were married inside the air-conditioned courthouse on April 14, 2000. Rhonda was twenty-nine. Gerry was thirty-three. A female justice of the peace from Jamaica officiated. They were Couple 73 that day at the courthouse.

Two new Florida friends joined the wedding party at the last minute. There were no family members. No rice-throwing, cake-smashing, or overt signs of celebration. Rhonda didn't want to tempt fate by having a splashy second wedding; she just wanted to be happily married to Gerry, flying under the radar of whatever cosmic forces had wrecked her first attempt at matrimony and motherhood. So she insisted on keeping their wedding simple, quiet, and just between them. She wore a little white sundress with spaghetti straps that she had hanging in her closet. The two couples went to Outback Steakhouse for the wedding banquet.

The Wiles had found a small temporary apartment in

nearby Miami Lakes. Rhonda had gotten a good job as a hospital nurse. They couldn't afford to buy wedding rings, because they were both still broke from their divorces, Rhonda's bankruptcy, and the move to Florida. So before they headed south, Gerry had combined all their old wedding jewelry, an engagement ring, and some miscellaneous gold and got a Niagara Falls jeweler to melt down the parts and mix them together. Rhonda and Gerry had two new wedding rings created from the fragments of their past lives.

Gerry found work at a local fire department. In 2003, he rejoined the military, the U.S. military this time. He enlisted as a reservist in the Coast Guard. As part of his service, Gerry was granted U.S. citizenship.

Together, Rhonda and Gerry were rebuilding their lives.

In 2004, Gerry was deployed to the Iraq-Kuwait border as part of Operation Iraqi Freedom. During his tour, he walked two miles each way to call Rhonda from a satellite phone. He did this every day for ten and a half months.

Gerry was coming home for good just weeks before Christmas—the best Christmas present Rhonda could hope for. During the phone calls between Kuwait and Miami, Rhonda and Gerry started plotting the rest of their lives. Once Gerry's Coast Guard duty was complete, they wouldn't need to stay in Florida. Neither Rhonda nor Gerry loved the place. They liked the heat, but abhorred the wet, heavy humidity of the summers. Her parents had been snowbird vacationers in Arizona for years, spending five months of winter soaking up the dry heat as an antidote to Canada's wet cold. Gerry and Rhonda joined them for short trips, and fell in love with the Sonoran Desert valley. They talked about moving to Mesa, a suburb about fifteen minutes east of Phoenix.

A year before, as Gerry and Rhonda shared their last, long embrace before Gerry left Florida for Iraq, he asked Rhonda to think about an important question. He had been frightened to have more children, Rhonda knew. He had explained, again and again, that he was terrified of having children because he was afraid of losing them—a repeat of what had happened with his first wife and his young daughters.

"You don't know what it's like, Rhonda," Gerry had shouted during their arguments about when they could start trying to have kids. His face would redden with pain and frustration. "You have no idea what it is like to lose your own children."

But Rhonda desperately wanted—needed—kids. She'd made that clear to Gerry from their earliest days together. In many ways, this was *the* question of Rhonda's life: when would she become a mother? It was the answer she had been trying to find—or avoid—since the long ago morning of her suicide attempt.

Holding Rhonda close as they said good-bye, Gerry had whispered, "Maybe we can start talking about starting a family when I get back?"

Soon he was coming back. They were mapping their future together. Rhonda and Gerry began to talk seriously about having a baby. Or babies.

*Once you have* absorbed the shock that you are infertile, assuming you still want children (and not everyone does), three major strategic modes await you. Combat analogies apply. Because becoming a parent when you are infertile is a battle that requires courage, wile, and determination.

Plus a very large war chest.

Option one: you can treat your infertility in hopes that you will conceive, carry, and birth a child.

Option two: you can adopt someone else's child.

Option three: you can have someone else bear a child for

you, with or without your genetic contribution, depending upon your exact medical afflictions.

Not that Rhonda and Gerry Wile knew anything about infertility, how to treat it, the challenges to adoption, or the risks and costs of surrogacy.

They just wanted a baby.

# Part 3

---

One Vasectomy, Two Vaginas

In the summer months, the only spot in the United States hotter than Mesa, Arizona, is Death Valley. The temperature in Mesa reaches or exceeds 100 degrees Fahrenheit on an average of 110 days each year. On June 26, 1990, the thermometer recorded an all-time high of 122 degrees, rivaling cities such as Riyadh and Baghdad in terms of shimmering heat.

Mesa and nearby Phoenix sit in a large, flat ancient river basin ringed by mountains, once headquarters for the Hohokam Indians. These days, the region is known—for good reason—as the Valley of the Sun. Phoenix, with 4.1 million metro area residents, is the sixth most populated city in the United States, and Mesa is one of the nation's fastest-growing cities. Mesa was officially settled by Mormon pioneers in 1878. Of course, long before the Mormons there were other hominoids, including the ancient Hohokams way back in 700 BC. The population today hovers around 500,000 people, including Gerry and Rhonda Wile.

About fifteen minutes east of Phoenix, Mesa has several spectacularly beautiful golf courses, public parks, and nearby Superstition Mountain, the most photographed site in the county. The Mesa sidewalks are smooth and wide. The black asphalt roads with their freshly painted white lines gleam in the sun. There are fifty-seven elementary schools, evenly spaced

Rhonda Wile

Gerry Wile

Rhonda's first child, Frankie

Frankie and Gerry on a hike in Arizona

so that each residential neighborhood has one within walking distance. Mesa feels as carefully constructed as Disney World. Driving around Mesa, you can't help but crave a minivan and a few kids to fill up the backseat.

Almost every day in Mesa is a beautiful day. The sky a blue wash, not a cloud anywhere, zero humidity. White sun, a breeze bringing the fresh scent of cactus flowers and sage down from the desert. Palm trees, cacti, and paloverde trees with their striking lime green bark line the cleanly swept streets and sidewalks.

Mesa is a very long way from the dirt, the throngs, the bright lights and cacophony, the culture, the history, the thrill and excitement and hustle of New York City, or Mumbai, or even nearby Phoenix.

In its ordinariness, Mesa looked like the perfect place to raise a family.

"We're ordinary people," Rhonda says, "who just wanted an ordinary baby."

But Mesa, Arizona, turned out to be a distinctly extraordinary, distinctly infertile place for Gerry and Rhonda Wile.

The first issue to address when Gerry and Rhonda started their baby making was Gerry's . . . ahem . . . vasectomy.

Astoundingly, he had not told Rhonda about the operation during their courtship, the early years of their marriage, or their many, many conversations about how much Rhonda wanted a family.

"It just never came up," Gerry says now, as if still trying to mask the significance of his omission. But really, what had stopped him from confiding in Rhonda for nearly six years was that he didn't want to risk losing her. He knew how much she longed for a family. He figured he would fix his vasectomy without the girl of his dreams ever finding out he'd had one.

In 2004, after he and Rhonda had started to talk seriously about starting a family, but while he was still deployed in Iraq, Gerry moved forward with a solution. Fourteen years before, the Canadian military doctors had performed a simple vasectomy, cutting the vas deferens tube, removing a small portion of it, and bending the cut section backward, as one would fold over the tip of a plastic straw. Gerry consulted a military doctor and made plans to have the surgery reversed. He didn't tell Rhonda. No confrontation, no tears, no betrayal. There was simply no need to upset her.

His vasectomy could be reversed with a relatively simple operation, the military doctor who'd examined Gerry explained, via a detailed official e-mail, sent to their home computer in Florida, read by . . .

Rhonda Wile.

Rhonda was stunned. And furious. And flabbergasted. Had she given her heart away, again, to a deceitful man? Not an easy way for a woman whose first husband had been a compulsive liar to learn that her second husband could not father the children she had always dreamed of having.

With Gerry still in Iraq, Rhonda bit back her instinct to confront him. This was not a conversation to have via satellite phone. Although she was experiencing an emotional war zone, Gerry lived every day in a real war zone. She simmered and wondered what the hell Gerry had been thinking. She tried to smile and chitchat during their daily phone calls for the next several months.

She felt sick at the thought of not being able to have children. Would she ever be able to forgive him? Did she love Gerry enough to stay with him, if that meant never having the babies she had dreamed of since she was a small girl watching *Happy Days*, playing dress-up, and devouring her Eat-More candy bars?

"I didn't know if I could," Rhonda explains today, closing her eyes and shaking her head silently.

What hurt even more than the devastating news about Gerry's vasectomy was that he had lied to her. Rhonda valued honesty above almost every other quality, in herself and her relationships. The betrayals in her first marriage had left her with an insistence on candor in every nook and cranny of her friendships, professional relationships, and most of all, in love. Without honesty, she couldn't trust Gerry, or how she felt about anything in their marriage.

The day Gerry came home, she was overjoyed to see him back safe and sound, despite her questions and deferred rage. Rhonda waited as long as she could. She lasted close to four hours.

As they sat next to each other on their bed, she silently handed him the doctor's note.

Gerry read a few lines. Then his face, filled with joy seconds before, crumpled. He buried his head in his large, calloused hands. He began to cry.

What he said next—the first words out of his mouth— deflated Rhonda's rage, because she knew it was the truth.

"I didn't want to lose you," Gerry said, with tears on his cheeks. "I love you more than anything in the world. I couldn't tell you, because I couldn't take the chance you'd leave."

Gerry wrapped his arms around Rhonda as if she were a life raft. Then he attended to her ire and wiped her tears, as well as his own. His brown eyes were soulful, his repeat apologies and explanations slightly bumbling—a cross between Brad Pitt and Fred Flintstone. He said he was sorry. He admitted he had acted like a jerk. He explained sincerely that she was the best woman in the world and he would do anything to make her happy, including give her babies since that's what she wanted. He smiled as only a six-foot movie-star-handsome, firefighting, two-Gulf-Wars veteran can smile.

Rhonda rallied. Bit by bit, forgiveness came. Like Rhonda's parents, they kept holding hands.

Although Gerry and Rhonda didn't know it, these days a vasectomy is actually not a huge problem, compared to other fertility challenges. In many ways, male snafus are *good* news today, far easier to remedy than female vexations. This isn't fair, but infertility is not a gender-neutral disease.

Sperm are the simplest component involved in conception, whether you are a surrogate, a fertility doctor, or an intended parent. You need one healthy spermatozoa cell to make a baby; the average human male ejaculation produces more than 20 million per milliliter of 'em. As most of us know firsthand, men can ejaculate daily or even several times a day. That makes sperm a relatively cheap commodity within the ART marketplace.

Sperm were first iced in 1776 in the mountains of northern Italy by Lazzaro Spallanzani, a Roman Catholic priest, kicking off over 250 years of data on freezing and thawing male sperm.[1] Sperm are reasonably happy to be frozen and thawed. If the conditions are right, these guys can survive for decades. Carefully tested and screened sperm used for surrogacy and ART cost only $100 per ounce—by far the least costly ingredient needed to make a baby.

When complications arise—a blocked vas deferens tube, a rise in temperature in the scrotum, scarring or infection from sexually transmitted illnesses, or lackluster "swimmers" with low motility—modern medical corrections can be fairly straightforward. The only semen-related problems that lead to outright rejection of a potential father's sperm are inherited deformities like sickle-cell anemia, revealed by genetic testing, or deadly communicable diseases such as HIV. When a man cannot achieve an erection or ejaculation—due to impotence, a war wound, paralysis, a terrible car accident, a coma—sperm today can be extracted directly from the testes, even in a man who has had a vasectomy, and delivered to the egg via artificial insemination or IVF.

When it comes to sperm today, there really is no such thing as infertility.

Sometimes even death does not prevent successful sperm retrieval—although ethics often preclude doing this in the absence of the man's consent. Hours after a man's death (or even years, if the semen has been frozen), the sperm can be called into action using turkey baster insemination or IVF. Fresh or thawed, warm, upwardly mobile sperm get shot directly into a woman's vaginal canal, or into an IVF petri dish, and sperm will naturally do their darndest to find an egg.

Therefore Gerry's big secret was, actually, a relatively simple problem to solve.

Rhonda and Gerry's next roadblock was a bigger one. The U.S. military doctor would willingly tackle the vasectomy reversal. But the government would not pay to undo an elective operation their Canadian brethren had performed so ably. The Wiles' health insurance policy would not cover the reversal.

Insurance reimbursement for fertility remedies presents a tricky moral and financial equation. Some government agencies, such as the Centers for Disease Control, as well as fertility advocates, consider infertility a disease—and a highly treatable one. The famous screen stars and musicians who advocate for surrogacy don't face financial challenges paying for it, so the high cost and lack of insurance coverage rarely warrant any ink in the glowing press about their miracle babies. There is no national consensus, or even public debate, on what infertility coverage the average American is entitled to—or how many treatments an individual must pay for by reaching into his or her own wallet.

Some states mandate infertility treatment coverage; others do not. War veterans like Gerry are not eligible for IVF, even if military injuries have caused them to become infertile.[2] In

2011, a New York court awarded a Brooklyn mother $1 million in a hospital malpractice verdict for a stillborn baby whose death was caused by medical neglect. Today's infertility sufferers ask, if a stillborn baby is worth $1 million, how much is a never-born baby worth?

Blue Cross and Blue Shield, a national federation of thirty-nine independent health insurance companies, provides health coverage for 100 million Americans—one in three. However, each affiliate and each employer individually chooses how much coverage to provide. Some companies reimburse for routine and preliminary treatments, such as ob-gyn appointments and hormone supplements. Other, more generous plans, cover IVF treatments, and offer a stipend toward adoption (but not surrogacy).

Back and forth the disputes simmer. Many infertility victims exhibit physical and psychological damage. Why shouldn't health insurance cover their treatment costs? Opponents would argue that Gerry's vasectomy, like many actions impacting fertility, had been voluntary, and was not endangering his physical survival. Shouldn't scarce medical dollars be allocated to alleviating truly serious, involuntary afflictions?

In the Wiles' case, at least there was clarity: their insurance policy would not cover having a voluntary vasectomy voluntarily reversed.

The Wiles plowed ahead anyway. They discovered the Tucson International Center for Vasectomy Reversal. The center's feel-good slogan was "We Make Dads Again." The Wiles liked the microsurgical specialist, Dr. Sheldon Marks. Especially when he told Gerry that back in high school, he had loved microscopic manipulation so much that, for fun, he wrote the Gettysburg Address on the back of a postage stamp using a high-powered magnifying glass. The health-care professional in Rhonda liked that Dr. Marks had been performing microsurgical vasectomy reversals since 1983, at the world-renowned

Mayo Clinic in Rochester, Minnesota, and had specialized in them since 1991.[3]

The surgery ran about $9,000. Rhonda and Gerry used up their savings, plus a hunk of credit card debt, to pay for it. Innocently, they thought that was all the money they would ever spend on fertility treatments.

They were wrong.

The Wiles got their money's worth, however. The operation was an unqualified success, perhaps the most successful vasectomy reversal in the history of mankind.

The average un-vasectomized human male releases a billion sperm a month. After a vasectomy, sperm are still produced in the male testicles, but zero sperm escape the tube leading to the tip of the penis. (This is why vasectomy is so reliable as birth control.) After a successful vasectomy reversal, the average man releases 20 million sperm during a single ejaculation. Anything less than 20 million per milliliter qualifies as defective spermatogenesis, or "low sperm count" in infertility jargon.

Twenty million spermatozoas is pretty good. Definitely enough to get the average thirty-five-year-old wife pregnant. Especially since statistically, Rhonda had a 66 percent chance she'd be happily pregnant within one year.

To be certain the operation was a success, Dr. Marks ran a sperm count test after the operation. He showed Gerry and Rhonda a magnified screen with Gerry's fresh sperm whizzing by, practically smiling. In one ejaculation, Gerry Wile released 220 million sperm, more than ten times the average. By any standard, that's a lot.

It is amazing, given the angst, expense, controversy, and Hollywood dirt that surrogacy generates, how little most adults know about conception and infertility. This includes people who have been trying to get pregnant for years. It even applies to surrogates themselves, many of whom consider pregnancy their calling, or at least their profession. What happens *after* what happens between the sheets remains a mystery to most adults. So it's actually not so surprising that human beings are shockingly naïve about infertility, given that we are clueless about fertility as well.

To understand why surrogacy can be such a miraculous solution to infertility—and why the fees paid to surrogates are justifiable—you need to understand what happens to make a baby, and the thousands of things that can go wrong in the attempt. Even surrogates and couples who are right this second trying to conceive (TTC in blog shorthand) don't necessarily understand how to get sperm, egg, and uterus all together in the right order to make a baby. What's most amazing, even today, is that most human beings do not understand this process and could not explain the details of conception—or inconception—to our own children.

First, infertility is far more common than most people realize. About 10 to 12 percent of the human population is infertile.[4] In the United States, this translates to roughly one in every seven or eight couples, or about seven to eight million American adults.[5] Anyone can be infertile—celibate priests, sexually active teenagers, virgins, gays, lesbians, and transgendered peoples. Technically, even a surrogate can be infertile; to be a successful gestational surrogate, you don't need viable eggs or unblocked fallopian tubes. All you need is a healthy uterus.

A woman has roughly the same chance of being infertile—11.8 percent[6]—as she does of getting breast cancer at some point in her life.[7] Infertility—the medical term is "impaired fecundity"—is generally defined as the inability to conceive or carry to term a baby after twelve months of no-birth-control sex between a man and a woman of childbearing ages, which the Centers for Disease Control defines as ages fifteen to forty-four.

The only reliable test for infertility is trying, and failing, to have a baby. Doctors cannot screen patients for infertility the way they might for scoliosis or hemophilia. Nor are there consumer-friendly pharmacy tests for infertility. Ironically, you often do not find out you are infertile until after you've spent years trying *not* to get pregnant.

One-third of the time, impaired fecundity is the man's "fault" and one-third of the time it's the woman's.[8] Sterility's causes are myriad—scarring from untreated sexually trans-mitted infections, missing or blocked reproductive tubes deep inside the body, fibroids growing on the uterus, low sperm motility, cigarette smoking.[9] Sometimes, doctors suspect in-fertility may be a baffling combination of male and female factors unique to the individual couple. Roughly 30 percent of the time doctors have no idea of sterility's genesis; the causes remain unsolved mysteries to infertility specialists and their patients.

As a result, many cases of infertility go undiagnosed, mis-understood, and untreated for decades. Or millennia.

For much of our history, there was no way to understand infertility's causes, because human beings had little informa-tion about the basics of conception. Prior to the twentieth cen-tury, our knowledge was limited to what could be seen from outside the body (an erect penis, a pregnant belly, enlarged breasts) and what doctors could deduce from performing crude autopsies on humans and animals.

However, in the first fifty years of the twentieth century, using nifty new inventions like X-rays, chemical analyses, and laparoscopes, doctors figured out, basically, what happens in-side women's bodies to create life. They decoded the importance of hormones—estrogen and progesterone are the two that control the female reproductive cycle, testosterone for men. A researcher discovered that if you removed a mouse's ovaries, she couldn't conceive. The first pregnancy tests were invented in the late 1920s, analyzing a pregnant woman's urine using mice, rabbits, and frogs.[10]

Eventually, research determined that conception boils down to three sequential actions: ejaculation of sperm, fertilization of egg, and implantation of the resulting embryo in a woman's uterus. It sounds simple, but a lot can go wrong.

Human eggs, or oocytes, are created inside the female body. A baby girl is born with all the eggs she will ever have in her lifetime. Following the onset of puberty, each month, a human egg is released from either of a woman's two ovaries. When the egg is mature, the ovary ships the tiny follicle up along one of two fallopian tubes—flexible, trumpet-shaped "pipes" connected to the upper section of the uterus. To prepare for a surrogate pregnancy, doctors stimulate egg production and extract multiple eggs, either from the intended mother or an egg donor.

A healthy uterus is a muscular, V-shaped organ about the size of an uninflated football. The baby, known when in utero as a fetus, grows inside the expanding football. And this uterus is what infertile couples hire a surrogate for—because no one, at this moment in time, has ever gestated a baby outside a human uterus.

But wait—we're getting ahead of the story. Back to conception.

We can all use a good visual when it comes to understanding complicated scientific matters. Since we're talking football, the Texas Longhorns logo comes in handy here.

Imagine you are looking straight at a surrogate's abdomen. Her belly button is just above the center of the longhorn head. The skull is the uterus. The horns are the two fallopian tubes stretching out to the ovaries (although the tubes are more narrow, squiggly, and downward curving than the horns shown here). The ears represent the two ovaries. The nose is the cervix, facing down to the vagina.

Got it? Okay. Here's the actual medical diagram:

## Female Reproductive System

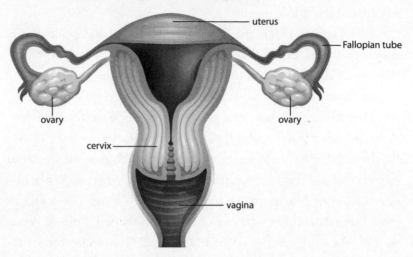

Illustration of female reproductive system © BlueRingMedia/Shutterstock.com

During intercourse and artificial insemination, sperm enter the vagina and travel up the cervix, and can live in the uterus and fallopian tubes for about seventy-two hours, waiting for a mature egg. If it is exactly the right time of the monthly menstrual cycle for conception—approximately halfway between menstrual periods in women with regular cycles—a mature, ready-to-be-fertilized egg meets up with the single-fastest-swimming sperm in one of the fallopian tubes. The "right" time for successful conception is surprisingly brief: each month, one ripe egg lives only for roughly twelve hours, kind of like a rock star diva with one fleeting Top 40 hit.

One lucky sperm—the first sperm to reach the egg—drills into the egg's outer membrane and creates a zygote, a single-celled organism that develops into a multicelled blastocyst.[11] The egg's outer membrane instantly hardens, preventing other sperm from breaking through.[12] (If more than one sperm pierce the membrane simultaneously and two or more sperm fertilize the egg, the egg invariably dies.)

110

When doctors are toiling to create a baby for a gestational surrogate to carry, all this magic is highly controlled. The healthiest sperm and egg are brought together in a laboratory petri dish. Specialists monitor every phase under a microscope and determine precisely when sperm and egg meet.

Often, on the road to creating a surrogate pregnancy, multiple eggs are fertilized. A different sperm fertilizes each egg. The results are dizygotic/fraternal, or nonidentical, off-spring, such as reality TV's Jon and Kate's plus eight (such high-order multiples are almost always created by IVF fertilization of multiple eggs in a lab; it's extremely rare for multiples above triplets to form naturally). This zygote-to-embryo transformation takes about eight days, and it all takes place inside a very nice petri dish instead of a woman's fallopian tube. These embryos can be frozen, for future use, once fertilization has taken place.

Finally, a doctor transfers the resulting fertilized embryo or embryos from the petri dish to the surrogate's uterus via a catheter. The embryo must implant inside the surrogate's uterine wall in order to live and grow into a fetus over the next nine months. The most complex and least understood step in successful human reproduction is how and why a healthy, fertilized egg implants in a woman's uterine wall. Natural conception, artificial insemination, and surrogate IVF—even when involving healthy, strong-swimming sperm and mature, viable eggs—often fail to produce an egg that successfully cleaves to the uterine wall.

The result is miscarriage, which occurs in 30 percent of natural human attempts, often before a woman even suspects she is pregnant.[13] In an early miscarriage, the fertilized embryo flushes out along with the discarded uterine lining of menstruation. The embryo is so small you cannot see it. In IVF attempts with women thirty-five and older, the embryo fails to implant even more often, nearly 70 percent of the time.[14]

If all goes smoothly after fertilization or IVF embryo transfer, the embryo burrows safely into the nutritious blood-rich uterine lining that has developed and thickened just for this purpose. Not getting a period is one of the first signs that a surrogate might be pregnant; the uterine lining, which is grown and discarded monthly, stays put to nourish the baby. Over the next nine months the embryo will gradually grow into a fetus and then a baby.

Now—congratulations—you are up to speed on successful natural and surrogate baby making.

Having dispatched Gerry's vasectomy, neither Rhonda nor Gerry had reason to think they would face any more problems conceiving. Rhonda was a healthy woman with no history of menstrual irregularities. Gerry had already fathered one child, a daughter now in her late teens.

"So we knew his little guys were good," Rhonda explains matter-of-factly, like the nurse she is.

At age thirty-five, Rhonda still had thousands of viable eggs. Most women do.

However, Rhonda had entered the least predictable decade of her life in terms of fertility. The only certainty was that she would become less fertile with every month that passed. From thirty-five to forty-five, there's great variability in women's ability to conceive naturally. Some get pregnant easily; some find getting pregnant difficult or impossible without medical intervention. By age forty-five, only one out of ten women can conceive naturally.[15] Remember this the next time you see a pregnant singer or actress in her late forties on a magazine cover—in all likelihood, she did *not* get pregnant without eggs from a younger donor, IVF, and several very expensive fertility doctors.

A study published in *Human Reproduction*[16] reports the following grim correlation between conception and a woman's age:

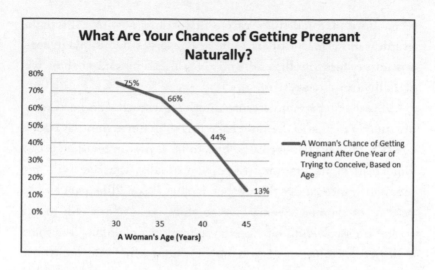

Roughly 70 percent of thirty-year-old women trying to conceive naturally will be pregnant within twelve months.

At age thirty-five, about 66 percent will conceive within a year.

At age forty, only 44 percent will be successful within a year.

At forty-five, nearly nine out of ten women are infertile. At forty-five! That's when most women are just beginning to discover how fabulous they really are.

This downward slope is driven both by the age of the eggs inside a woman's body, and their diminishing number. Older women have more trouble getting pregnant, and more trouble staying pregnant. Messing up the odds even further is the fact that the older the egg, the less able it seems to be to divide normally, an essential task during fertilization and the subsequent growth of the embryo.

But what's most bizarre and puzzling about these statistics is that few women, even our country's most educated ones, know the reality about how dramatically our ability to conceive diminishes with age.[17] It's been well documented that American women are plagued by negative distortions of our self-worth. Studies show many of us believe ourselves to be fatter, less attractive, less intelligent, and worth less in salary than we actually are.

However, the majority of American women—75 percent— drastically *over*estimate how easy it is to get pregnant, at every age. We blithely believe ourselves to be superior, fertility-wise: almost all of us assume, overoptimistically, that we will get pregnant more easily than other women. In a 2011 survey, 90 percent of women twenty-five to thirty-five years old, at all education levels, had no clue that a forty-year-old has less than a 10 percent chance of getting pregnant after one month of unprotected sex.

*Once Gerry's vasectomy* had been undone, Rhonda got jazzed about getting pregnant. She window-shopped for maternity clothes online. She researched the nutritional benefits of breast-feeding for the first year. She bought pregnancy magazines and hoped and planned. She went to see her ob-gyn for advice. What prenatal vitamins should she take? Any other health issues she should address?

Rhonda's doctor offered standard ob-gyn advice: "Rhonda, since you are thirty-five and healthy, there's no reason why you two shouldn't start trying right away."

So Gerry and Rhonda did.

Like 75 percent of sexually active women not using birth control, Rhonda Wile did not get pregnant the first month she and Gerry tried to conceive. Statistically, some women will get pregnant the first month—even the first day—they have intercourse without using birth control. But on average, it can take a year to conceive.

A year of high hopes and nerve-wracking uncertainty.

When couples face trouble conceiving a child, whether in

India or America or Argentina, they don't immediately rush out to the nearest surrogacy clinic. First, most turn to an ob-gyn expert. Roughly 20 percent need support and advice, but no medical intervention.[18] Given that obstetrics and gynecology are by definition female medical specialties, infertility treatments almost always initially focus on the female partner, skewing the emphasis and investigative effort from the start.

It's only when you try, and fail to conceive over time, that you learn the awful statistics: that one in eight people have trouble conceiving. That you always had a 10 to 12 percent chance of being one of them.

You also do not know, until you have to know, that every case of infertility is individual. There are a few general categories of infertility: blocked tubes, low sperm count, polycystic ovarian syndrome, and the like. However, couples with these diagnoses still manage at times to conceive—just as other couples with no diagnoses fail to have children. The genesis and prognosis of every single infertility case is unique.

This explains why, in part, treating infertility is so expensive, so experimental, so unpredictable, and so terribly lonely. It is almost as if each case of infertility creates its own private affliction. As a result, an infertility diagnosis can rattle, and then terrify, each sufferer. No doctor or clinic can give you a guaranteed treatment plan or reliable statistics on your particular chance of success. The insistent, 2 A.M. bombshell questions quickly become: *Will I ever become a mother, a father? Will I never see myself reflected in a child's face? Never hold a grandchild in my arms? Am I, of all people, destined not to have my own children?*

*The Wiles' conception*—like most conceptions—took months of trying. When she finally skipped a period in early 2006 and got a positive result on a pharmacy pregnancy test, Rhonda was surprisingly surprised. The news felt almost too good to be true. She was as thrilled as a six-year-old on her birthday. Gerry was even happier. He handed out a dozen bubble-gum cigars to friends and neighbors.

In February 2006, they went to Rhonda's ob-gyn for the second sonogram, to hear the baby's heartbeat for the first time. Inside the darkened exam room, Rhonda lay, mostly naked, on the narrow vinyl table. Gerry reached for her hand in the dark.

The sonogram technician lubed up the sonic probe and turned on the machine. She stared at the backlit monitor. There was a long moment of quiet.

The technician paused. She looked at the ceiling instead of looking at the Wiles. Then she said, "I need to get the doctor."

This is never what you want to hear the ultrasound technician say.

Rhonda knew what this meant. Gerry looked at Rhonda's face. He started to cry.

The doctor came in and checked the sonogram. He confirmed what Rhonda and Gerry already knew: there was no heartbeat on the ultrasound. Their baby had died.

Like 30 percent of pregnant women, Rhonda had miscarried.[19]

It was seven and a half weeks into the first pregnancy of her life.

"I didn't know then," Rhonda says now, "that it would be the only pregnancy of my life."

Generally speaking, the causes of infertility in women are complex and hard to treat, increasing the value of gestational surrogacy as a treatment option for millions of women devastated by their bodies' limitations.

Eggs are vastly more intricate than sperm. They are hard to access, given their location embedded inside the ovaries within a woman's pelvis. Eggs are tricky and temperamental.

Easily damaged by heat and cold. Not terrifically amenable to being frozen or thawed even once.

Some might say like women ourselves.

Another problem is that an hour-old baby girl has a lifetime supply of 300,000 to one million oocytes, which sounds like a lot. But not in comparison to the 20 million sperm a man produces in every milliliter of semen. Plus, eggs are fragile. They get damaged and die easily.

Reproductive scientists believe that the female body does not, cannot, *will not* generate more eggs in its lifetime.

At least at this moment in medical history. Given how critical egg supply is to creating babies, vanguards such as biologist Jonathan L. Tilly at Massachusetts General Hospital have been experimenting with extracting stem cells from human ovaries and tinkering with them to produce human egg cells.[20] Success re-creating oocytes from mice stem cells was announced in 2012, but it's not clear how far into the future success with human eggs lies.

So the scarceness of eggs presents an impenetrable roadblock when it comes to female fertility.

Age also matters. What counts is the age of the eggs, not the age of a woman's body. The CDC has found that women of nearly any age can get pregnant as long as they use young, freshly donated eggs from women under age thirty. Dr. William Schoolcraft, founder of the Colorado Center for Reproductive Medicine, says the majority of the female infertility he sees is due primarily to the age of a patient's eggs.[21]

"People kind of think now at forty what they used to think at thirty," Schoolcraft told NBC News. "People do yoga and they run and they do all these healthy things. They assume that means 'I'm not aging.' But their eggs don't know that."[22]

The importance of young eggs also explains why most donors are under thirty, and why medical researchers are intent upon harvesting and freezing fertilized embryos *and* unfertilized eggs from women in their twenties when follicles rock. Frozen eggs can be thawed ten, twenty, or thirty years later, fertilized and implanted back into their donor or a surrogate, potentially silencing women's biological clocks and vastly extending a woman's fertility window. Initial egg freezing success rates were only about 10 percent. Doctors now claim up to 80 percent success rates with flash-freezing of unfertilized eggs using a process called "vitrification," which costs about $10,000 to $15,000.[23]

This is what Sofia Vergara, the sexy brunette Colombian actress from *Modern Family*, did before undergoing radiation for thyroid cancer, enabling her to have a baby via surrogate in her forties using her own eggs and her fiancé Nick Loeb's sperm.[24]

For eggs, it's all downhill after age twenty-nine. The average woman has lost 90 percent of her "ovarian reserve" by the time she turns thirty.[25] Of the hundreds of thousands of oocytes a woman is born with, most have died by the time she hits her mid-thirties. At thirty-seven, a woman has roughly 25,000 oocytes in her ovaries. At forty, she has 3 percent remaining. By the time she turns fifty, there are only about one thousand eggs left.[26]

Many pregnancies end naturally in the first trimester, much of the time before a pregnancy has even been confirmed. So Rhonda's miscarriage was nothing unusual. Except to her and Gerry, whose hearts it broke.

Most ob-gyns suggest waiting three months to try to get pregnant again following a routine miscarriage. Perhaps because of her training as a nurse and familiarity with doctors, instead Rhonda decided to investigate what had happened inside her body. It was part of Rhonda's preoccupation with honesty: she wanted her body to be honest with her, too. So she asked her doctor to conduct a thorough inspection.

And here is where Rhonda goes from being an ordinary nurse and wife who wanted a baby, to the winner—or loser—of a bizarre reproductive lottery. Her ob-gyn, poking around her female plumbing, lifted a small flap of skin near her vaginal opening. He made a startling discovery. If Rhonda had been born one hundred years before, even thirty years before, what her doctor uncovered that day would have dealt a death blow to her hopes of becoming a mother.

This is what her doc found: underneath her creamy white belly, her freckled abdomen, her bikini line, Rhonda had two vaginas.

If a couple does not become pregnant after exploring standard, relatively low-cost fertility treatments, they still do not call in the surrogates. Hiring a surrogate doesn't even occur to most people at this stage. A full diagnostic workup on the female partner is usually what comes next.

Complex diagnoses quickly get you into the expensive, exhausting, time-consuming, and frequently experimental medical terrain known as assisted reproductive technology. The American Society for Reproductive Medicine lists 189 different infertility-related medical definitions in the topics section of their Web site: hyperprolactinemia, premature ovarian failure, uterine polyps, dysfunctional uterine bleeding, hydrosalpinx, dyspareunia. These diagnoses usually lead straight to IVF.

Then your doctor prescribes subcutaneous hormone shots to trigger ovulation and to stimulate additional egg production. An embryologist surgically extracts your eggs, combines egg and sperm in a medical laboratory, and transfers the fertilized eggs back into your, or a surrogate's, uterus. That means more shots to help the fertilized egg implant, and more hormones to keep the egg in the uterus following implantation.

And more uncertainty.

And lots of money.

One IVF cycle can take several months and cost upwards of $12,400, according to the American Society of Reproductive Medicine. Each cycle can involve several invasive medical procedures as well as dozens of hormone injections and medications; treatment is not usually covered by health insurance. In other words, most people pay for their own fertility treatments.

And the bleak reality: there is never a guarantee of a baby.

Like female fertility overall, IVF success diminishes with age. For a woman in her early forties, the American Pregnancy Association estimates the chances of success with IVF are only 6 to 10 percent.[27] The Centers for Disease Control, headquartered in Atlanta, by law must track and report IVF pregnancy success rates from the nearly five hundred ART clinics in the United States. In 2009, the average chance of success from one ART cycle sloped downward as the intended mother's age increased:

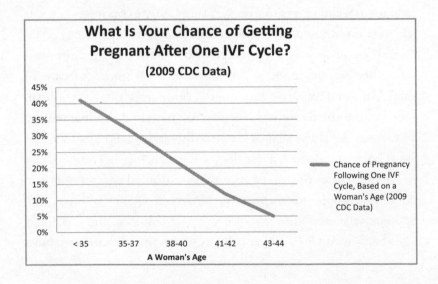

**What Is Your Chance of Getting Pregnant After One IVF Cycle?**
(2009 CDC Data)

Chance of Pregnancy Following One IVF Cycle, Based on a Woman's Age (2009 CDC Data)

A Woman's Age

This means that the chances of your getting pregnant, from one ART cycle using your own eggs, are as follows, based on how old you are when you do IVF:

41 percent chance of getting pregnant if you are younger than thirty-five

32 percent chance of getting pregnant if you are thirty-five to thirty-seven

22 percent chance of getting pregnant if you are thirty-eight to forty

12 percent chance of getting pregnant if you are forty-one to forty-two

5 percent chance of getting pregnant if you are forty-three to forty-four

Most of the decreasing luck getting pregnant comes because as you get older, you have fewer healthy eggs. But part of the explanation is that IVF miscarriages increase with age, too. According to the CDC's 2009 data, miscarriage occurred in only roughly 14 percent of ART cycles among women younger than 35.[28] However, nearly one in three ART cycles in women at age forty end in miscarriage. Almost two in three ART cycles in women older than forty-four fail.

When people in your office and friends in the neighborhood toss around IVF success stories, these stats never get mentioned. *People* magazine doesn't feature celebrities' failure-to-conceive stories on its covers; you only hear about actresses like Kelly Preston having a baby at forty-nine. Most people don't hear about the heartbreaks.

As a result, the vast majority of women who delay childbirth, or face infertility, blindly assume IVF will be a reliable, albeit costly, cure-all.

Just as women overestimate our fertility, the majority have no idea that by our mid-forties, we will have close to a 95 percent chance of failure with ART. A 2011 poll showed that women radically miscalculate IVF's success rates, no matter a woman's age, with a majority guessing that IVF results in pregnancy 50 to 60 percent of the time.[29] Even in the best of circumstances, with young eggs and young bodies, ART is successful only 40 percent of the time.

So, after years of disenchanted hopes and depleted bank accounts, what if repeat IVF cycles and other forms of ART *all* fail? Could you accept never having your own biological child? Never having a child at all? Often, cruelly, the years of setbacks make people crave a baby even more passionately.

In late 2006, a few months after her miscarriage, the ob-gyn doctor confirmed it: Rhonda Wile had two vaginas.

Yes, two vaginas. Or more precisely, two vaginal canals, two cervixes, and two uteruses.

On her right side, Rhonda had a normal "primary" vagina that she had put to good and regular use. It showed signs of sexual activity, a broken hymen, and a routine trip north to a uterus.

Branching off from her primary vagina on the left side, like a saguaro cactus arm sprouting diagonally in its quest to bear fruit, was another, smaller, virgin vagina. Beneath a flap of moist tissue was a secret vaginal canal that had not been used, leading to a second uterus.

An extremely rare didelphus uterus.

Two vaginas. Two uteruses.

Rhonda was stunned by the news. For days she looked down at her abdomen as if to confirm the shocking, invisible reality between her hips. She had two vaginas? Her doctor's discovery felt like a simultaneous betrayal and a startling revelation.

She felt as if her body had been keeping a secret from her. How could she ever have known? All the magic was occurring on the inside.

You might think that in terms of fertility, two vaginas and two uteruses would be pretty nifty. Rhonda Wile was fertile—technically. Doubly fertile. Perhaps that is why she conceived relatively quickly at age thirty-five. In India, the land of multiple gods, perhaps Rhonda would be worshiped like the powerful fertility goddess Devi, the Great Mother goddess, with many arms and enormous breasts, far more impressive than Barbie.

But the problem, the deadly problem in terms of fertility, is not always conception. Many infertile women can get pregnant easily. The problem for some is staying pregnant for nine months. Ironically, the root of Gerry and Rhonda's infertility was not Gerry's vasectomy, as they'd originally thought. The problem was inside Rhonda.

Each of Rhonda's uteruses was 60 percent the size of a regular uterus. She could conceive naturally using her right-hand vagina multiple times until her eggs ran out in five or ten years. But she would probably never carry a healthy fetus past twelve weeks, her ob-gyn explained. A twelve-week-old fetus cannot live in a 60 percent sized uterus or survive outside the womb. So Rhonda's miraculous internal plumbing, her double vaginas and double uteruses, in all likelihood condemned her to a lifetime of miscarriages.

But today, doctors can treat hundreds of different causes and symptoms of infertility. And she'd already proven she could get pregnant. Rhonda had so many medical options.

Didn't she?

A *big question* with ethical and societal reverberations: Who is entitled to have a baby via surrogate?

A world-famous actress who doesn't want to gain thirty
  pounds while pregnant?
A brilliant musician who yearns for parenthood but is
  terrified of sexual intimacy?
An ambitious woman who wants to experience parenthood
  while campaigning to be president of her company—or
  our country—by forty-five?
Anyone who can afford it?

The consensus within the ART medical community is that
surrogacy is justified only under strict medical circumstances.
If the intended mother doesn't have a uterus or if her uterus is
malformed, like Rhonda Wile. If her eggs are too old or otherwise not viable. If she suffers from a physical or psychiatric
condition that requires medication incompatible with pregnancy. If she has had recurrent miscarriages or repeat IVF
implantation failures.

Or increasingly, if "she" is a man who wants a baby.

*Naturally, the exorbitant* expense causes some parents to
give up on surrogacy as an option. Only 3 percent of Americans have a household income greater than $125,000 per per-
son. Even the wealthiest U.S. citizens, the financial elite, may
have trouble devoting $80,000 to $100,000 to the conception of
a baby, knowing they still need to be able to afford the care,
feeding, clothing, and education of a child in the United States
for the next 20 years.[30]

How practical—how morally just—is surrogacy as a solution to infertility, when 97 percent of Americans can't afford it?

The cost and complexity of surrogacy also cause some to
turn to private, potentially risky, and at times illegal, arrangements. Sometimes, these deals work out beautifully. Other
times, the consequences are dire. Intended parents and unborn

children are vulnerable, and some surrogacy and ART insiders fall victim to their own greed.

In August 2011, the world learned a name that nearly everyone in the surrogacy community had known for years: Theresa Erickson. Erickson was a forty-three-year-old San Diego attorney who had specialized in reproductive rights law, one of a handful of high-profile, expensive lawyers whose practice was dedicated to solving prospective parents' unique fertility problems.

Perhaps it is not a surprise that the biggest U.S. surrogacy scandal broke in California, the state that pioneered surrogacy and assisted reproductive technology.

Theresa Erickson had an impressive reputation in the surrogacy field. She'd written the bible on U.S. surrogacy, a handbook called *Assisted Reproduction: The Complete Guide to Having a Baby with the Help of a Third Party*. She had been interviewed by Bill O'Reilly, Greta Van Susteren, Ted Koppel, and other celebrity TV anchors.

In early 2011, the FBI began secretly investigating Theresa Erickson. New York authorities enlisted the undercover aid of Manhattan socialite Taylor Stein, the daughter of rock promoter Howard Stein and ex-girlfriend of William Lauder of Estée Lauder fortune and fame. Taylor was on the verge of paying $180,000 for an infant supplied by Erickson's agency when the FBI exposed the scheme and pressured Taylor to help bring down the illegal baby-selling ring.[31]

The Bureau believed Erickson had been using her inside knowledge of U.S. and international surrogacy laws to run an elaborate baby-selling ring for six years.[32] Along with two other lawyers, Hilary Neiman, a thirty-two-year-old attorney based in Maryland, and Carla Chambers, fifty-one, based in Las Vegas, Erickson's scheme involved hiring surrogates and implanting the women with fertilized embryos *before* adoptive parents were found. Chambers allegedly bragged about carrying at least a half-dozen surrogate babies herself for the ring's wealthy, and naïve, clients.

This practice is illegal in the U.S., for good reason. U.S. laws require doctors to document a surrogacy agreement before implanting an embryo, to insure that every fetus has parents before gestation begins. To duck this regulation, Erickson had surrogates travel to the Ukraine for the embryo implantation, where she used anonymous sperm and egg donors, taking advantage of lower medical costs and lax ART laws.

Once a surrogate became pregnant, Erickson would devise a story for potential clients such as Taylor Stein. She would apologetically explain that the original IPs had reneged on a contractual surrogacy agreement—which in reality is extremely rare. She pitched prospective parents an emotional "this baby needs a family" appeal, along with the added incentive that they could have a baby quickly and without meeting the traditional surrogacy guidelines. Two warning signs that the desperate intended parents either missed or ignored were that Erickson never let them meet their surrogate, and at times she let parents "choose" the sex of their future baby.

Erickson also filed fraudulent paperwork in San Diego courts to back up her story. Her firm then auctioned each baby to the highest bidder. Ironically, clients ended up paying *more* for an illegal baby than they would have through a legitimate surrogacy agreement; the incentive seems to have been getting a baby with a minimum of interviews, legal wrangling, and contracts. Surrogates who completed a pregnancy were paid roughly $40,000.

The FBI had received a tip from one of Erickson's illegal gestational carriers. Although she was twenty-three weeks pregnant, the surrogate hadn't been paid anything, hadn't received a formal surrogacy contract, and hadn't met any prospective parents.[33] Erickson pleaded guilty in August 2011.

The story splashed across newspaper front pages, burned up the Internet, and rocked the ART community.

Erickson's practice was illegal in at least three ways. The first was noncompliance with California laws requiring intended parents to sign a contract before the embryo implantation.[34] The second was conspiracy to commit wire fraud by transmitting fabricated documents to the State of California. The third foul was falsifying information to the couples whose babies were born through the surrogates she recruited for the scheme.

All three lawyers pleaded guilty in October 2011.[35] Along with a $70,000 federal fine, Erickson may be ordered to pay up to $1 million in restitution to the twelve families she deceived and the hospitals where the babies were born. She also spent five months in prison and nine months under home confinement.[36] Erickson surrendered her law license in August 2011 when she initially pleaded guilty. She never contested the charges, admitting in court that she had "truly lost" her moral compass.

In the wake of the scandal, Taylor Stein hired the surrogate who was pregnant with "her" baby. The child was born in March 2011, in Los Angeles, where Stein moved in part for the legal protection California laws afford intended parents of surrogate children. "I went and got [the surrogate], brought her to my home in L.A. . . . paid her health bills, took care of her, and she gave me the most beautiful son ever," Stein told the *New York Post*.[37]

The dozen other babies Erickson sold remained with their families, hopefully untouched by the scandal that had made their lives possible.

*Back in Arizona,* soon after her ob-gyn diagnosed Rhonda's didelphus uterus, two different fertility specialists dashed

Rhonda and Gerry's dreams. Determined to get help, they went to see four more doctors. Before each new visit, they held hands in the waiting room, hoping for a different prognosis. Rhonda wanted to be a mother, *needed* to be a mother, more than she had ever wanted anything in her life. There had to be a way for her dream—such an ordinary dream—to come true.

Five of the six reproductive specialists agreed: with two small-sized uteruses, all the mainstream, proven infertility remedies were not viable options. Standard treatments—Clomid, IVF, intrauterine insemination (IUI)—might help Rhonda get pregnant. But nothing could help her *stay* pregnant.

Only one fetal and maternal medicine expert—an internationally respected physician who specialized in high-risk pregnancies and preterm deliveries—held out hope. Listening to the MD's assessment in an office crowded with scientific journals and a pink plastic replica of a woman's uterus, Rhonda's and Gerry's hearts expanded with optimism.

The doctor confidently explained that no study had ever proven that a woman with two uteruses could not gestate a baby. Rhonda had gotten pregnant fairly easily, hadn't she? Of course, she would not be able to carry more than one embryo, making IVF tricky, and even then hers would be a very high-risk pregnancy. But doable given his skill.

Then, almost as an afterthought, the doctor cautioned the Wiles that Rhonda would probably carry the fetus until only nineteen or twenty weeks, half a normal pregnancy. The result would almost certainly be a mentally or physically handicapped child. He made it sound like this was good news.

Gerry gripped Rhonda's hand. They had already discussed this. Both had agreed they could never, in good conscience, bring a child into the world knowing he or she would suffer from lifelong birth defects. The doctor's solution was not a solution for the Wiles. They left their hope on his office floor.

If Rhonda had been born earlier in history, her childbearing life would have been a baffling roller coaster of conception and miscarriage, as many as three to six loops of hope and despair per year. No one would have been able to accurately diagnose, or treat, her infertility.

Many people, including perhaps Rhonda herself, would have blamed her for her barrenness. If she had grown up in countries with extreme Islamic influences such as India, Afghanistan, or Saudi Arabia, her husband and in-laws may have abandoned her, with societal sanction. Rhonda's life would have been characterized by the death of fetus after fetus, and the end of the hope that she would ever be able to bear a single healthy baby.

The reason, even in today's world of ART miracles, that the Wiles could only find one specialist with any hope for Rhonda was that, to date, most of ART has focused on eggs— extracting them, fertilizing them, and getting them to grow. Far less research has explored re-creating, repairing, or expanding a woman's uterus. Rhonda—or eggs extracted from Rhonda's ovaries—might create a baby one day. But due to her small uteruses, Rhonda would never be able to carry a baby from conception to full-term birth.

Rhonda didn't know it, but around the world, doctors had tentatively begun uterine transplants for women with defective or missing uteruses. In 2000, Saudi Arabian doctors transplanted the womb of a forty-six-year-old woman into a twenty-six-year-old, whose uterus had been removed after excessive bleeding following a Cesarean delivery. In early 2007, a New York hospital attempted to transfer the womb of a recently deceased, but otherwise reproductively healthy woman who'd died in an accident into a thirty-eight-year-old cancer survivor.

Neither transplant was successful.

A team led by Mats Brännström of the University of Gothenburg's Sahlgrenska Hospital in Sweden was laying the research groundwork to conduct experimental transplants. A

British mother named Eva Ottosson was lobbying doctors around Europe to donate her womb to her daughter, Sara, who had a condition called Mayer-Rokitansky-Küster-Hauser syndrome, which meant she had no uterus and was missing parts of her vagina.

Promising experiments. Hopeful research. Too unproven to help Rhonda and Gerry.

The good news, in 2007, was that doctors understood human fertility thoroughly enough to tell Rhonda and Gerry what was going wrong inside Rhonda's body. But no matter how many miraculous innovations the world's finest fertility doctors had come up with, none of them could help Rhonda Wile have a baby.

# Part 4

---

Heartbreak, Miracles,
and Money

Long before Rhonda Reycraft and Gerry Wile visited a single fertility specialist, an auspicious first date of sorts took place, over eight thousand miles away in Mumbai, India.

The year was 2005.

The setting: the polished marble halls of a world-class hospital in the city still known by many as Bombay.

On one side: a seasoned, respected female ob-gyn doctor.

On the other: an arrogant male whiz kid fresh out of medical and business school.

Both were Indian doctors. The similarities ended there.

Dr. Yashodhara Mhatre practices Buddhism. Dr. Sudhir Ajja is Hindu.

She was born in 1967. He is nine years younger.

Dr. Sudhir's parents arranged a traditional Indian marriage for their son. Dr. Yashodhara chose a love match.

He is loud and mercurial, with a flashing white smile that can disappear in an instant when he is angered. She rarely loses her temper.

At five foot one, Dr. Yashodhara Mhatre, petite, demure, and dark-haired, always waits for her patients to speak first, like a priest hearing confession. She listens patiently and sympathetically to the stories of their troubles getting pregnant. She's disarmingly soft-spoken, at least upon first impression. An outstanding doctor, she has excelled in her field of obstetrics and gynecology, her talent and work ethic amplified by an unusual compassion, which is critical for the psychological element of her specialty.

Wherever Dr. Yashodhara goes in Mumbai—one of her favorite restaurants, Mainland China; the crowded Hiranandani Hospital waiting room; the waterfall in the sleek lobby of the Grand Hyatt hotel—her patients and medical colleagues jump up to hug her. Even women lying in their hospital beds after delivering babies have been known to struggle to stand to embrace Dr. Yash, as she is called affectionately. They know her placid smile hides a fighter's determination to defend her opinions and advocate for other women. Dr. Yashodhara comes from a Dalit family, one generation removed from the "untouchable" Mumbai slum dwellers. Like many Indian women, she is tough despite all her pretty ways.

Dr. Sudhir Ajja is often moving too fast for anyone to hug him. Dr. Sudhir descends from a Hyderabad family whose roots can be traced to an ancient weavers caste, his deep brown skin indicative of his southern ancestors. Like many Indians from educated families in a country that reveres doctors, he earned a medical degree in his early twenties. During the year of rural medical service required by the government, he searched for a specialty for his career, a challenge that would hold the interest of his restless, inquisitive mind. He surprised his breathlessly hopeful family by going to business school. After graduating with an MBA in 2005, he joined Hiranandani Hospital as an administrative director.

Despite their differences, what Dr. Yashodhara and Dr. Sudhir discovered they have in common, although they express it in different ways, is a passion for helping infertile couples from around the world have babies in India.

––––––––

*Can you assign* a monetary value to a baby?

While India has too many babies, and factions of Indian culture whittle the value of female infants down to zero, American society continues to grapple with the precise monetary value of any infant, male or female. Courts have handed down payouts up to $1 million when hospital negligence causes a stillborn birth. State laws mandating infertility insurance coverage vary widely on whether conceiving a baby is a human right or "elective treatment." Insurance companies and their membership battle furiously over what baby-making attempts justify financial reimbursement.

Rhonda and Gerry Wile, like other infertile couples, wouldn't, and probably couldn't, attempt to capture their fertility trials or longing for a child with monetary measurements. Dollars are too crude a scale. When yearning for a baby ravages you, monetary limits do not curb your desire. The value of money becomes, for many, more or less irrelevant, especially as a gauge for how deeply you want a baby.

This didn't stop money from being one of the Wiles' biggest challenges to repairing their impaired fertility. From the moment they discovered their infertility, money dictated how aggressively they could treat it. All ART treatments, including hiring a surrogate, are, by medical definition, experimental.

"Nothing we tried was guaranteed to produce a child," Rhonda explains now, looking back.

Treating infertility was a money pit for Gerry and Rhonda, as it is for most infertile couples; perhaps especially painfully for the Wiles, because Gerry and Rhonda, as a firefighter and a nurse, had both chosen professions based on their desire to help others, not to enrich themselves.

In the Phoenix metro area, a registered nurse's average hourly wage is $30.55.[1] A nurse's annual salary ranges from roughly $48,000 to $78,000. The total take-home pay depends on hours worked per shift, number of shifts, and whether the employer is a hospital, a rehabilitative nursing home, or a geri-atric care facility.

A firefighter in Maricopa County can make $20 to $30 an hour. Total annual firefighter salaries average from $53,000 to $75,000, based on hours, shifts, and seniority.

Before taxes, Rhonda and Gerry Wile's annual household income in any given year fluctuated between $100,000 and $150,000, give or take a few bucks. A steady, reliable, generous living for a family.

As long as any children in that family are conceived and carried free of charge.

To place their earnings in perspective, the Wiles' annual income puts them squarely within the demographic of candi-dates to be surrogates—rather than the top 3 percent of wealthy Americans who can afford to hire them. There was no way Rhonda and Gerry could afford an American surrogate or prolonged infertility treatments at American prices.

Almost all fertility treatments are astonishingly expensive. IVF cycles at $12,000 to $30,000 a pop. Hormone treatments that run $1,000 a day. Adoption, the selfless act that can cost you $60,000. Almost none of the costs are reimbursed through insurance, and no bank will lend you the money in advance.

Few medical options are available—realistically—to the 97 percent of Americans who cannot afford infertility's most ex-pensive treatments. Having a baby through any of these innova-tive fertility pathways would eat away the Wiles' entire annual after-tax household income, several times over.

Not to mention the final alternative: paying another woman to carry your baby.

Surrogacy remains the most expensive cure for infertility.

In the United States, that is.

---

In a country of 700,000 physicians, you might think it hard for an individual doctor to stand out. Dr. L. H. Hiranandani never had that problem.

Lakhumal Hiranand Khiara was born in 1917 in Thatta, Sind, long before the British Raj left his country, in a northern region of India that is now Pakistan. As World War II approached, he traveled to England to study medicine. He returned to India and became a prominent surgeon as his country gained independence from the British and modernized itself and its medical system. An outspoken opponent of capital punishment and euthanasia, Dr. Hiranandani successfully campaigned to make buying human organs a crime in India.

Many eighty-year-olds are content to look back on their lives and play with their grandchildren. In his ninth decade on earth, Hiranandani decided he wanted more: to create a world-class Indian hospital, on par with the finest medical institutions in the world, in the heart of Mumbai, the country's largest city.

Today, the Dr. L. H. Hiranandani Hospital perches on Hill Side Avenue in Hiranandani Gardens in one of Mumbai's newest suburbs, Powai. The regal sandstone building sits astride a hill in the middle of modern Powai, which means "picnic by the lake." There is, in fact, a large lake nearby, one of the few in Mumbai. Built in 2004, the massive 200,000-square-foot hospital has two hundred beds and six specialty departments. The ground-floor lobby, as large as four basketball courts, includes waiting rooms, a pharmacy, and checkout stations. Like most buildings in Mumbai, the six-story hospital is surrounded by thousands of neatly ordered illegal slums, small tin shacks covered with bright blue waterproof plastic.

In the United States, most hospitals have a local government, a university, or a religious organization providing financial and administrative backing. Most people pay their bills through health insurance. Not at Hiranandani. By the glass exit doors in the spotless marble lobby, patients line up to settle their bills at cash registers. Hiranandani is 100 percent private. There are no insurance receipts, credit card payments, or government reimbursement forms at Hiranandani. Health care here is strictly a cash business.

Dr. Yashodhara Mhatre grew up not far from where Hiranandani sits today, in a family of four girls, risky business in a country where a common blessing is "May you be the mother of one hundred sons." However, her father, Janardan Jadhav, was one of Mumbai's modern heroes. He knew firsthand about Indian discrimination, having grown up in a slum himself, as part of India's Dalit class of sweepers and servants performing the city's dirtiest tasks. His father switched the train signals along Mumbai's dirty, noisy, dangerous train tracks, working for the Great Indian Peninsula Railway and the Mumbai Port Trust Railway. His mother sold fruits and vegetables in a makeshift outdoor stand by the Central Railway Workshop in the Wadala neighborhood. As a small child, Dr. Yash's father spent his days riding Mumbai's sweltering, rattling trains, selling trinkets and snacks to passengers.

Inspired by "untouchable" Dr. B. R. Ambedkar, a visionary equal rights leader on par with Martin Luther King Jr., Dr. Yashodhara's father was determined to educate himself and to rise above the slums and the caste hierarchy. After days spent working alongside his family, "Janu" stayed up every night studying and preparing for the country's standardized educational exams. He taught his younger siblings the Roman alphabet in the lamplight.

In the tenement, or chawl, where his family lived, there was only one electric light: the outdoor bulb by the communal toilet. So that is where Janu studied at night, sitting in the dirt, and standing for hours when the dirt turned to mud in the monsoon season. His studies paid off. He was accepted to

Chhabildas School, which required a four-mile walk every day. Later, he attended Elphinstone College and went to Siddharth College on a government scholarship. He joined the prestigious Indian Administrative Service (IAS) in 1963. Dr. Yashodhara was born four years later.

Having overcome caste discrimination, he was determined that his daughters would battle India's widespread sexism. To him, four daughters were a blessing of a different kind. Janu frequently told his daughters he did not believe in India's age-old practice of dowry any more than he accepted the caste stratification. He made sure all four received the finest education available in Mumbai.

"Your education is your dowry," he often told the girls.

Dr. Yashodhara earned her bachelors and medical degrees from Seth Gordhandas Sunderdas Medical College and King Edward Memorial Hospital at the University of Mumbai. After her ob-gyn residency, she completed a fellowship in reproductive medicine at KKH, the Kandang Kerbau Hospital in Singapore, one of Asia's oldest and largest hospitals specializing in health care for women and children. She's got all the right credentials: she's a member of the Mumbai Obstetric and Gynaecological Society (MOGS) and a fellow of the Gynecological and Obstetrical Society of India. Not too shabby for a girl born of the lowest Indian caste. She joined the medical team at Hiranandani's Centre for Human Reproduction in January 2005.[2]

Dr. Sudhir Ajja and Dr. Yashodhara Mhatre crossed paths frequently at Hiranandani. Dr. Sudhir was casting about for a good idea for a medical business. Dr. Yash was recovering from years of her own infertility battles. She'd been through seven IVF attempts—as a successful Indian doctor, she could afford the costly treatments. The last IVF cycle, luckily, had resulted in one daughter, born in 2000. But Dr. Yash knew most women probably could not afford to try so many times.

Together, Dr. Yashodhara and Dr. Sudhir came up with the concept of creating a clinic in Mumbai devoted exclusively to helping infertile couples have babies through surrogacy.

Paid gestational surrogacy had become legal in India only in 2002. India's skilled doctors, accommodating laws, vast number of low-income, fertile women, and relatively low health-care costs made surrogacy an ideal global medical business. Additionally, India was the only region in Asia that permitted commercial surrogacy, offering a coveted geographic advantage.

In 2005, most infertility clinics in Mumbai and throughout India catered to upper-caste Indian clients who could pay handsomely for discreet solutions to fertility challenges. A few Indian doctors had begun dabbling in marketing ART to wealthy foreigners, particularly Americans, Europeans, and Australians— people with the money to travel overseas for fertility treatments that were prohibitively expensive, and sometimes illegal, in their native countries. Global medical "tourism" was becoming more common around the world. But only a handful of Indian fertility clinics offered surrogacy as a treatment option. None focused exclusively on gestational surrogacy.

Dr. Sudhir's vision for the new business was practically psychic. The number of births resulting from surrogates in India was rising dramatically by 10 to 15 percent a year. India, a country with too many people and too many babies born every day, was on its way to becoming the largest supplier of babies for the world's infertile.

Riding to work on his motorbike, Sudhir saw baffled, sometimes panicked, sometimes disgusted, pale-skinned European, Australian, and American tourists in Mumbai every day. He knew that coming to India for two to three weeks of sightseeing, shopping, and picture-taking as a Western tourist was often overwhelming. He knew coming to India to make a baby would be beyond overwhelming.

So Dr. Sudhir set out to make surrogacy in India as comfortable and "natural" as he could. His marketing goal was to offer infertile international couples peace of mind—along with the latest ART treatments and gestational surrogacy. The slogan he created was "Making Babies Possible." As easily—and affordably—as could be.

Dr. Yashodhara and Dr. Sudhir's first disagreement was over the clinic's name. There were no medical practices in Mumbai that openly touted surrogacy—and only a few in India who quietly offered it. Dr. Yash felt the clinic's name should opaquely suggest joy and happiness; trumpeting surrogacy was anathema. Dr. Sudhir felt a bolder, more honest approach was best.

They argued for months.

Finally, Dr. Sudhir prevailed. The clinic would be called Surrogacy India. The next step was to establish a Web site. This Dr. Sudhir did from a noisy Internet café, because in November 2007, Surrogacy India did not yet have an office.

As 2007 drew to a close, Rhonda and Gerry Wile had gotten to the end of their fertility highway. Only adoption, surrogacy, and giving up remained as alternatives.

As the executive director of RESOLVE: The National Infertility Association, the United States' leading infertility advocacy group, Barbara Collura often first meets couples at this painful stage. Like the pretty Dr. Yashodhara Mhatre in Mumbai, Barbara Collura knows infertility's desperation firsthand. She was thirty-two when she was diagnosed with one of the simplest, most thoroughly understood causes of failure to conceive: blocked fallopian tubes. It was the same affliction Lesley Brown, the mother of the first IVF baby, experienced over twenty years before.

Collura's doctors were cheerfully blasé: "You are only thirty-two! You have thousands of eggs! You have an 80 percent chance of conceiving!"

Collura underwent IVF four times from 1997 to 1998. Her doctor harvested thirty-nine healthy eggs on his first try—which is like finding a $100 bill fluttering on a deserted sidewalk.

Every embryo failed to implant in her uterus.

"I was at the wrong end of every statistic," Collura explains today in her office in McLean, Virginia.

She experienced a cascade of isolation, shame, and grief. In the late 1990s, there were no *Oprah* shows explaining the heartbreak of failure to conceive. She knew of no support groups. She had no idea that millions of other women across the country were experiencing identical alarm and despair.

Her doctors were baffled and frustrated. "Nobody pulled me aside and offered sympathy or understanding," she recalls. She felt like a pariah among her baby-making sisters and friends, who had all conceived easily and often.

Finally, Collura got pregnant—naturally. Her doctors were confounded: how could blocked fallopian tubes result in a positive pregnancy? Barbara was overjoyed. Then one Friday night she was rushed to her local emergency room in an ambulance. The embryo had implanted in one of her narrow, scarred fallopian tubes. An ectopic pregnancy. Emergency termination of the pregnancy saved Barbara Collura's life.

She never attempted to get pregnant again.

Today, Surrogacy India is headquartered in the Bhandup West neighborhood of Mumbai. The wide, four-lane LBS road winds past dozens of narrow slum alleyways filled with wild dogs trotting alongside rickshaws the size of golf carts, barefoot children in faded blue and white school uniforms, and women in bright kurtas balancing folded laundry on the crowns of their heads. Bhandup West becomes more upscale as you approach the gleaming steel and glass Dreams shopping center, modest by U.S. standards, but a local landmark in Mumbai.

At the next red light, Tank Road, there sits a tidy white two-story cement strip mall on the right. It boasts an Axis Bank, a tiny food market, a store selling orange and green patterned saris, another stocked with men's brown vinyl shoes. The five-room office on the second floor that houses Surrogacy India might as well be called "Dreams," too. Here, infertile couples chase visions more elusive, and more enduring, than the ones available at the mall up the street.

Surrogacy India has grown steadily since their first surrogate baby was born in 2009. Fifty-eight babies followed in 2010. Halfway through 2011, the clinic celebrated their one hundredth baby. It was a magical milestone the doctors, at times, thought they'd never reach.

The second-floor hallway is stuffy, humid, and hot. Behind two frosted glass doors lies SI's inviting, air-conditioned reception room. The walls are painted a soft orangey-pink. The sofas are butter yellow. The pastel color scheme mimics the type of meticulously decorated nursery created by excited expectant parents who don't yet know the sex of their coming baby.

Past another set of sliding glass doors, the directors of Surrogacy India, Dr. Sudhir and Dr. Yashodhara, sit next to each other at one long glass-topped mahogany desk. Outside, across the hall, is a cool gray conference room, as well as an exam area with an ob-gyn table, sink, speculum, latex gloves, and gauze towels.

Adjacent to the office is another long rectangular room. To the left of its arched wooden entrance sits a neat pile of visitors' shoes—tattered men's loafers and children's sandals. The foyer and large room are kept cool and breezy with two large ceiling fans whirring on their highest settings. Twelve neatly made narrow iron beds line the room. It feels like the sleeping quarters of a girls' boarding school, bringing to life the illustrations of the French children's book *Madeline*.

Except that all twelve of the laughing, dark-skinned women sitting on the beds are pregnant.

Outside the open windows the Mumbai symphony of honking auto-rickshaws, cars, and motorbikes drones on. Although Surrogacy India's egg donors and clients come from all over the world, SI's surrogates are drawn locally from Mumbai itself and its nearby slums. The women are a mix of Hindu, Buddhist, and Muslim. Most are between twenty and thirty years old. They all have children, usually two or more. Although a few are single or widowed, most have been in traditional, arranged marriages since age sixteen or seventeen.

The surrogates are poor by Western standards, living in slums without significant income, savings, or property. However, by Indian standards, they are not the country's most desperate. They are the majority, living in the city's vast slums alongside 55 percent of Mumbai residents. Many can read and write; they are healthy, with glowing skin and shining white teeth; they are well clothed and their lives are, relatively speaking, economically stable. There are millions of women beneath them on lower poverty rungs, begging for food on a daily basis, forced to work as four-dollar-a-trick prostitutes, sleeping at night with their children on patches of city pavement, envious of slum residents who, like SI's surrogates, instead go home to small shacks with electricity and running water.

The women living in SI's Mumbai "surrogate house" come there for one of three reasons. Many are waiting for a positive pregnancy test following in vitro. Others, already pregnant, have some minor complication that requires daily medication, ultrasound monitoring, or a special diet. The rest are waiting out their third trimester of pregnancy; all surrogates live in SI quarters for their final trimester because the forced rest decreases premature births, increases infants' birth weights, and cuts down on the average length of babies' neonatal intensive care.

Often the surrogates' homes are an hour or more commuting distance from Surrogacy India's headquarters. The clinic requires that surrogates, once pregnant, must reside within thirty minutes of SI for monitoring and medical care. Many surrogates then choose to live on-site, or rent rooms or tiny apartments near the clinic. For the length of the pregnancy and postdelivery recuperation, relatives care for surrogates' own children. Husbands and children visit the surrogate houses every day.

Some surrogates also live away from home in order to hide their for-profit pregnancies from inquisitive and judgmental neighbors and relatives. Surrogates often leave out the incriminating details when telling neighbors and relatives that they are leaving the slum for a temporary job. Others stress the medical fact that they did not sleep with another man in order to get pregnant. Some fear they will be questioned and shamed about being surrogates, although surrogates insist they themselves do not feel embarrassed about the job.

Each surrogate has a dedicated mentor who has been a surrogate herself. This handler makes sure each surrogate takes her prenatal vitamins, eats nutritiously, and refrains from strenuous work or exercise. Other SI regulations—which surrogates agree to via written contract—include no smoking and no sex during the conception phase and throughout the pregnancy. Surrogacy India's payment schedule is similar to U.S. agencies. A 10 percent deposit is paid to the surrogate when she gets pregnant. Fifteen percent is paid at the end of each trimester. The remaining 45 percent is paid immediately after delivery.

The difference is the amount of money. In the United States, the surrogate fee runs from $25,000 to $50,000. In India, the range is roughly $5,000 to $8,000.

Groups opposed to surrogacy consider the surrogates' work distasteful, dissolute, a cog in an exploitative baby-manufacturing enterprise. *Organ donors for the rich.* But from the view of the surrogates themselves, they are mothers doing a difficult and remunerative job. By providing children for people who cannot have them, they are furthering their own children's futures.

*Most couples seeking* a surrogate have survived sustained emotional agony. They've ached for a baby to love and nurture. Dreaded never experiencing parenthood. Their trials can bring out their innate kindness, sympathy, and openness of heart.

When one Surrogacy India client's surrogate miscarried, the intended mother immediately flew 6,440 miles from London. She held the dead male fetus in the Mumbai morgue and sang him lullabies. She came back several months later to try surrogacy again. Today, she is raising a baby girl created through Surrogacy India.

However, some clients and clinics are less thoughtful about creating a baby.

Dr. Sudhir picked up the phone one day at his glass-topped desk in Bhandup West. On the line was a California man who wanted Surrogacy India's help. He explained that his wife had an especially gorgeous figure. He did not want to "ruin" it through pregnancy. (She didn't know he was calling.) Could Dr. Sudhir help?

An e-mail came from a New York doctor who informed Dr. Sudhir that her medical residency kept her too busy to carry a baby—as if she might order a few online infants along with her groceries.

Elsewhere in India, Australian parents independently hired a surrogate they had met through a clinic in order to skirt the agency fee. Once pregnant with twins, the surrogate threatened the intended couple with an abortion unless they made additional payments. She reportedly got what she demanded.

Nearly nine hundred miles away from Mumbai in Delhi, a clinic promised a Rhode Island couple their skilled doctors could use the woman's eggs, despite the fact that reputable U.S. and Indian clinics believed she was too old to produce enough high-quality ovum for IVF. Once the couple had traveled to Delhi, the clinic reneged—and offered a last-minute egg donor. With the surrogate standing by, having taken hormones for weeks, the couple agreed.

Nine months later, once their baby was born and they had picked her up, DNA testing showed she was not related to the intended mother or the intended father. The clinic, intentionally or accidentally, had used the wrong sperm. Their baby was not their baby. But the clinic refused to admit fault, or speculate about whose baby it might be. Without a genetic link, the American couple could not get a U.S. passport for their baby, and they could not legally take her out of India. The intended mother remained in India with the baby; her husband returned to Rhode Island to earn money to wage a complicated legal and diplomatic battle. The case remains unresolved as of the writing of this book.

Surrogacy India politely rebuffed both the California businessman and the workaholic New York doctor. The clinic regularly turns away the overzealous. Dr. Sudhir takes seriously one of the murkiest areas of assisted reproduction: his obligation not only to prospective parents, but to their unborn children as well.

At times he wonders: does his commitment to babies make him morally obligated *not* to help couples who strike him as narcissistic, mean-spirited, arrogant, or pathologically workaholic? Infertility does not discriminate for, or against, the world's predators. Do apparently self-centered people have as much of a right to be parents as the British mom rocking her dead son in the morgue?

Do unborn babies have a right to doctors who screen potential parents? Aren't the babies that result from his work SI's patients, too?

What stops Dr. Sudhir and Dr. Yashodhara from judging whom to help is simple: it is not their decision who gets to have babies. Infertile couples experience extreme stress and distress. They do not present their best selves to their doctors—they usually present their most honest, raw selves struggling with a deeply disappointing, cruel, and baffling predicament.

Surrogacy India and most other principled fertility doctors have embraced a common ethos: they tend to be nonjudgmental, within reason, in regard to potential parents. A fertility clinic is not in the business of deciding who will make the best guardians. Neither is a cancer doctor or an orthopedic surgeon expected to assess his patient's worth to the human race before he operates.

Many fertility clinics have elaborate guidelines, policies, and rules, a natural response to still-evolving medical best practices. High standards are especially critical in this market, with its vulnerable clients, emotional opponents, and rife lawsuit potential. Reputable clinics, in India and other countries, know how important ethics and guidelines are to potential clients and regulators.

However, to keep things simple, Surrogacy India tries basically to keep things simple. They investigate clients carefully for health and emotional issues. Most of their surrogates come to them through other surrogates. This and the small size of the clinic helps them choose clients and surrogates wisely. Like most ART clinics, Surrogacy India sets age limits for patients and other objective guidelines concerning their physical and emotional health. They require clients to follow a succinct number of rules: no contact with the surrogate or donors, except through SI, and no outside payments. Clients must sign a contractual agreement with SI. They must also sign a seventeen-page contract with their surrogate, and make a deposit. Surrogates and their husbands must sign contracts and affidavits as well, which are explained to them because many surrogates have limited literacy.

But no one has to pass a parenting test.

It took two years following Barbara Collura's life-threatening ectopic pregnancy for her to find her own resolution. For her, it wasn't surrogacy. She spent a year of crying once a week in an infertility social worker's office. Hundreds of hours logged in RESOLVE support group meetings and educational events—long before she became a RESOLVE employee herself.

"Infertility makes you very, very indecisive," she explains. "And very, very depressed. The constant waiting for the positive pregnancy test around the corner. The endless treatment cycles. The stories of other infertile couples and their doctors' expositions. Years of dashed hopes rob you of the connection between decisions and solutions."

For some, the never-ending uncertainty of not knowing when, or even if, you will become a parent can be more emotionally crippling than infertility itself. RESOLVE, which was founded by a group of nurses in 1974, presents an array of choices to their members—surrogacy, adoption, ART, living child-free. Each couple is encouraged to decide, or "resolve" their infertility, on a personal level, in the way that feels right for them.

For Collura, resolution came through separating pregnancy and parenthood.

"I couldn't give up my dreams of becoming a parent just because I could not get pregnant," she says today, over ten years later. She and her husband decided they didn't need the biological connection offered by surrogacy. Today, Collura is the happy mother of a son adopted from Guatemala in 2001.

"Infertility took away my ability to get pregnant. Not my ability to become a parent."

Pregnancy is, for most parents, the critical first step toward parenthood. But it's only a few months out of the lifetime it takes to raise a child. How much does it matter who is pregnant for those nine months?

For Gerry and Rhonda Wile, the answer, they reluctantly realized as 2007 drew to a close, was to find someone else to be the one who was pregnant for them. Rhonda began, painfully, to abandon the emotional milestones of seeing her own positive pregnancy test, buying maternity clothes, or watching her belly grow. She tried to refocus her hopes on the larger goal of becoming a mother, one way or another.

First, Rhonda went, excitedly, to a local adoption seminar at a nearby Scottsdale hotel. What most struck Rhonda was the main speaker, an Arizona woman who'd adopted a girl from Ethiopia. The woman stood on the stage and explained all she'd learned about countries that welcomed American adoptive parents, and matter-of-factly listed the rules and regulations agencies used. She rattled off body mass index and age requirements, courses one had to take to become sensitive to adopting an African child; no diabetes, no heart disease, no physical imperfections.

The restrictions echoed like dissonant musical notes in Rhonda's ears. The woman didn't say anything about how important it was to want a child, to be willing to love any child as your own.

The speaker explained that many adoption agencies—especially private and religious organizations—have stringent requirements for prospective parents. Some agencies serve only married heterosexual couples. Some agencies have strict health standards for prospective adopters; others are more lenient. Some require that adoptive parents be active members of a particular religion. Some specify how much money a couple must have saved—bank statements proving a baseline of $50,000 are often required. Medical conditions—even something as common as high blood pressure or breast cancer—can eliminate couples from the application process.

This discrimination—which would be actionable in practically any American workplace—is legal when it comes to adoption. High demand for babies—thirty-five times the number of babies available—means birth mothers and their agencies can be very, very picky.

And expensive. Rhonda took careful notes about the cost of adoption, which varies widely and is dependent on agency fees, the number of hours billed by attorneys and counselors, and the medical expenses of the birth mother and child. Fees paid to agencies range from nothing for foster care adoption, to more than $30,000 for private agency assistance, with no guarantee of a successful or binding adoption. The birth mother's medical costs can range from $10,000 to $20,000. Her rent, food, and clothing expenses can climb to an additional $12,000 for nine months, with counseling adding another $2,000. Company or state health insurance reimbursement for adoption expenses is rare, and when it exists, is minimal compared to maternity coverage that would kick in for "natural" conception and delivery. The total out-of-pocket for an independent U.S. adoption can run to $60,000 or more per baby.

But the worst part was when the woman blithely noted that people with a history of antidepressant use or a suicide attempt would not be considered as potential parents. You had to undergo psychological testing to be approved as an adoptive parent. If you'd ever taken antidepressant medication, you had to be off it for two years before the agencies would consider you as a potential parent.

Sitting in the dark, theater-like hotel auditorium, Rhonda knew medication had saved her life. It still provided her a critical foundation of biochemical stability. She couldn't go off her meds for two months—much less two years—and expect to be a good mother.

It had been twelve years since that bleak February morning in Florida when Rhonda, devastated by her first marriage's dissolution, had tried to end her own life. In the years since, she'd faced her grief and unrealistic expectations and rebuilt her self-esteem and her approach to marriage and life. Yes, she took antidepressants. She knew dozens of people—dozens of *parents*—who took the exact same medication. They helped her to stay positive and emotionally grounded. Rhonda had seen a National Institute of Mental Health (NIMH) estimation that over 27 million Americans took antidepressant medications. How could medication and a failed suicide attempt over a decade before automatically eliminate her from consideration as an adoptive parent?

She made it out to the car before breaking down. She called Gerry, bawling hysterically.

"It's all my fault," she wailed. "We're never getting a baby because of *me!*"

Driving back to Gerry and Frankie, Rhonda thought about lying. Who would know? The suicide attempt had taken place in Florida. Her brother had never checked her into the prevention facility. Would an agency actually call her doctor about her prescriptions? Even if they did, Rhonda knew doctors and pharmacists were legally prevented from releasing this private information. Rhonda could lie.

Except that she couldn't. Or more precisely, she wouldn't. She would be a good mother, as is. Every day at work Rhonda tended responsibly to sick and dying patients. For twelve years she'd been a caring owner to Frankie. She knew she would be a loving, unselfish mother.

Rhonda gripped her car steering wheel hard as she drove down the highway back to Mesa. She wasn't going to lie to anyone. That wasn't how she wanted to build a family. There had to be a way to become a mother, good enough just as she was.

Giving up was not viable, either. Gerry and Rhonda wanted a baby more than ever.

There was only one solution, the Wiles gradually realized.

Rhonda began researching surrogacy online. Her nursing knowledge, and access to medical sources through her work, gave her an avalanche of information overnight. She quickly discovered that surrogacy's legality was uncertain in Arizona, and blatantly prohibited in ten other states and the District of Columbia. Paid, or commercial, surrogacy was prohibited throughout Canada. Discouraging news. They would need to look farther afield and educate themselves on state-by-state surrogacy laws. The Wiles would have to leave home to create their family.

At that point, they thought they'd have to travel a few states' distance. A long drive or a short plane ride away. It never occurred to them they might have to leave their *country* to have a baby.

The truth hit Rhonda when she began researching how much surrogates, and their lawyers, are paid in the United States. Rhonda rarely considered herself to be spiritual or religious. But as she calculated the $100,000 a surrogate baby would cost, she started to wonder: Was God trying to tell her something? All her life, from her earliest childhood memories, she had known she wanted to be a mother. Nothing mattered more to her.

She had been through so many painful detours. Her first marriage. Her suicide attempt and depression. The slow evolution of her trust in Gerry. The expensive reversal of his vasectomy. The discovery of her didelphus uterus. The impossibility of adoption. The sky-high expense of surrogacy. Maybe these mammoth roadblocks all added up to a karmic message from nature or God for Rhonda Wile: You are not meant to be a mother.

Gerry told her again and again that she *was* meant to be a mother, a good one. But doubt wormed its way into her mind, woke her at night when she was sleeping, troubled her with its harsh message every time she saw a pregnant woman at Walmart or a baby at the supermarket near her Mesa home. She couldn't shake her misgivings, no matter how much Gerry reassured her.

Seeking her own resolution, one day in late 2007, Rhonda searched the Internet for the one remaining option that she and Gerry could afford: hiring a surrogate from another country. Her approach was pragmatic, but felt duplicitous, as if she were a traitor to her adopted country. Plus, she'd never been outside North America. But she and Gerry needed a surrogate and a clinic they could afford on a nurse and firefighter's combined annual household income. The only way they could do that would be to look outside the United States.

She typed "global surrogacy" into her Google search window. You can Google anything. Even a baby.

Three countries popped up again and again: Panama, Ukraine, and India. Rhonda knew very little about any of them. She was drawn to India because, as a nurse, the one thing she did know about the country was the reputation of its highly skilled, well-trained doctors.

She dug deeper. India had over five hundred clinics that offered surrogacy. Thousands of babies had been created for infertile couples there. It struck Rhonda as ironic that such an overpopulated, impoverished country was one of the world's leading providers of surrogate babies. But she liked that, too—she knew, again through her nursing experience, that volume carries its own inherent quality. You want the doc who has done the most appendectomies to perform yours. Indian doctors probably knew as much, or more, about creating and delivering babies than doctors anywhere in the world.

Her night-owl computer research showed that India's laws, unlike Arizona's, accommodated intended parents. In India, Rhonda discovered, surrogacy is legal as long as the surrogate has no genetic connection to the baby she carries, and the adoptive family has at least one genetic link through sperm or egg.

One particular Web site appealed to her. The "Making Babies Possible" slogan on Surrogacy India's simple, friendly pink and blue Web site seemed to reach out directly to Rhonda. She went back again and again to the Surrogacy India site, wondering: Could the people behind these sunny cyber pages help her create a baby?

Her hand trembled on the computer mouse the night she sat at her desk in her pj's and searched for information about the cost. Surrogacy India did not post anything about costs. Only a few Web sites published anything about expenses and payment schedules. She finally found one lone article that estimated the entire expense, including round-trip travel to India from the United States, was less than $25,000.

Rhonda's heart did a cartwheel. Twenty-five thousand dollars was more than the down payment on their house. As she'd struggled to establish her reputation during the first decade of her nursing career, $25,000 had been more than her annual take-home pay. But the total cost to have a baby via surrogate in India was less than the American surrogate's fee alone. With years of solid experience in her field and in Gerry's, maybe they could come up with $25,000.

She told Gerry everything. He was skeptical. He had never met anyone from India. Did they speak English? Did they have real hospitals?

They looked up India on the map on Rhonda's computer. It seemed absurd—and somehow wrong, unfair—that they would have to travel halfway around the world for a baby when most people just made one in their bedroom. But for the first time in a long time, Rhonda and Gerry felt the stirrings of real hope.

155

*Dr. Sudhir and* Dr. Yashodhara had founded Surrogacy India at the end of 2007—just as Rhonda and Gerry came to the somber realization that Rhonda would never carry a baby herself. Since then, SI had struggled to attract American clients. Surrogacy India had lined up surrogates, egg donors, embryo transfer specialists; Lilavati Hospital for egg harvest, fertilization, and transfer; and the Hiranandani maternity ward.

All waiting for business.

Yet, like every new enterprise, Surrogacy India needed more clients, greater cash inflow, more tantalizing word-of-mouth success stories. The United States dwarfs other markets, including Australia and Europe, in terms of money spent on fertility treatments, adoption, and surrogacy. To survive as a clinic, more than anything else, Surrogacy India needed American clients.

Several Americans had called and inquired via e-mail after visiting the Surrogacy India Web site. Everyone asked for references. SI had top-notch affiliates, including infertility expert Dr. Anita Soni at Hiranandani and a slew of Dr. Yash's former patients. But SI faced a Catch-22: potential American clients wanted recommendations from other Americans, people they could call and speak to for personal reassurance. And they preferred ones who had left India and returned home with healthy, screaming U.S. citizens in their arms.

By early 2008, Surrogacy India had yet to have an American couple as a client.

Then Rhonda and Gerry Wile called.

*Now, Gerry loves* to slalom around the Net looking for data, maps, and useful downloadable government forms. But when it comes to connecting with people, he prefers old-fashioned tools such as the telephone. So one evening he picked up his phone. *What the hell*, he thought. He punched in the long string of numbers Rhonda had written down from the Surrogacy India Web site.

Dr. Sudhir happened to be riding his motorbike to work when the phone rang. He answered. He heard Gerry Wile's booming voice. Gerry Wile heard a bunch of Mumbai street noise.

Almost instantly, across 8,847 miles of sand and ocean, a friendship was born between a fertility entrepreneur putt-putting to work in the middle of the most crowded island in the world, and a Canadian-American firefighter calling from a desert an ocean away. Like their predecessors Dr. Steptoe and Dr. Edwards, in that moment, the two men came together to try to make a baby.

"Gerry and Rhonda were the only ones who didn't ask for references," Dr. Sudhir explains now with his unzip-your-heart smile. "They said they liked us, and that that was more important than any reference."

In order to proceed with the initial testing procedures, Surrogacy India required a $150 wire transfer from the Wiles' Arizona bank to their Mumbai bank. Gerry felt terrible when the bank deducted $5 in fees. SI received only $145. He worried Dr. Sudhir would doubt his and Rhonda's interest.

When he called Dr. Sudhir to explain, the doctor laughed. "It is a sign of great trust that you sent anything."

And their journey together began.

Since Surrogacy India was founded in 2007, India has become the largest global provider of gestational surrogates outside the United States. The factors behind India's emergence as a supplier of gestational carriers are simple. An abundance of healthy, fertile women who are willing to become paid surrogates for a fee that international clients can afford. An excellent national health-care system that includes world-class experts in all forms of assisted reproduction. Widespread English fluency. Accommodating government regulations.

To couples desperate for a child, the five hundred surrogacy clinics sprinkled throughout India offer priceless, life-changing fertility assistance.

To Indian women eager to work as surrogates, many of whom—like Gauri—are uneducated women from Indian slums, what international clients offer is equally life-changing and priceless.

The $5,000 to $8,000 U.S. dollars paid to a female surrogate in India sounds like a relatively modest sum to most Westerners, especially compared to American surrogate fees. However, it translates to five to eight times the average annual household income in India. An Indian surrogate being offered $5,000 is akin to an American woman being offered approximately $200,000—four years of annual household income for nine months of work.[3]

To place an Indian surrogate's payment in perspective, consider gross national income. GNI—which measures both an individual's income and government spending per person—is roughly $1,170 U.S. dollars in India, according to 2009 UNICEF data. In the United States, GNI is $46,360. In other words, the average person in the United States is forty times wealthier than the average person in India, most of whom survive on less than two dollars a day.[4]

India ranks 148th out of roughly 200 countries in terms of GNI. People in Afghanistan, Ethiopia, and Sierra Leone are poorer than those in India, but not by much. And like everywhere in the world, women in India are, on average, far poorer than men. Most Indian women could not accumulate $5,000 in ten lifetimes.

Indian surrogates find out about the curious concept of

surrogacy, and the huge payments offered, through word of mouth. Unlike Rhonda, they can't Google "surrogacy" because most do not have access to computers or the Internet. Instead, their communication network consists of friends, acquaintances, and relatives who have served as surrogates.

When Gauri finally came to Surrogacy India to explore the strange, lucrative idea of having a baby for another couple, Dr. Yashodhara explained the process, and in turn asked Gauri many questions. These are the queries all potential surrogates are asked to consider before becoming what Surrogacy India calls in their pamphlet a "Special Woman," but others—perhaps even the surrogates themselves—would call helping an infertile couple's dream come true in exchange for a large pile of money.

We thank you and are proud of you, if you have made the decision to become a Surrogate or are thinking of becoming a Surrogate. You need to be:

Special Woman between the ages of 21–35 years, having a sincere desire to help infertile couple achieve parenthood

Special Woman who has experienced the joy of having a child and nurturing the young life

Special Woman with a positive approach and willing to undergo psychological evaluation

Special Woman who did not experience any major pregnancy complications

Special Woman who believes in families and has full emotional support from your husband/partner, who also understands the implications of the surrogacy program and is willing to participate in any which way required.

Special Woman, who understands the pain of a childless couple, is dedicated to the surrogacy program and also understands her responsibility toward the intended parents helping them fulfill their dreams. Thus she will not drop out of the program midway leaving the couples dreams unfulfilled.

Surrogacy India doesn't include payment details in the Special Woman pamphlet. But the money is what draws potential surrogates.

Now . . . your children are hungry. Your parents and grandparents are hungry. You are hungry. Your home is a corrugated tin shack covered with plastic to keep out the rain. The surrogacy payment means everyone in your family will eat, live in a house, and go to school. You have no other means to earn money. In less than a year, you can transform your life, your children's lives, and your grandchildren's lives—forever.

Now would you be interested in carrying someone else's baby?

For Gauri, the answer was yes.

Surrogacy India operates on a combination of interlocking factors. A thorough understanding of infertility's psychological scar tissue. Consumer-friendly capitalism. Access to elite medical expertise at one-tenth the U.S. expense.

Dr. Yashodhara and Dr. Sudhir present clients from around the globe with a range of fertility treatments nearly identical to those offered by the finest U.S. fertility clinics and hospitals—at enormous discounts, even when you factor in the cost of traveling to India. SI offers gestational surrogates, donor eggs, donor sperm, in vitro fertilization, frozen embryo transfer, assisted "hatching," blastocyst culture, and referrals to other specialized fertility clinics in India. SI also provides genetic testing. Of your DNA. The egg donor's DNA. The sperm donor's DNA. The surrogate's DNA. Your baby's DNA.

But what Surrogacy India really offers parents is peace of mind. Every SI touchpoint seeks to assuage trepidatious clients contemplating the disconcerting idea of creating a child in an unfamiliar country thousands of miles away from home. Surrogacy India tries very hard to make the prospect of having a baby via a complete stranger in a foreign land seem almost . . . easy.

At least that's how it sounded over the phone when Gerry first called Dr. Sudhir.

*Most people trying* to wrap their heads around hiring a surrogate to carry a baby for them in a faraway country don't, at first, tackle all the critical questions they need to answer. Considered simultaneously, the possibilities can be even more overwhelming than the original idea of having a baby in a foreign country, via a foreign gestational carrier. Gerry and Dr. Sudhir didn't dig into any of the dozens of mandatory decisions during that first conversation. But here is small sampling of what Surrogacy India needs to know:

- Do you need an egg donor?
- Do you need a sperm donor?
- Do you need a gestational surrogate or do you want to try to carry the baby yourself?
- Who will be the baby's guardians in case of the death of the intended parents?
- What choice will you make if the ultrasound shows a significant birth defect?
- Do you want vaginal or Cesarean delivery?
- Are you coming for the twenty-week sonogram?
- What date would you like to arrive for the birth?

Although many intended parents find these questions hard to absorb, especially all at once, Surrogacy India's goal is to take care of all medical, legal, and practical details efficiently, so clients can focus on the emotional aspects of having a baby. SI provides travel and hotel arrangements, as well as a checklist for all the documents ART travelers need, but may not know they need—such as a marriage license, proof of citizenship, and India's seemingly endless bureaucratic forms.

SI handles all financial transactions, including gratuities, payments, and commissions. Additionally they provide the surrogacy agreement template and Indian legal support to customize the surrogacy contract. Surrogacy India provides advice for passport and exit visas, as well as a knowledgeable "fixer" who can help manage the notoriously byzantine and corrupt Indian government to avoid last-minute roadblocks.

Here, Mumbai's business climate and large population work in favor of foreign intended parents. Visa and passport processing are both far more quixotic and unpredictable in India's smaller cities. Mumbai benefits from its proximity to the U.S. Consulate and the Foreigners Regional Registration Office (FRRO), both of which provide travel documentation to the millions of foreign travelers who come through the city annually.

All this is critical, because naturally clients want to leave India once the baby is born—with their baby.

Surrogacy India's clients don't worry about getting from the airport to the hotel. SI arranges pickup, transportation, sightseeing, and a travel fixer. They even give each client a local cell phone.

Surrogacy India is like a Disney cruise-ship provider. Doctors Yash and Sudhir have thought of every possibility. They take care of everything.

Except on this trip, instead of coming home with some expensive photos and a Tinker Bell pin, you come home with a baby.

*Your* baby.

*Out of the* two million American citizens of Indian descent who live in the United States, there are only a handful in

Mesa, Arizona. Just enough to sustain two Indian grocery stores and five Indian restaurants. In early spring 2008, in preparation for their first trip to India, Rhonda and Gerry asked friends to take them to an Indian movie. They sat through the newly released, epic four-hour Hindi extravaganza *Jodhaa Akbar* in a Tempe theater, watching in bemusement as dozens of sari-clad women danced in the aisles.

Their friends also introduced them to a few favorite restaurants. Their favorite quickly became Guru Palace on South Gilbert Road, owned by Rana Singh Sodhi, a Sikh man in his forties from northern India. The Wiles tried an Indian cheese called *paneer*, spicy chicken tikka cooked in a clay tandoor oven, and *gulab jamun*, hot fragrant balls of pastry in a sweet syrup.

Gerry loved everything. Rhonda liked the bread.

Gerry being Gerry, he struck up a warm friendship with the easygoing owner of Guru Palace. Rana Singh Sodhi was forty-five, the youngest of three Sikh brothers who had emigrated from northern India to the United States. Rana and his brothers wore turbans and sported thick black beards as expressions of their Sikh beliefs.

His oldest brother, Balbir, had also settled in the Phoenix area. Balbir had owned a local gas station. He was well known for giving children candy from his convenience store if they lacked money.

Gerry and Rhonda were horrified to learn that on September 15, 2001—four days after the Pentagon and World Trade Center towers were attacked—a Mesa man had shot Rana's brother five times as he worked at his gas station. The assailant, Frank Roque, mistook Balbir for a Middle Eastern terrorist because of his dark skin and turban. A local jury sentenced Roque to death; a high court later commuted the sentence to life in prison. Rhonda and Gerry learned that, in the hysteria following the 9/11 attacks, as many as seventeen Sikhs living in America were murdered by deranged "patriots," simply for being Indian in America.

"Of course," Rhonda explained on her blog in the spring of 2008, "Gerry and I know we won't be coming home from our first trip to India with an actual baby."

Instead, they would bring home what they craved almost as dearly: hope for a baby. A baby in the very near future. They would in fact leave their baby, created from one of Rhonda's eggs and Gerry's sperm, in India, growing in another woman's uterus. So what if the baby grew for the first nine months inside another woman's uterus? Rhonda tried to shrug this off as a detail, driven by the reality that a baby needed an affordable uterus larger than either of hers.

On Tuesday, April 1, 2008, Rhonda wrote the first entry of her blog describing her infertility journey. She called it "Steps of Our Journey." She started blogging to share her anguish, excitement, and doubt in the search to become the mother she felt she was meant to be. She never dreamed that one day, her blog would be one of the most widely read in the surrogacy community, encompassing over 95,000 hits and four hundred pages of entries, photos, and medical results.

Rhonda and Gerry landed in Mumbai on Sunday, April 6, 2008. The doctors from Surrogacy India met them, their first American clients, at the international airport. Once the Wiles were settled at their hotel, the focus turned quickly to baby making, with examinations, hormone shots, and blood tests. Dr. Yash, with her soft-spoken, sensitive ways, tried to make Rhonda feel like a sister, not a medical patient.

"She came here for a baby," Dr. Yash cautioned her staff. "Not a treatment to 'fix' her."

The first medical procedure took place on April 14, 2008— the Wiles' eighth wedding anniversary—at Lilavati Hospital in downtown Mumbai. Dr. Yashodhara held Rhonda's hand during the entire operation, nodding frequently, reassuring and encouraging her with soft words and her calm gray-brown eyes as IVF specialists Dr. Hrishikesh Pai and Dr. Nandita Palshetkar performed the laparoscopy to extract ten follicles from Rhonda's ovaries.

Ten potential babies!

Rhonda had been injecting hormones for the past two weeks to stimulate egg production in preparation for IVF. Given that eggs vary in quality, the doctors could not rely on her usual monthly cycle. Ten eggs represented a fine yield; the doctors and the Wiles were excited by the take. They were on their way to making a baby.

Next door to Rhonda at Lilavati Hospital, a slight, dark-skinned male employee in a pale blue smock silently led Gerry to a small room off the larger hospital waiting area. He wordlessly handed Gerry a tiny paper Dixie cup. The little room had paint peeling from the walls, a cot with a wool blanket, and a notable absence of magazines with naked ladies on the cover. Gerry had to poke his head back into the hallway to ask Rhonda to join him for "inspiration."

*Happy anniversary, honey!*

Soon enough, Gerry provided his contribution. Some of his swimmers would be used immediately; the rest frozen and stored, safely and cheaply, should they be needed for future attempts. It only took a few short minutes for Gerry Wile to complete his half of all current and future Wile family conception equations.

The doctors examined Rhonda's ten harvested follicles under a powerful microscope and ranked them. They looked for the highest-grade eggs for fertilization. They chose eight to fertilize into embryos, and added Gerry's sperm to the sterile petri dish. Then the doctors let nature work her magic.

With nothing to do but wait, during the next few days,

Leslie Morgan Steiner

Gerry and Rhonda explored the Gateway of India, the Taj Mahal Palace Hotel, and the colorful washday orchestra at Mahalaxmi Dhobi Ghat, where more than five thousand laundrymen clean and iron thousands of pieces of clothing and textiles each day, since manual labor in India is still cheaper than machinery. The Wiles bought kurtas and gifts and sampled Indian food. People on the streets marveled at Rhonda's thick blond hair and in broken English asked to touch her fair skin. The Wiles ate at Mumbai's Pizza Hut and KFC, both restaurants so wildly popular that local Indians choose them for marriage proposals, and where security guards hold sway at the entrances.

Mumbai was hot, crowded, smelly, filled with honking horns and stray animals. Overwhelming. But the Wiles embraced every idiosyncrasy.

"This is the country where my child has been conceived," Rhonda thought every time she saw a stray dog run through a mud puddle or a sacred Brahman cow stop traffic. "I will be proud to say this and share this with them. No country is perfect. No culture is ideal. But these people are one of the most kind and loving and generous societies I have come across. I will have a lifelong tie to this culture, my home-away-from-home."

Three days later, on April 17, back at Lilavati Hospital, Rhonda put on the same kind of surgical scrubs and mask she wore every day at work in Arizona. The Lilavati doctors let her into the small, undecorated surgery room to hold the hand of an Indian surrogate named Tanisha.

This was the most critical step in gestational surrogacy: the transfer of the fertilized embryos from petri dish to the surrogate's uterus. Rhonda and Gerry had chosen Tanisha from Surrogacy India's online roster of potential surrogates several weeks before their trip. Tanisha, a diminutive Hindu woman with two children, had been taking hormones to simulate pregnancy and ready her uterus to accept the embryos.

While Tanisha lay on the examining table as if preparing for a Pap smear, her feet in stirrups and her hand held by Rhonda, Dr. Pai threaded a narrow tube called an embryo transfer catheter through Tanisha's cervical opening to the middle of the uterine cavity.

The catheter was loaded with five of Rhonda and Gerry's fertilized embryos. Dr. Pai normally transfers only three embryos during IVF. However, based on his past experience, Rhonda's age, and Surrogacy India's determination to help the Wiles, he chose to increase the number to five. He had painstakingly "hatched" each of the five embryos with a laser, creating a gap in the outer area of the embryo called the zona, a special technique Dr. Pai believed would help the embryos implant in Tanisha's uterine lining. Using an abdominal ultrasound, Dr. Pai guided the catheter tip to the proper location in Tanisha's uterus. Then he tipped the catheter to release the embryos onto the endometrial lining of her uterus. The procedure was fairly painless, not requiring sedation or pain medication, because a woman's cervix and uterus have minimal nerve endings.

Rhonda kissed Tanisha's cheek and whispered one of the only Hindi words she knew. She said *"Shukria,"* which means thank you. Tanisha's job for the next hour was to lie still. Then she would be escorted back to Surrogacy India's special "surrogate home" for fifteen days of rest and minimal activity, a luxury Tanisha had often provided for others, but never experienced herself. Her husband and sons would remain at their tiny home in the slum, cared for by female relatives. A special caretaker, in this case Dr. Meenakshi Puranik, would oversee Tanisha's care, making sure she took her prenatal vitamins and did little else until the pregnancy was confirmed.

Everyone involved knew that if more than two embryos cleaved to Tanisha's uterine wall, the doctors would "reduce"

The Wiles with the two founders of Surrogacy India. *(Left to right)* Dr. Sudhir Ajja, Dr. Yashodhara Mhatre, Rhonda Wile, and Gerry Wile.

the number of growing fetuses to maximize a healthy pregnancy and birth. In India, unlike the United States, the law forbids surrogates to carry more than two babies at once, given the danger to the surrogate mother and the babies she carries. Everyone also knew it was possible that no embryos would

Although Gerry and Rhonda traveled to India in search of a baby, they unexpectedly fell in love with the country, its people, and the many wonders they found there.

implant successfully, although there was no reason to think this likely.

To show the Wiles a sampling of India, Dr. Yashodhara and Dr. Sudhir took them north to Agra. Gerry and Rhonda rode camels. They visited the famous Taj Mahal temple. They flew south to Goa, to see the gorgeous white-sand beaches. The Wiles, who had never sightseen outside North America, rode in rickshaws, on elephants, in rickety buses, and on small Indian commuter planes. They loved it all.

On Sunday, April 20, Rhonda and Gerry headed back home. Their luggage spent an extra day in India, but eventually made it back to Arizona. Frankie badly needed a bath. They were all very happy to see each other.

Then began the wait for the positive pregnancy news. Despite their exhaustion, in their hearts, both Rhonda and Gerry already could feel that the embryos had implanted in their Indian surrogate eight thousand miles away. They *knew* they were pregnant. The only real question, in their minds, was how many of their five fertilized embryos would implant.

Surrogacy India's protocol is to wait two weeks before administering a pregnancy test. During this time, Gerry had to head to San Angelo, Texas, for a three-month Fire and Emergency Services training course conducted by the U.S. Department of Defense at Goodfellow Air Force Base. Rhonda started a new job at a new hospital. After everything they had been through, fourteen short days seemed like a reasonable time to wait for the good word.

Neither Rhonda nor Gerry had an inkling of how much longer than two weeks they would have to wait for a positive pregnancy test.

In India, where the vastness of the population means bureaucracy rarely parallels logic, the laws governing surrogacy all make unexpectedly good sense. Regulations are straightforward and pointedly designed to prevent three specific abuses: exploitation of women, destruction of female fetuses, and bribery of foreign clients. Another surprise is that India's ART rules are, in fact, far more stringent than U.S. regulations.

Guidelines stipulate that the surrogate must be an Indian citizen, between twenty-one and thirty-five years of age. If she is married, the consent of her husband is required. No woman can undergo embryo transfer for the same client more than three times. She may not have more than five live births, including the births of her own children. If a surrogate miscarries, she cannot work as a surrogate again.

Treatments specifically focused on producing a male or female baby are prohibited—critical in a country where seven thousand female fetuses are aborted every day. Commercial, or paid, egg donation is legal. Ditto for commercial surrogacy. Both have been permitted in India since 2002.

Traditional surrogacy is prohibited—only gestational surrogacy is allowed. The surrogate may not have a biological link to the child she carries. The baby or babies must be created through IVF, to provide the surrogate as much emotional and psychological separation as possible. Creating a baby via surrogacy is a medical procedure and a paid job, distinctly different from traditional motherhood. The intended parents must have a genetic link to the child the surrogate carries—either through sperm or egg—to avoid a eugenics marketplace where parents seek to purchase a barbaric ideal of physical or genetic superiority.

In India, if a surrogate becomes pregnant with more than two fertilized embryos, no matter how willing the surrogate and intended parents may be, selective reduction must be performed. Contracts between surrogate, clinic, and client are mandatory. Surrogacy is a business transaction, albeit a highly emotional, deeply personal, and at times controversial one.

U.S. Department of State citizenship regulations governing American babies born in India and other countries are also straightforward and conducive to international ART and surrogacy. Any baby born outside the United States to American parents is considered a U.S. citizen born abroad, no matter how that child is conceived or gestated. Just like Rhonda and Gerry's Arizona senator John McCain, who was born in Panama in 1936 where his father was stationed as a naval officer. For any baby born to U.S. citizens serving in the military, living or traveling abroad for any reason, the process is simple: the local hospital provides a birth certificate, the local U.S. Consulate issues a Certificate of Birth Abroad, and once parents prove their parentage and U.S. citizenship, the baby is issued a U.S. passport.

Within the United States, much of surrogacy and ART

remains unregulated, untracked, contested, and debated. Sure, the CDC's Division of Reproductive Health tracks and publishes fertility clinic success rates. Nonprofit organizations ASRM and SART publish guidelines on the suggested number of embryos and prices for donated eggs. RESOLVE and venerable clinics and agencies across the country publish recommendations and share their collective expertise at conferences and think tanks around the world.

But no legal or government entity enforces these principles and best practices. Even though the Centers for Disease Control estimates that 1 percent of babies born in 2010 were conceived through some form of assisted reproduction, when it comes to sperm, eggs, and the surrogate uteruses that host embryos, assisted baby making remains virtually unregulated by the U.S. government or private industry watchdog groups.

Take sperm donors. On May 25, 2005, the U.S. Food and Drug Administration (FDA) implemented national human tissue donor screening rules.[5] Many states have additional certificate and licensing regulations for clinics that collect, store, and sell sperm. As a result, commercial sperm donations are now tested for HIV and other life-threatening contagious illnesses.

However, tracking sperm donors—and their medical histories—remains a dodgy pursuit. There are over one million people alive today in the United States who were conceived through donated sperm. It is a Sisyphean task to organize and enforce access to donor identity, genetic history, and medical records for the roughly 30,000 to 60,000 U.S. babies born each year using donor sperm. The donors themselves, who are paid only about fifty dollars per donation, and babies born from their donations, are not registered or tracked by any government agencies or private sperm donation enterprises.

Sperm donors often want to remain anonymous. The transaction is usually, for the donors, purely financial. Many donors want it to be completely forgettable. Quite often intended parents want the donors to stay anonymous as well; close to 80 percent of heterosexual parents do not ever tell their children or families that a child was conceived using donor sperm.[6]

A limited number of random FDA inspections cannot possibly guarantee compliance with the 2005 regulations across the sperm bank industry. There is one independent agency, the American Association of Tissue Banks (AATB), that inspects and accredits sperm banks—but accreditation with the AATB is voluntary. American mothers of donor children are not required to report a child's birth to the sperm bank they used or to specify donated sperm on the infant's birth certificate. Less than four in ten parents voluntarily do so, making the number of babies born using donated sperm impossible to accurately estimate or track.

Unlike Britain, France, Australia, and Sweden, which cap the number of children one donor can father at ten, the United States has no limits on the number of babies born to any one individual donor. (There are also no restrictions on the number of eggs a woman can donate, the number of times she can be a surrogate, or the number of babies a surrogate can carry at one time.) Six out of ten sperm donors donate more than fifty times.[7] Due to the establishment of registries to connect families of sperm donors, such as Donor Sibling Registry, we now know that some popular sperm donors have fathered more than 150 children.[8] Parent advocates now encourage children born using donors to memorize their sperm father's "number" as part of their overall sex education, so that as teenagers and adults they do not inadvertently end up dating or marrying their half siblings. Practical advice, yes. And also completely whack-job crazy.

Back in Arizona—where laws were unclear about whether Gerry and Rhonda could hire a surrogate, and where a federal judge in 2013 found a notorious Maricopa Country sheriff named Joe Arpaio and his virulent one hundred deputies guilty of racial profiling against immigrants from Mexico and Central America—any babies born to Gerry and Rhonda abroad via surrogate would be treated as legal U.S. citizens. No questions asked. Or at least, only a few questions to make sure each baby was lawfully born to parents who are U.S. citizens.

Not all countries are so accommodating to babies born via surrogate. Two of Europe's largest, wealthiest countries, France and Germany, both adamantly oppose commercial surrogacy. Paid surrogacy within each country's borders is illegal. Additionally, in some cases, citizens' biological offspring, born via surrogate mothers in other countries, are prevented from coming home with the intended parents via visa restrictions and passport red tape. In other instances, children born via surrogate in other countries are not allowed to become citizens in their parents' home country.

Nine years before the Wiles began exploring surrogacy, a French national living in Paris, Sylvie Mennesson, finally faced the end of her fertility road and accepted that she was unable to bear children. She and her husband, Dominique Mennesson, turned to a surrogate mother in California. The surrogate conceived using Dominique's sperm and donor eggs. The surrogate mother gave birth to twin girls in California in 2000; like any babies born in America, the girls were granted U.S. citizenship. Dominique and Sylvie Mennesson are recognized as the twins' parents on the U.S. birth certificate.

However, France, which bans commercial surrogacy, refused to recognize the Mennesson children as the legal offspring of French nationals. In 2011, after years of lower court battles, France's top court ruled that the Mennesson twins are not French citizens. The twins' names were stripped from France's national civil registry. Being listed on the national registry is a requirement for obtaining identity cards and passports, documents the girls may now never have in their family's home country.

The United States is their only legal residence. As long as the girls are children they will be allowed to live in France with their parents. But their future nationality is in question. The Mennesson twins are immigrants, and one day will be illegal immigrants, in the only home country they have ever known.

*The news came* on Wednesday, April 30, 2008. Ten days after they stepped off the plane back in Phoenix. Gerry was still training in Texas.

Doctors Yash and Sudhir called Rhonda at home in Arizona. They had no choice but to be blunt.

Tanisha was not pregnant. A "negative" in surrogacy shorthand. Blog insiders lash the dreaded result derisively as a BFN or "Big Fat Negative."

Despite Rhonda's healthy eggs, Gerry's robust sperm, and the surrogate's receptive uterus, and despite the fact that the Wiles had traveled all the way to India to make a baby on the day of their eighth wedding anniversary, none of Dr. Pai's five carefully laser-hatched embryos had implanted into Tanisha's uterine wall.

Not a single one.

Rhonda, home alone in Mesa with Frankie at her feet, felt her heart detonate. She had been so sure Tanisha would get pregnant. That she and Gerry would be holding their baby in their arms in nine months.

They had been through four years of trying to conceive. They'd spent almost $25,000 on Gerry's vasectomy reversal, hormone drugs, doctors' fees, and travel expenses. They had ventured over eight thousand miles away to have a child.

She'd been such a good girl. She had been unflaggingly hopeful, cheerful, patient, and optimistic at every turn. When many tourists complained about how filthy, poverty-stricken, chaotic, and polluted Mumbai was, she and Gerry had embraced the dirt as the earth where their child would be born.

Maybe God was not listening to her. Maybe she was not meant to be a mother.

She posted the negative news on her blog under the headline, "Our Journey Ends Here."

*Two weeks later,* Rhonda spent Mother's Day alone.

On May 22, 2008, Rhonda became a U.S. citizen.

On June 17, Rhonda turned thirty-eight.

Her biological clock was ticking. Very loudly.

*One might assume* that our nation's insurance companies would pay for the treatment of the disease of infertility, no matter its genesis.

Not so.

In most cases, infertility strikes randomly. Fertility doctors consider impaired fecundity a physical disease, on par with a brain tumor or leukemia. When the sufferer may arguably be to blame, because she's over- or underweight, or she postponed having children until her late thirties, this does not lessen her suffering any more than a smoker stricken with emphysema or a diabetic whose obesity has worsened the disease.

However, only fifteen out of fifty states require employers' insurance policies to cover infertility treatments. Four states— Rhode Island, New York, New Jersey, and Connecticut— mandate coverage only until women are a set age, ranging from forty to forty-six. Many states do not provide infertility treatments to their poorest citizens, the recipients of Medicaid, state medical assistance, or the State Children's Health Insurance Program. And the nearly 50 million Americans without any insurance obviously do not receive treatment if they are infertile.

No states cover surrogacy as a remedy for infertility.

The federal government has stepped in, in small but symbolic fashion, with the S. 965: Family Act of 2011, reintroduced in May 2013 as S. 881, which offers couples a tax credit for fertility treatments similar to the break offered couples who adopt.

Even in states that mandate insurance coverage for infertility, most coverage policies apply only to married couples. This means that single parents and homosexual couples are excluded. Many states allow exemptions for employers whose religious beliefs conflict with infertility treatment. Many states cap the number and type of treatments to be reimbursed—for instance, Illinois restricts egg retrievals to four attempts for a first birth, and two attempts for a second birth.

It's hard to imagine state laws written to say, *Sorry about that brain tumor, but because you're gay, your insurance policy doesn't cover your chemo.* Or you have lupus—but since you are over forty-five, you have to pay for your own medication. Or that you must be married in order to have a broken leg set and put in a cast.

Writ large on these state-by-state restrictions are our country's collective prejudices against certain kinds of people becoming parents. You cannot be too old, or too poor, or already have children, or be in a sexual or cultural minority, or be too religious or not religious enough. You must be married. And you definitely are not eligible to have a baby if you work for a company with fewer than fifty employees.

U.S. health insurance policies also routinely deny support to surrogates.

Just as intended parents, understandably, are often blinded by an intense emotional craving for parenthood, so too surrogates can be overwhelmed by their wish to help infertile couples. Some inexperienced surrogates assume that because they are doing a good deed for another family, "everything" will work out, including insurance coverage. Few surrogates know, or understand, that these financial risks can be just as real as the emotional high dive of carrying someone else's baby.

Most people cannot predict their own routine insurance coverage with certainty. Surrogacy coverage is rare, and rarely explicitly included or excluded in writing. The risks to surrogates are monumental, illustrating the complex issues surrogacy presents to American society.

Until recently, insurance underwriters viewed surrogate pregnancy as identical to regular pregnancy. The assumption from the underwriter was that if a woman was pregnant, she was pregnant with her own baby. The surrogate's health insurance policy automatically covered her medical expenses. There was no need to investigate any pregnancy claims.

Today, underwriters are increasingly wary of unintentionally reimbursing medical expenses incurred by commercial surrogate pregnancies. Policies increasingly differentiate between *maternity* coverage and *surrogacy* coverage.[9] Frequent changes are common: TRICARE, the health-care program covering military families, abruptly altered its policy language in 2010 to restrict surrogacy coverage,[10] a blow to the industry since military wives made up roughly 35 percent of American surrogate mothers.

More and more insurers refuse to pay claims when a baby is conceived and delivered under a surrogacy agreement, explains Trish Taylor, the founder of New Life Agency, the world's leading full-service assisted reproduction insurance provider. From the insurer's viewpoint, the policy is being stretched to cover the medical costs of a contractual business agreement—which they see as distinctly different from providing health-care coverage for a "natural" pregnancy. There are many legal ways for insurance companies to deny coverage or void a surrogate's policy. Companies have every right to be suspicious of potential fraud incurred if a surrogate lies on her insurance forms, no matter how well meaning the surrogate's intentions.

In the end, the surrogate herself, and her family, are legally responsible to pay her ob-gyn expenses, and both her and her baby's hospital bills—no matter what any surrogacy contract says. In cases of a premature birth, a newborn death, a complicated delivery, or an extended neonatal intensive care unit (NICU) stay, the hospital expenses can run to hundreds of thousands of dollars. If intended parents cannot or will not pay, the surrogate can be held liable for medical expenses by the insurance company and the medical providers involved.

And finally, many insurance companies have lifetime caps on reimbursement. Even if her insurance company covers her delivery, a surrogate may unwittingly use up this reimbursement with an expensive surrogate baby delivery, forfeiting her or her family's future insurance coverage as a result.

*Surrogacy India conceived* their first international surrogate baby via IVF in the summer of 2008, just a few weeks after Rhonda and Gerry's Big Fat Negative. The baby, created for a New Zealand couple, would safely and joyfully arrive at Hiranandani on March 30, 2009. Dr. Yashodhara and Dr. Sudhir did not, initially, tell the Wiles about the Kiwis' Big Fat Positive; in fact, they weren't sure they were ever going to hear from the Wiles again. Everyone had hoped, so deeply, that the friendly American firefighter and his beautiful nurse wife would be SI's first international parents.

Most especially the Wiles themselves.

*Rhonda was done.* Gerry could see it in her thousand-yard gaze. She'd given up. She stopped posting on the blog. She refused to discuss trying again. She looked away when she saw a baby perched in another family's cart at the grocery store. She closed her lips when they passed a pregnant woman walking in the park near their house.

A new neighbor dropped by. Rhonda, who was home alone, invited her into the kitchen for a glass of iced tea. Sitting on Rhonda's kitchen stool, the pretty young woman told Rhonda all about herself. She was eighteen. Her husband was in prison. And—she cupped her hand sweetly on her belly—she had just found out she was pregnant.

Rhonda responded viscerally, more like a rabid coyote baring its teeth than a neighbor serving iced tea on a hot day. She clenched her jaw and smiled, without showing her teeth, transferring her fury to her iced tea, gripping the plastic tumbler so tightly she nearly broke it. Keeping her smile plastered on, she told the neighbor how very, very happy she and Gerry were for her.

Gerry waited. For four months. Then he confided to Rhonda the questions that troubled his nights.

Gerry tried to make the solution sound easy. The only suggestion he could come up with was to try again.

Could the next time be "the one"? They couldn't get any more broke. Why not try just once more?

Feeling battle-scarred, brave, and buoyant, like a pair of Marines rallying for the next overseas deployment, Rhonda and Gerry planned a second trip to Mumbai, this one for early September 2008. Both their employers gave them the time off they needed—not easy, considering their professions. The Wiles' neighbors agreed to care for Frankie again. Maybe this time, Frankie would consent to a bath from someone besides Rhonda.

Another 4:45 A.M. departure out of Phoenix Sky Harbor Airport, with a pit stop and a change of planes at JFK in New York. The Wiles arrived in Chhatrapati Shivaji International

Airport twenty-seven hours later. It had been five months since Tanisha's BFN.

Mumbai, despite all its chaos and commotion, its paradox of hope and disappointment, was beginning to feel like their second home.

Gerry and Rhonda started unpacking, and took naps and showers at the VITS Hotel on Andheri Kurla Road not far from the airport and Annawadi, the massive slum that lies on either side of the large international runways. Then Dr. Yashodhara and Dr. Sudhir picked them up in the lobby and took them out to Mainland China for dinner. They ate their favorite dishes: honey chicken, jasmine rice made with real jasmine flowers, pan-grilled crab cakes. Unlike their prior visit, which fell toward the humid buildup to the monsoon season, Mumbai was dry and breezy, as it is every fall, with bright blue skies, no humidity, intact roads, and neat, smooth dirt sidewalks.

Along with Mumbai's fresh autumn breeze, Rhonda and Gerry felt faint hints of hope.

Dr. Yashodhara's first decision was to increase Rhonda's daily dose of Gonal-f, the hormone that stimulates ovarian production of egg follicles. She knew how crushed Rhonda had been by the negative. No one from Surrogacy India wanted the Wiles, their first and still only American clients, to go back to the United States again without leaving a pregnant surrogate behind.

Women take Gonal-f, or other forms of follicle stimulating hormone (FSH), to increase ovary production, in preparation for egg donation, egg freezing, IVF, IUI, or embryo creation. Many take it to harvest eggs for immediate fertilization and transfer into a surrogate, as in Rhonda and Gerry's case. Gonal-f, officially known as follitropin alfa injection, is made from purified recombinant genetically modified Chinese hamster ovary cells cultured in bioreactors.

A remarkable drug.

However, the most remarkable thing about Gonal-f and other FSH drugs is not where or from what they are synthesized, or even the fact that they stimulate egg creation and thus get human life started. What's most remarkable about Gonal-f is its cost. FSHs are phenomenally expensive drugs, costing over $1,000 per daily dose. A woman needs to take the drug for fourteen days, so the cost for one extraction cycle can run to $15,000. Insurance companies often do not cover FSH drugs.

To save money, Rhonda and Gerry had been buying Gonal-f secondhand off a Web site in the States, from couples who no longer needed FSH. Rhonda had been taking a daily dose for eleven days prior to coming to Mumbai. Almost $11,000 worth at retail prices.

The drug, which comes in liquid form, is injected via a needle pen under the skin of the belly. Some women inject themselves, finding the daily prick fairly easy and pain free. As a nurse, Rhonda certainly had the medical skills to inject herself, but mostly it was Gerry who did the injecting, just so he could be a part of it all. He got out the needle every morning as soon as Rhonda woke up, sometimes doing two injections a day. The Wiles' most memorable injection took place in the miniature bathroom of the Boeing 777 flying them to India.

The team of doctors at Lilavati harvested six follicles from Rhonda during this second extraction. It was a fairly good crop, although not as good as the first extraction of ten follicles five months before, when Rhonda had been a few, critical months younger. The docs would have preferred a dozen eggs from which to choose the healthiest to fertilize. Rhonda and Gerry watched from a lab window as Dr. Pai, wearing gloves, scrubs, and a mask, laser-hatched their future babies under a microscope.

Through Surrogacy India, the Wiles had picked another surrogate. This one was named Pushpa. She was a petite, dark-haired, Hindu woman with a red bindi in the middle of her forehead, the traditional mark signifying that she was a devout married woman. She had an easy, warm smile showing a mouthful of white teeth that looked almost too large for her slim brown jaw. Gerry and Rhonda gave her a silver and turquoise necklace from Arizona—explaining that they wanted her to have something from their world. She immediately began introducing them to the doctors and nurses as "my friends."

Pushpa invited them to visit her, her young son and daughter, her husband, and her mother, at their small home in a rural, tree-lined village outside of Mumbai. Despite the fact that Rhonda and Gerry did not speak Hindi and Pushpa did not speak English, the families communicated effectively with smiles, hand gestures, and laughter. This would be Pushpa's second time serving as a gestational surrogate. Pushpa's husband had been very supportive during her first surrogate experience for another couple, cooking and cleaning during the pregnancy so that Pushpa could rest.

On Wednesday, September 10, 2008, the doctors prepared to transplant five fertilized, healthy "embies," created from Rhonda's eggs and Gerry's sperm, into Pushpa's uterus. Pushpa may have been devout but she was also unusually outspoken for a poor Indian woman. Her husband was at work, so he could not be there for the transfer. Instead, fingering the turquoise stones around her neck, she asked Gerry to hold her hand during the procedure. The SI doctors explained that no Caucasian man had ever sat next to an Indian woman during an embryo transfer at Lilavati. Wearing a pale green hospital gown, Gerry held Pushpa's hand with tears dripping down his cheeks as the doctors intently went about creating a baby for him and Rhonda.

For the next few days following the transfer, Rhonda and Gerry explored Mumbai. They passed the time visiting temples and shopping for gifts for Pushpa, a gold-flecked sari for Rhonda, souvenirs for friends at home, and a Punjabi suit for

Gerry. It was not easy to find one of the traditional, long-sleeved, below-the-knee silk jackets for a man of Gerry's height and girth. Strangers frequently assumed Gerry was a WWF wrestler; Indians claimed he looked similar to a character from American wrestling television reruns. One rickshaw driver even asked for his autograph. The Wiles had a Punjabi suit custom sewn for Gerry. His measurements created much amusement for the tiny, dark-skinned tailor, half his size.

Back home in Mesa, five months after their first negative result, on Wednesday, September 24, 2008, Rhonda and Gerry Wile got the call from Surrogacy India.

Over a six-month period, they'd spent over thirty-five days in India on their baby quest. They'd forked over more than $30,000 for their two trips to Mumbai, two rounds with Surrogacy India, and the out-of-pocket money they'd spent on doctors and specialists in the United States. They'd traveled 24,000 miles, foregone nearly a dozen weeks' income.

All for nothing. Pushpa was not pregnant. None of the five fertilized embryos had successfully implanted. Another Big Fat Negative.

As Rhonda cried on the brown couch in their living room, Frankie licked her arm. All Rhonda wanted in the world was to hold her baby in her arms.

She knew she would never be a mother.

She also knew she couldn't bear never being a mother.

The theory of surrogacy—hiring someone to carry a baby for you and then expecting that woman to surrender the child at birth, forever—strikes many as unusual, repellant, or even morally reprehensible. Those who embrace "shared motherhood" are in the minority in American culture. Even the people who support surrogacy as a viable solution to infertility often were initially leery.

Most mainstream religious authorities oppose surrogacy and egg and sperm (gamete) donation. Most conservative Protestant congregations, the Anglicans, the Eastern Orthodox Church, Christian Science, and many other religious organizations condemn the practice as unnatural and far removed from biblical procreation. Mormonism officially "discourages" surrogacy,[11] although notable Mormon Mitt Romney's seventeenth and eighteenth grandchildren were born via surrogate mother in 2012.[12] Jerry Falwell, the colorful evangelical Southern Baptist pastor, spoke out against surrogacy before he died in 2007.[13] Judaism is one of the few religions that allow the practice of all techniques of assisted reproduction, as long as the egg and sperm originate from the wife and husband respectively.[14]

At the extreme end of the negative opinion spectrum are the views of the Catholic Church. On February 22, 1987—nearly ten years after Louise Joy Brown's astonishing arrival in England—Pope John Paul II issued *Donum Vitae*, Latin for "Gift of Life." The Catholic doctrinal letter made explicit the Catholic Church's opposition to artificial reproductive technology for the 1.2 billion Roman Catholic couples, pharmacists, doctors, ethicists, theologians, politicians, teachers, and financiers around the world. The church's message was precise: the in vitro fertilization technology that made Louise Brown's existence possible was ethically and morally intolerable, and in direct opposition to Catholic beliefs.[15] In February 2012, Pope Benedict XVI hosted a three-day Vatican conference on infertility, reiterating the church's opposition to all forms of surrogacy and ART as forms of arrogance against God's will.[16]

The Catholic Church's logic can be perplexing. It is difficult to find people who are more pro-family and pro-life than infertility sufferers. The Old Testament itself, in Genesis, instructs the faithful to "Be fruitful and multiply." The Bible is sympathetic to, and open-minded about, infertility and potential solutions. Surrogacy, after all, is mentioned in the Old Testament—twenty-one times.[17]

And yet the Catholic Church unambiguously opposes parents willing to go to emotional, financial, and medical extremes to procreate via assisted reproduction. Unlike infertility sufferers, the men of God—and they are all men—who crafted the church's pedagogy on reproduction have consciously and voluntarily decided to devote themselves to God. Of similarly free will, certainly guided by spiritual callings, they chose not to have children.

But infertility is never a choice.

Take the Waters family. A dedicated oncology nurse and a high school English teacher whose exaltation of James Joyce exasperated most of his students, the Waters met in Ohio in the mid-1960s, where they both had been raised in large, middle-class second-generation Irish immigrant families whose connections to their Roman Catholic roots remained strong. The young couple—Mr. Waters tall and lanky, with floppy dark red hair, Mrs. Waters shorter, plumper, blonder—settled in Arlington, Virginia, a rapidly growing suburb of Washington, D.C., where they both found good jobs, given the plethora of new hospitals and schools in the area.

The Waters set about raising a family in the early 1970s, long before surrogacy and IVF became mainstream infertility treatments. It never occurred to either of them that they would face trouble creating the family they dreamed of, and their religion encouraged. The Waters' ancestors were all from Ireland, where many forms of reproductive interference, including abortion and surrogacy, were illegal in the 1970s and remain illegal today. In Ireland, the Latin maxim *mater semper certa est* is still enforced, meaning the birth mother is always the real mother. In March 2013, for the first time, a High Court judge in Dublin ruled that a woman whose sister had gestated twins for her was, in this particular instance, the "real" mother, based on proof that she and her husband had provided the sperm and egg that created the child and were thus the genetic parents.[18] However, the Roman Catholic Church doctrine, and its condemnation of IVF and surrogacy, still carries legal and moral weight.

By the mid-1970s, the Waters had five children—infertility was not their immediate problem. By another biological quirk, all five children were angelically attractive, with curly reddish blond hair and freckles, each surpassing their parents in sheer beauty. American society was changing rapidly in ways their Irish relatives couldn't comprehend. One of the Waters daughters came out as a lesbian during her teens; their youngest son as a gay man in his twenties. Their daughter Eileen had an emergency appendectomy in eighth grade. Unbeknownst to anyone, including her doctors, Eileen's burst appendix also scarred her fallopian tubes, rendering her infertile before she had even kissed a boy. Their second oldest son, Sean, became a bartender and married a teacher like his father. His wife had several miscarriages in the first three years of their marriage.

The Waters children eventually all managed to have children, but they faced obstacles only ART could rectify. Their homosexual son and his partner adopted two American infants. Their infertile daughter Eileen utilized IVF to have twins using her own eggs and her husband's sperm. Their lesbian daughter had one child, using a friend as a sperm donor. Happily, Sean and his wife weathered the mysterious miscarriages; their ob-gyn eventually diagnosed the problem as reproductive incompatibility between the couple. Under this doctor's care, they went on to have three healthy girls in six years. During visits back to Ireland, the Waters stayed quiet about the details of the babies' conceptions, and avoided all discussions of ART, out of dismay that their Old Country friends and relatives would condemn the decisions to interfere with "God's will."

If the Waters had not left Ireland, none of this reproductive creativity would have been permitted. As practicing Catholics, they would have faced religious, legal, and societal condemnation for supporting their children's desire to have children, and their own natural wish for grandchildren. Which raises a heartbreaking question for the world's devout Catholics: Is it logical—is it moral—for religious leaders to pass judgment on the infertile, to mandate that they not treat their infertility, without experiencing and understanding infertility themselves?

Although *Donum Vitae* caused much head spinning and some eye rolling, the logic rings true to many, Catholic or not. *Donum Vitae* creates a vexatious moral dilemma for the devout who also devoutly want children (and grandchildren).

The desire to conceive, bear, and raise children is natural. Infertility is natural, too. Is counseling couples not to treat infertility akin to advising people not to treat cancer, diabetes, or other disabling diseases? How much do these religious teachings and arguments matter if your body and your heart are craving a child, passionately, intensely, and single-mindedly, exactly as God and nature intended?

Would church doctrine extinguish your longing and despair? Assuage decades of loneliness and disappointment? Could your faith stand up to centuries of evolutionary biology?

Or would the burn to have a child lead you away from a religion that disallowed treating infertility?

Even if your church or your God said it was wrong, would you still try to have a baby by any means possible?

———

*By early October* 2008, Rhonda and Gerry had rallied each other, once more. They decided, somewhat grimly, to try to conceive again. However, their tunnel-vision hope was tempered by pragmatism, wrought by the bitter disappointment of their two negatives. This time, they would use two surrogates simultaneously—an expensive, risky, double-or-nothing gamble only the most desperate clients attempt. Success could mean as many as four babies born at roughly the same time. Pushpa would be one surrogate, and they would have to pick another with Surrogacy India's guidance.

After their two failures transferring Rhonda's eggs to surrogates, both Gerry and Rhonda knew something else: they had to consider abandoning Rhonda's dream of having her own biological child, and using donor eggs instead.

Using fresh donor eggs from women under thirty, IVF positive pregnancy rates can run as high as 80 percent on the first transfer.[19] After the two devastating negatives with Rhonda's eggs, anything close to 80 percent sounded wonderfully excessive. They could use Gerry's frozen sperm, chilling in cold storage at Surrogacy India's clinic, donated during their visit to India in April.

Gerry asked what mattered most—having a baby, or having a baby specifically from Rhonda's eggs. "Do you want *a* child, or do you want *your* child?" he asked her, holding her hands, sympathy in his eyes. He knew that, starting with the news of his vasectomy, Rhonda had struggled with the fear that they would never have children. For years she had feared that it would somehow be her fault, some kind of inexplicable karmic punishment, if they didn't.

For Rhonda the argument was bittersweet.

"I have some hesitation about it not being 'my' baby," Rhonda explained to everyone via her blog, which she had started writing again faithfully. How could she bond without a biological connection? Would she be a true mother? Rhonda's own parents sided with Gerry and the statistics. They were 100 percent enthusiastic, insisting they would love their grandchild no matter whose egg or body created the baby.

Rhonda, of course, knew all about the pros and cons of using donor eggs, from her own research and the thousands of infertility sufferers who shared their experiences on her blog. She'd just always assumed that, given her relative youth and her healthy ovaries, her eggs would work. It seemed doubly cruel that, in addition to her uterus, her eggs had failed, too.

It was hard enough for Rhonda, after all she'd been through, to imagine another woman carrying her baby. It was even harder to imagine another woman carrying her baby when the baby wasn't biologically "hers." At least that's how Rhonda saw it as she wrestled with the decision.

Rhonda remained unsure, heartbroken, wondering what to do. She felt, at her bleakest moments, like a failure as a woman. Was she not meant to be a mother? Would she, could she, feel like a mother with a baby that was not hers genetically? Would her baby sense that she wasn't as "real" a mother as other women? What if she held herself back from her child because of all the voices, in her head and throughout our society, that would question her validity as a mom?

Advice from a blog friend finally clicked.

"You love Frankie to bits," she reminded Rhonda. "She has no genetics from either you or Gerry. She's not even human. She's a *dog*. Do you love her any less because of it?"

Rhonda figured that if she could have loved a $25 puppy like her own child for the past thirteen years, chances were good she'd have no trouble with a real live baby.

The decision to use an Indian egg donor, instead of a Caucasian one, came easily.

Many international couples who turn to Indian gestational surrogates use their own eggs, or pick international egg donors from online catalogs. They want their child to look as much like them as possible; physical resemblance is a key component of family unity to many folks, perhaps for natural, Darwinist reasons. To meet this demand, Surrogacy India hires young, white women from Europe and South Africa to donate eggs. Western donors usually charge more for their eggs than Indian women, and the donor must fly to India and spend at least two weeks in a hotel during the final hormonal injections and follicle extraction; the eggs must be fresh to maximize the chances of fertilization and implantation.

Many intended parents travel to Mumbai solely for the birth of their baby, eating every meal in their hotel and venturing out only to Surrogacy India, Hiranandani Hospital, and the necessary government offices to retrieve a passport and exit visa for their baby. They hole up in their hotel until they can leave India, for good, with their child. Most have no plans to ever return.

Not Rhonda and Gerry. They had embraced—and felt embraced by—India from the moment their first plane landed at Chhatrapati. During their two trips to India they'd explored many corners of Mumbai. They'd traveled to Agra in the north and to Goa's southern beaches. They'd visited small villages and several of India's largest cities. They had come to love the country and its people. They were grateful, beyond words or dollars, for the opportunity India offered them to become parents together. It seemed natural to both Rhonda and Gerry that their baby's genetic mother, in addition to the gestational surrogate, would be Indian.

After spending the weekend of October 18 and 19 in the Arizona mountain retreat of Pinetop with Frankie, fishing, hiking, and lounging in front of their cabin fireplace, they came home to Mesa and picked an egg donor from SI's online profiles. She was a beautiful twenty-one-year-old Muslim girl from the north of India. Her picture showed long black wavy hair, dark brown eyes, and small facial features similar to Rhonda's. She had an easy smile like Gerry's. She was far more petite than either Rhonda or Gerry; finding a woman in India as tall as the Wiles is a challenge. On her questionnaire she wrote she was a housewife who enjoyed singing and cooking.

Once they finalized their decision, the egg donor, the Wiles' surrogate Pushpa, and another "backup" surrogate hired by Dr. Sudhir and Dr. Yashodhara began hormonal injections to synchronize three sets of reproductive organs. Surrogacy India was not taking any chances this time around.

The Wiles hoped for an embryo transfer sometime in December.

A question worth asking: Why didn't the Wiles, and infertile couples around the world, try to adopt India's unwanted female babies? There are 11 million of them, after all. American couples want babies. Female Indian infants need homes. India could supply the entire globe with babies. It's an equation with an obvious solution. Right?

Not exactly.

One of India's contradictions is that although the country has too many babies, bureaucratic regulation and lack of government support have made foreign adoptions of Indian babies dauntingly difficult.

The first obstacle is a powerful Indian prejudice against adoption. It is extremely rare for Indian couples, infertile or not, to adopt children—or for Indian parents to offer children up for adoption. There are biases against adoption of children with lighter or darker skin. Barriers exist against adopting children of a different religion or caste. There is a stubborn cultural preference toward children and grandchildren with a biological link to their families.

Some Indian families prefer childlessness to adoption of someone else's offspring.

Some, out of pride and cultural pressures, will abandon their children before asking another family to care for them.

Additionally, although India is one of the eighty-one countries participating in the Hague Adoption Convention consortium established in 1993, intercountry adoptions of Indian children remains extremely frustrating, expensive, and time-consuming. To adopt an Indian child, non-Indian couples must submit proof that they have been married for more than five years. They must be between thirty and fifty-five, with a combined age of less than ninety. Single people are eligible but same-sex couples are not.[20] The median fee charged for adopting an Indian baby in 2010 was $15,617, not counting travel, legal, or medical expenses.[21]

Additionally, a child cannot be eligible for foreign adoption unless there has been a legitimate attempt to place the child within an Indian family. After these hurdles have been cleared, adoption hypothetically takes a year. In reality, very little happens in Indian bureaucracy in less than two to five years.

Facilitating foreign adoptions has not been one of India's national priorities. Promoting international adoptions of female infants would, in fact, be hugely risky politically. No one in the government has been foolhardy enough to acknowledge the magnitude of India's genocide and abandonment of unwanted infants. The peril of the Indian sex trade of girls is very real. No politician wants to risk the accusation that India would sell its daughters to foreigners, even those who would love and care for the babies India cannot raise.

Finally, most unwelcome babies are born into poor, uneducated, illiterate families—families who probably have no idea that couples outside India would provide for their female children. Without grand-scale, proactive government intervention and outreach to impoverished communities—including education, marketing, establishment of orphanages, and multilingual agencies tasked with connecting needy babies with foreign adoptive families—it is impossible for the families with too many daughters to reach out to non-Indians desperately looking for children.

As a result, it was a small miracle that this country of 1.3 billion people, with 11 million unwanted female babies, allowed a number of Indian children to become U.S. citizens in 2010. A very small miracle, to be precise: American families were permitted to adopt 243 Indian girls in 2010.[22]

*Thursday, November 27,* 2008, was Dr. Yashodhara's forty-first birthday. She celebrated at her Mumbai home with her eight-year-old daughter, her miracle baby created after seven IVF attempts.

Twelve hours later, the Wiles awoke to Thanksgiving in the United States. Both Gerry and Rhonda had to work, so they were up early that morning. In anguish, they watched the TV screen in their family room. Smoke poured out the windows of the gorgeous, historic red-and-white domed Taj Mahal Palace Hotel, where Rhonda and Gerry had taken a starry-eyed ride in a hammered tin, horse-drawn carriage two months before.

Over a century prior, Jamsetji Tata, one of Bombay's most successful native businessmen, had built the Taj hotel. In the late 1800s, his motivation, reportedly, was defiance of the British Raj "whites only" policies that forbade Indian guests in their city's grandest hotels. The elegant Taj opened on December 16, 1903.

Over one hundred years later on Thanksgiving morning

2008, the Wiles' TV screen showed India's oldest, most iconic luxury hotel in flames. Pakistani extremists of the Lashkar-i-Taiba terrorist group, assisted by an American, David Headley, had arrived by boat in Front Bay harbor next to the eighty-five-foot-high Gateway of India. They breached the gates surrounding the Taj's lavish outdoor swimming pool courtyard. During a three-day spree, the terrorists would kill 166 bystanders in the Taj lobby and restaurants, and injure 308.[23]

The terror exploded miles from Surrogacy India's headquarters. Dr. Yash, Dr. Sudhir, and the other clinic employees Gerry and Rhonda had come to know were all safe. But Rhonda and Gerry still felt the pain of having their baby cradle invaded by terrorists, particularly a group headed by an American. Thousands of miles away from Mumbai, in the hot Sonoran Desert, they felt solidarity with their new family at SI.

The next day, Friday, Gerry and Rhonda celebrated a somber Thanksgiving holiday. They ate a quiet meal at home with Rhonda's parents, Shirley and Ron. The only light note was Frankie. Rhonda had outfitted her twelve-year-old white Catahoula in one of her many holiday outfits, this time as a canine Pocahontas in black Indian braids, a brown leather doggy dress, and four matching beaded faux-leather ankle bracelets. The finishing touch was a small plastic tomahawk strapped to Frankie's side.

December's drawn-out holiday season proved an ordeal. Couples struggling with infertility often find Christmas agonizing. The constant reminders of the season's magical, childlike appeal shine a red-and-green spotlight on their own dearth of children. Santa at the mall. Reindeer and sleigh decorations blanketing Mesa's commercial and residential neighborhoods. Christmas cartoon specials on TV. Every burst of holiday spirit seemed to mock the Wiles' hopes and dreams, silently whispering: *Christmas is for children. Too bad you don't have any.*

*On January 10,* 2009, at 3:32 A.M., the phone rang in Rhonda and Gerry's Mesa, Arizona, home.

It was late Saturday afternoon in Mumbai—but the middle of Friday night in Mesa. Rhonda and Gerry were asleep in their pajamas. Frankie was curled happily at the foot of their bed.

They were both afraid to answer the phone. They knew who was calling.

Twice they had gotten bad news in the middle of the night from India.

They turned to look at each other while the phone rang.

Frankie sat up, shook her black ear, and yawned.

Without saying a word, Rhonda picked up the receiver next to her pillow. She heard a crackle of the long-distance lines, as if the phone cord were actually under the ocean connecting the United States and Mumbai.

"Hello? This is Rhonda." Her groggy voice couldn't totally mask her trepidation.

Dr. Yashodhara and Dr. Sudhir spoke at once, each one trying to make their voice heard over the other. They sounded like schoolchildren clustered outside the ice cream truck, clamoring to get the Good Humor man's attention. They explained that they had just gotten the day's results from their lab.

Next, Rhonda heard hateful words, the precise two sentences she had heard months before, on another phone call with Surrogacy India, a brief conversation she would never be able to forget.

"Pushpa is not pregnant. Her pregnancy test was negative."

Rhonda felt the phone slip. She never wanted to talk to

196

anyone, about anything, via the telephone again. Gerry saw her lean back into the pillow. Her eyes lost focus.

But the doctors were still talking. They were explaining something about the backup surrogate, whose name was Shashi. Gerry could hear their voices through the receiver still clutched in Rhonda's limp hand.

"Shashi's test came back positive. You are pregnant," the doctors said simultaneously.

Time stopped for a minute. Rhonda sat up and gripped the phone until her knuckles turned white. She started to cry. Because he'd known Rhonda for almost eleven years, Gerry understood these were tears of joy.

Four years had passed since Gerry's vasectomy had been reversed.

Three years had passed since Rhonda's miscarriage.

Nearly a year after their first trip to India, at ages thirty-eight and forty-two, Rhonda and Gerry Wile were finally having a baby.

Now here's the part of the story where Gerry Wile goes a little crazy.

In a good way.

Gerry told everyone about the baby, which, at a few weeks' gestation, measured the size of the tip of a ballpoint pen.[24] First, logically, he announced the positive to relatives, friends, and his coworkers at the firehouse. Knowing what he and Rhonda had been through, everyone was especially pleased with the good news.

Then the neighbors. Of course he had to tell the owners of Guru Palace, still one of the Wiles' favorite restaurants, located in a nearby strip mall along South Gilbert Road. Then the elderly couple at the next table at Paradise Bakery Café.

Customers pumping gas at McKellips Chevron. The cashier at Fry's supermarket. A teenaged sales clerk at the local electronics store.

He didn't just share the good word about a baby on the way. In all his six-foot, 200-plus-pound masculine glory, he effusively explained to myriad passersby all about Surrogacy India, their new gestational surrogate named Shashi, the beautiful young Muslim egg donor, Dr. Pai's laser assisted techniques, and how to buy Gonal-f on the secondary Web market. Gerry commonly spent twenty to thirty minutes at a stretch, gesturing with his hands, clutching a stranger's shoulder, drawing air diagrams with his pointer finger, pontificating on the joys of surrogacy to dazzled bystanders.

Surrogacy India had set up a confidential, password-protected Web site for Rhonda and Gerry to track the pregnancy. They could view every test result, sonogram, ultrasound, and paper trail online. This gave Gerry a lot of detail to share.

The most important: there was one healthy baby inside Shashi's single yolk sac. The baby was due September 23, 2009. Although amniocentesis or a trained ultrasound technician would eventually be able to determine the sex of the baby, no one—including the staff at Surrogacy India, the gestational surrogate, or Rhonda and Gerry—would know the baby's gender until the baby was born. Indian laws forbid tests to determine the sex of a fetus, as a result of the high number of gender-driven abortions plaguing the country.

Gerry explained this to people, too.

He started collecting surrogacy T-shirts. One smiling man. Two smiling women. A sign that read joyfully *WE'RE HAVING A BABY!*

Gerry loved detailing to strangers why there were two women on the shirt.

Within two weeks of the call from Surrogacy India, Gerry covered the windows of his Dodge Durango with three large, custom-made window films. He and Rhonda drew their idea, and a friend with an artistic touch brought the visuals to life. Gerry printed translucent films for the two side windows and the large rear one—images that were transparent inside the truck but looked like large billboards from the outside.

The window films featured a picture of a sleeping baby. The headlines read:

> LONGING FOR A CHILD OF YOUR OWN?
> STRUGGLING WITH FERTILITY ISSUES?
> WE CAN HELP. YOU ARE NOT ALONE.

Every four days, Gerry drove fifty-three miles from home to the Tucson–Maricopa firehouse where he worked forty-eight-hour shifts. Gerry's cell phone number and the Surrogacy India Web site were listed in large black type below the baby's blanket. He figured hundreds of drivers saw his car windows during each trip.

The makeshift billboards were Gerry's declaration that he and Rhonda had overcome infertility. After more than five years, it seemed only natural to let the whole world—or at least a chunk of Arizona—know the good news.

*Gestational surrogacy,* at its core, relies upon, and exploits, the separation of the three building blocks of fertility—egg, sperm, and uterus. Once these have been successfully decoupled, the biological imperative to reproduce can, perhaps, be split from the cultural imperative to marry or otherwise establish a long-term bond with another adult. If a specific woman and a man do not need to have sex—do not need each other as parenting partners—in order to procreate and raise children, do men and women need one another at all?

Gestational surrogacy thus has the potential to destroy

heterosexual marriage as an entrenched institution, a practice established thousands of years ago to maximize the chances of human survival.

Any woman seeking to conceive a baby can hypothetically rely on anonymous frozen sperm, harvested decades or even centuries earlier. Surrogacy and IVF also release men from long-term connections with specific female mates. With IVF and surrogacy, a man can create a baby with a woman he has never even met.

If gestational surrogacy becomes widespread and affordable— a viable alternative not just to infertility but also to traditional coupling—what will happen to marriage, the social, legal, and financial bedrock of American society? Can traditional male-female interdependency survive the loss of the biological connection that children foster between adults? To what extent will the state-by-state legalization of gay marriage pick up the slack?

Throughout history, marriage and parenthood have been profoundly linked. Not coincidentally, weddings and births are two of the life events most strongly sanctioned and celebrated by traditional Judeo-Christian religions, Western legal code, and even financial incentives such as IRS joint filing for married couples and deductions for "dependents" within one's family.

However, marriage is declining in the United States. In 1960, 68 percent of all adults in their twenties were married. In 2008, just 26 percent were.[25] Barely half of all adults in the United States—a record low—are currently married. The median age at first marriage has never been higher for brides (26.5 years) and grooms (28.7), according to Pew analysis of U.S. Census data.

A 2010 Pew Research survey found that 52 percent of today's eighteen- to twenty-nine-year-olds, the so-called Millennials, say that being a good parent is "one of the most important things" in life. In comparison, just 30 percent say the same about having a successful marriage, resulting in a 22 percentage point gap in Millennials' views of the link between parenthood and marriage. Surveys also find that Millennials are less likely than adults ages thirty and older to say that a child needs a home with both a father and mother to grow up happily. They are also less likely to view single parenthood and unmarried couple parenthood as "bad" for society.[26]

If current trends continue, the share of adults who are currently married will drop to below half within a few years. In the 2010 Pew Research survey, 39 percent of Americans said they agree that marriage as an institution is becoming obsolete. Back in the 1970s, only 28 percent agreed with that premise.[27] The imperative to establish a long-term traditional marriage and family is clearly weakening, even as gay couples push for legalization of their unions.

ART and gestational surrogacy, rare experiments only two generations ago, have become precious in terms of making more American families possible. At the same time, the advances have the power to threaten the institution of family as we have known it for centuries.

*"Why don't you* just adopt?"

Even after they had announced that they *finally* had a pregnant surrogate, Rhonda and Gerry were asked this question on an almost-daily basis. Well-meaning friends, coworkers, and family members broached surprisingly personal issues—a common phenomenon when a couple is openly struggling with infertility. American cultural norms, often rigid when it comes to *not* discussing sex, seem to permit intense, confrontational (and often clueless) interrogation when it comes to baby making.

Rhonda and Gerry would have happily adopted a baby. Any baby. Neither one cared anymore about the lack of genetic connection or whether the baby looked like either one of them.

No one seemed to understand how unfeasible it would have been for the Wiles to adopt a child.

"Spend five minutes searching the Internet under 'Domestic and International Adoption,'" Rhonda, still bitter with frustration years later, explains. "You'll realize how torturous and cruel adoption can be to potential parents. The birth mom gets to change her mind at the last minute. Social workers invade your house. I understand—no one wants a baby to go to an abusive home or a place where he won't be loved or properly cared for.

"But look at the requirements. You need to be a certain age. You have to have been married for a certain time. You can't be obese. You can't have a heart condition or diabetes or have ever taken antidepressants. If you have a dog, you have to submit the dog's tag number and rabies vaccination. It's not enough that you are going to love the baby and do everything for him or her. You have to meet all these restrictions—rules people conceiving naturally never even *think* about. And for years, social workers are allowed to inspect your home for the smallest problems. It's not right. It's like it's never really going to be your baby. There is no 'just' in adoption these days."

To the uninitiated, adoption, not surrogacy, is the clear solution to childlessness. Adoption offers unique joys, of course. To some parents and their kids, adoption feels every bit as natural and fateful as old-fashioned conception and birth. *Meant to be.*

However, adoption, by definition, always starts with loss. And although adoption solves childlessness, for some parents and children, it does not erase the longing for biological connection. It's perhaps specious for anyone to believe that either secrecy or openness could diminish this gravitas.

Roughly 500,000 American women (1 percent of women ages 18–44) are currently looking to adopt a child, according to the National Survey of Family Growth.[28] Most want babies. There are only 13,000 to 14,000 infants available for adoption in the United States every year. This translates to thirty-five adoption seekers for every adoptable baby in the United States. Driven by lack of American infants, U.S. citizens adopted roughly 11,000 infants from other countries in 2010.[29] It is arduously difficult, unpredictable, and expensive to adopt the babies who need homes. Adoption has changed from an inspirational, life-changing event into an impersonal, at times cruel, marketplace.

Today, open adoptions are standard in the United States. Intended parents are expected to fill out applications, present financial and health data, send their fingerprints to the FBI, and fly across the country for interviews, as if applying for an extremely prestigious corporate job (which, in many ways, adoptive parenthood has become). The birth mother often selects the parents herself. This shift in control creates more comfort and peace of mind for the birth mother.

However, today's candor and control for the birth mother inflict an emotionally fraught, competitive process upon intended parents desperate for a child. It is massively unfair, sadistic even, that people suffering from a disease that prevents them from conceiving or giving birth are subject to a grueling application process other parents never even know exists. Applying for, and being selected as, one American mother's first choice is harder than getting into Harvard, and it costs a lot more.

And you wanted a large family?

Although foreign adoptions offer couples more certainty and choice, they are no cakewalk. The average cost can run between $25,000 and $50,000. International travel expenses can equal or exceed the agency costs.[30] International adoptions are often less rigorously regulated, at times resulting in American couples adopting babies who were never officially surrendered by their birth families. Couples adopting internationally must satisfy U.S. Immigration and Naturalization

Service regulations, including a federal security check, and be deemed eligible by the departments of Homeland Security and Citizenship and Immigration Services. The Child Citizenship Act of 2000 allows the child to automatically become a U.S. citizen if at least one parent is a U.S. citizen; the naturalization process is independent of the adoption and typically occurs after the adoption has been finalized.

Adoption can be a beautiful and wondrous solution both to infertility and unplanned pregnancy. But anyone who compares adoption to biological conception and birth, or dismisses it as a casual solution to infertility, is naïve to today's reality that adoption, with its uncertainty, expense, and competition, has almost nothing in common with "natural" reproduction anymore—if it ever did. Which explains why so many people find gestational surrogacy, despite its costs and complications, far preferable to adoption today.

Even so, Rhonda listened attentively, soon after Shashi's positive pregnancy result, when a nurse who occasionally temped at the rehabilitation center where Rhonda worked started asking questions about the Wiles' interest in a baby.

"I know you feel it can be risky to try to adopt," the friend, Anne-Marie, told Rhonda. "But what if you were guaranteed, completely promised, that the birth mother wanted to give up the baby? That she would never, ever change her mind? Would you want the baby?"

Rhonda stared back. "Of course we would. We want a baby more than anything in the world."

Anne-Marie explained the situation. Her son's ex-girlfriend was a student in college. She was Catholic. She was pregnant. She was nineteen years old. She wanted to stay in college, to graduate, to get a good job. She could not have an abortion due to her strong religious beliefs. She was determined to have a healthy pregnancy, to find the baby a good home. She insisted she was going to give the baby a good start with a loving family to make up for her mistake of getting pregnant before she was ready to raise a child herself.

The ex-girlfriend was Caucasian. The father—not Anne-Marie's son—was Filipino and African American. The baby, which the young biological mother knew already was a boy, would be biracial.

Rhonda knew all too well that the adoption process would be lengthy, bureaucratic, and unpredictable, consisting of months or even years of paperwork and interviews. She understood that she and Gerry could not adopt the child until it was born, no matter what the birth parents promised. The birth mother would have the right to change her mind at any point during the pregnancy and for a set period after the birth until she legally relinquished her rights as a mother. The birth father could intervene, too. Both biological parents would have to terminate their parental rights, voluntarily or involuntarily in cases of neglect or abandonment. It was even possible that all four biological grandparents might have certain rights, too.[31]

Anne-Marie knew all about Rhonda's struggles with infertility. She figured that two people willing to travel to India for a baby might be amenable to a baby closer to home, no matter the obstacles. Rhonda said she would talk to Gerry that night after work.

"I didn't think Gerry would go for it. We both didn't want to go through the paperwork and waiting of adoption, especially given everything we'd been through already."

To her surprise, Gerry agreed immediately. "That baby needs a home," he insisted.

Rhonda told Anne-Marie they wanted the baby. The Wiles started the small mountain of adoption paperwork. An Arizona state social worker scheduled a visit to their home, explaining that before she came, the Wiles needed to install a fence around their small pool and to get a dog license for Frankie from Maricopa County Animal Care and Control.

Anne-Marie hosted a baby shower. The birth mother gave Rhonda a long, passionate letter, explaining how ashamed she was about getting pregnant, telling her how happy she was that the baby would have a loving home. Rhonda and Gerry picked out a name for the baby boy. In everyone's hearts and minds, it was the Wiles' baby.

It made no difference to Gerry and Rhonda that this meant they would have two babies born only a few weeks apart. One, sex unknown, from India. The other, a biracial boy from teenaged parents. They would find the strength to give both babies all the love they'd been storing up for the past decade.

*Two months before* the baby was due, Rhonda received a heartrending and terrifying message from Anne-Marie. The birth mother had overdosed. She was in a California hospital. State child welfare authorities, alerted by the hospital emergency room administrator, had charged her with child neglect for endangering the fetus. Once born, the baby would be turned over to the state of California's foster care system for a year instead of being put up for adoption to the Wiles in Arizona.

"It was a bad sign," Rhonda says now, "that the news came via text message."

Gerry cried when she told him. Rhonda pleaded with Anne-Marie over the phone to let them contact the birth mother. They would go to California. They would convince the foster care authorities that they wanted this child, that they would give him a loving, happy, stable home. They would beg.

Rhonda and Gerry spent several sleepless weeks trying to figure out what to do.

This unborn child's future had gone from loving security to completely unpredictable instability. He needed them more than ever now. This baby, after all, was their baby, too.

The state of California did not agree. Anne-Marie halted all contact with Rhonda and Gerry. They had nowhere to turn.

Eventually Rhonda and Gerry, like so many parents hoping to adopt, had to accept that this baby they had already come to love was not their baby after all.

Sometimes, it doesn't rain in Mesa for ten months straight. There are only two months per year where the rainfall tops one inch.

You could say that Mesa—not just for Rhonda and Gerry Wile, but also for every living thing—is not technically a fertile place.

Unless you are a saguaro cactus. Saguaro cacti grow only in the Sonoran Desert where Gerry and Rhonda live, a 120,000-square-mile "living desert" of unique plants and animals spreading out over Arizona, and parts of California and Mexico. Flora ecologists theorize that saguaros grow only in the Sonoran due to a unique confluence of soil deposits, rainfall patterns, and arid conditions.

The cacti are slow developers, with growth rates highly dependent upon precipitation. Saguaros take their sweet time maturing, often taking seventy-five years to grow a single side arm. Each saguaro is unique, like a family. Some have several arms branching out crazily like children born close together. Others have two lone arms, carefully balanced across from each other.

Saguaros grow only from seeds, never from cuttings of the adult cactus. Unlike many desert plants, they are not self-pollinators; they require fertility assistance from nocturnal long-nosed bats. The yellow and white saguaro flowers bloom from April through June, at night only, emitting a seductive fragrance. The bats, unknowingly acting out their role as saguaro conception aides, drink the nectar and transmit the

Saguaro cactus © Lane V. Erickson/Shutterstock.com

seeds to cross-pollinate with other saguaro seeds in the sandy dirt of the desert floor.

When Gerry and Rhonda bought their one-story desert home on the edge of Mesa in 2006, Gerry planted seven or eight different cacti in his small, rocky front yard. A round golden barrel, a spiky aloe, a fuzzy white "Old Man," a sprawling prickly pear, a floppy purple cactus with arms shaped like Ping-Pong paddles.

As a lover of the iconic saguaros long before he knew they, too, needed outside assistance to reproduce, Gerry applied for permits to transplant two of the environmentally protected plants. He moved them from the desert to his small, rock-covered front yard next to his black Durango parked in the slanted cement driveway. Each saguaro was about two feet tall when he planted them.

He decided to experiment by watering one, and leaving the second to natural precipitation and growth. Three years later, the unwatered cactus was still about two feet tall, a dark green color. The watered cactus was a paler green, its trunk visibly swollen with moisture. It had grown to be over five feet tall. If he kept watering it, like a son who outgrows his father, one day soon the cactus would tower even over Gerry.

# Part 5

---

## Operation Birth in India

*Rhonda and Gerry* made the trek from Arizona to India, once again. Their fourth trip inside sixteen months. This journey took place in late August 2009. Mumbai was in the middle of another hot, humid monsoon season. The heavy, constant rain felt as dirty as the polluted city air. Mud pulled off one of Rhonda's sneakers as she got into the taxi at the airport. The Mumbai streets were as loud and chaotic as ever.

Gerry and Rhonda were both thrilled to be back.

The Wiles arrived in Mumbai with plenty of time to witness every twinge of their surrogate's labor. After waiting nearly six years to have a baby, they were determined not to miss a single contraction—even one they couldn't feel in another woman's body. On her blog, Rhonda called the trip "Operation Birth in India."

Hiranandani Hospital, the private medical center where all Surrogacy India surrogates give birth, operates within a patriarchal country. A man founded it; his sons run it today. But one floor at Hiranandani—the maternity ward—is all about women. The nurses, or "sisters," who care for patients are all women. Most of the ob-gyn doctors and pediatricians are female. Almost all of the men on the ward are slim "boys" who clean the rooms and perform routine unskilled tasks. And naturally, the patients are all women.

Dr. Yashodhara, of course, fit right in.

The Queen of Hiranandani is the woman running the maternity ward—or some argue, the whole hospital: Dr. Anita Soni, who received her medical training alongside Dr. Yashodhara at King Edward Memorial Hospital. Dr. Soni, like many Indian women, comes off to foreigners as a mix of contradictions. She barrels into her small, paper-strewn office like a fifty-year-old four-star military general, leading with her chest, shouting orders to the patient trying to make herself as small as possible in a chair across her desk. This patient has been waiting to see Dr. Soni for over an hour. Dr. Soni sits abruptly in her swivel chair and leans forward, wagging a finger manicured with red polish, holding up a sheaf of medical printouts.

"Now, dear, your doctor says you are not using the needles! Not taking your prenatal vitamins! Your counts are too low. We are going to make you a baby. But you have to follow your doctor's orders."

She pauses, takes a deep breath, and gently cradles the abashed woman's hands in hers.

"Look at me. I know how deeply you want a baby, my sweetheart. Get over your fear of those needles!"

And she pushes away the woman's hands. Dismissed!

Dr. Soni and Dr. Yashodhara made a very strong team. Together, they once delivered one hundred babies in twenty-four hours. It was during another monsoon season, on a day when all public hospital employees in Mumbai went on strike. Hiranandani Hospital opened its doors to all patients in need, regardless of their ability to pay. Dr. Soni and Dr. Yashodhara filled every bed lining the hallways of the maternity ward; they refused to let Hiranandani turn away a single pregnant woman. Although they didn't fulfill the Indian prophecy, "May you be the mother of one hundred sons," these two women together came awfully close by ensuring the birth of one hundred healthy Indian babies in one (very long) day.

In August 2009, Dr. Soni and Dr. Yash were ready to deliver one more baby. This one was an especially special delivery: Surrogacy India's first American baby. Surrogacy India's policy is to induce labor between thirty-seven and forty weeks, based on Dr. Soni's evaluation of the health of the surrogate and baby. The night before their surrogate was given a Pitocin drip to bring on labor, Rhonda and Gerry visited Shashi, who was already settled on Hiranandani Hospital's maternity floor.

It had been four months since the Wiles' last trip to Mumbai, when they had come to join Shashi for her twenty-week ultrasound. A very long, costly distance to travel for a routine medical exam, the results of which Surrogacy India normally sends to parents via e-mail attachments. But Gerry and Rhonda, forced to miss most of "their" pregnancy, would not have missed the live sight of their baby, on the ultrasound computer screen, for any reason in the world.

Now, on the eve of delivery, Shashi's husband was also at Hiranandani. He had missed the labor and delivery of their two sons. He too was determined not to leave his wife's side for a minute of this unique birth.

Shashi sat cross-legged and slim on the hospital bed in her green cotton hospital gown. She and her family lived in a Mumbai slum called Malad, about a ninety-minute bus ride from Hiranandani. Her large brown eyes were wise and confident— and shrewd beyond her years. She had married at sixteen, and given birth to two sons by the time she turned eighteen. Now, six years later, she looked barely pregnant, more like a carefree teenager with a small stone piercing her nose, instead of a mother about to give birth for the third time.

Rhonda and Gerry put all four of their hands on Shashi's abdomen. They felt their baby kick. They listened to the heartbeat with Dr. Yashodhara's stethoscope. The baby was in the ideal position for an easy delivery, head down.

Dr. Yashodhara and Dr. Soni checked in every few hours.

Dr. Sudhir was ill with malaria; he was in a hospital bed at Hiranandani himself, trying to rally so he could witness the birth of SI's first American baby. Rhonda tried to keep the blog updated hourly for friends and family who were counting down the minutes. This would be an especially closely watched and joyous arrival, long awaited by thousands of captivated friends, family, and infertile onlookers who followed Rhonda's blog from around the world.

The day Rhonda's baby was due, like any expectant mother heading to the hospital, Rhonda packed her bag—with the baby's first outfit, newborn diapers, and other essential goodies and small comforts. She and Gerry checked into Room 415 at Hiranandani at 2:30 P.M. The Pitocin drip began and Shashi had Cerviprime gel applied to her cervix to help with dilation.

And then Rhonda and Gerry had to wait. First they waited in their room, which felt smaller and smaller as the minutes ticked by. At 9 P.M., they inched closer to the second-floor labor and delivery ward, ultimately stationing themselves next to the central nurses' desk, as close as they were allowed to be. Dr. Anita Soni came out from Shashi's room, only a few feet away but behind swinging hospital doors, to give them regular updates from behind her green hospital mask. Ditto for Dr. Yashodhara.

Every five minutes felt like an entire day.

At 10:15 P.M., Dr. Sudhir, his veins filled with adrenaline and a final dose of IV antibiotics, rushed past the nurses' station and Gerry and Rhonda, shouting "I didn't miss it, did I?"

He disappeared through the swinging doors that led to Shashi's delivery room before anyone could answer him.

Rhonda and Gerry both felt like antsy expectant fathers from the 1950s. They did laps around the nurses' station, nervously listening for a newborn cry until their eardrums ached. There were no pictures on the walls, no magazines, no waiting-room TV. Just Gerry, Rhonda, and a small wicker bench.

At least they had each other to comfort (and to drive a little crazy).

The Wiles' first child, a son, Blaze Xennon Wile, was born on the second floor of Hiranandani Hospital at 10:22 P.M. India Standard Time. The date was Wednesday, August 26, 2009. After cleaning off the baby, Dr. Soni brought him out to Gerry and Rhonda. Blaze was small and red and moist, with his eyes shut tight against the new experience of light, wrapped in a soft jade-green baby blanket.

Rhonda—in her first mesmerized moments as a mom— looked as if she had forgotten how to breathe. Gerry stood motionless next to her, holding her hand. Tears ran down both their cheeks. Neither one moved, as if their newborn son were a neon aurora instead of a baby. Dr. Yashodhara and Dr. Sudhir were beaming. A small crowd of sisters and orderlies came together quietly, as silent witnesses to everyone's joy.

Gerry broke the silence. "Hi, Blaze. Welcome to the family."

When he heard Gerry's deep voice, Blaze turned his head toward his father and opened his eyes.

By American baby norms, Blaze was a somewhat small newborn—five pounds nine ounces—especially for someone with a six-foot-tall father. But by Indian standards, Blaze was thriving, especially given that he was born at thirty-seven weeks. Rhonda and Gerry chose Xennon for his middle name. It meant "from a faraway land," underscoring the distances, both geographic and emotional, they had traveled to make his life possible.

At first, only Rhonda was allowed into the NICU to hold and feed Blaze. Most Indian maternity wards have a strict "moms only" policy. When Dr. Yash first explained the rule, it took Rhonda a moment to understand she was the mom now; *she* was the one allowed through the magical swinging doors. For so many years, Rhonda had felt like the one woman on earth exiled from the corridors of motherhood. But now, she was, undeniably, part of the club.

You can imagine how much Gerry appreciated this "no dads" rule. Gerry had a few minutes to hold Blaze immediately after his birth. Then he was demoted to pacing outside the swinging NICU door for hours, a large and frustrated American man filling the small hallway.

The other person at Hiranandani not permitted to see Blaze was Shashi. The woman who had carried him for nine months was now alone in her narrow hospital bed. The seemingly harsh separation of surrogate and infant is standard Surrogacy India policy. SI has found that immediate bifurcation makes the transition easier for surrogates in the long run. After Blaze was born and taken to the NICU, Dr. Yash showed Shashi a picture on her cell phone to assure her of the baby's health.

A few hours after Blaze's birth, Rhonda went to find Shashi in her recovery room. The Indian woman looked exhausted, pained, empty. Her husband, who had stayed through the delivery, was now at home taking care of their two boys. Rhonda was the one to tell Shashi the baby she'd delivered was also a boy; Shashi had not comprehended the baby's gender, in the exuberance and chaos of the delivery room, amid all the excited cries in English. For the next several days, Shashi would receive recuperative in-hospital care at Hiranandani, and then would move to the SI clinic for psychological counseling afterward. If she wished, after several weeks had passed, she could later "meet" the baby she had carried for nine months.

Not all surrogates choose to.

The Hiranandani pediatrician demonstrated particular caution about releasing Blaze from the NICU, because Dr. Soni had performed an emergency C-section when she discovered Blaze's thick umbilical cord had wrapped around his neck. After Dr. Sudhir finally intervened, the resident pediatrician allowed Gerry free access to his son on August 27th, twenty-four hours after his birth. Gerry spoke softly as he held Blaze, wrapped tightly in a blue-and-white checked blanket, big blue-brown eyes wide open under a small yellow cotton cap. Blaze's entire body fit in Gerry's right hand. Gerry did not put him down once for the next two hours.

After forty-eight hours of observation to be certain his health had stabilized, the youngest Wile was released from the NICU. Blaze continued to flourish, drinking 20 cc's of formula at every feeding, peeing, pooping, hiccuping, burping, and crying, delighting Rhonda and Gerry.

They took hundreds of photographs in just the first seventy-two hours. Every picture proved that they'd done it: despite nature's odds stacked against them, Rhonda and Gerry had finally made a baby. A beautiful, happy, healthy baby.

Blaze Xennon Wile was discharged from Hiranandani on Saturday, August 29, 2009. He was three days old.

Rhonda and Gerry Wile holding their newborn baby boy, Blaze, at Hiranandani Hospital in Mumbai, India, on August 26, 2009. Rhonda says this is her favorite picture of herself with Blaze; this moment was when she finally knew she had realized her lifelong dream of becoming a mother after years of fertility obstacles.

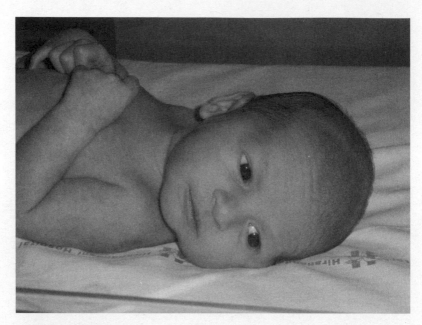

Blaze Xennon Wile

Two sets of dreams came true with Blaze's birth in 2009: Gerry and Rhonda
Wile became parents, and the founders of Surrogacy India had their first
American baby born via Indian surrogate.

After twenty-four hours of abiding by Hiranandani Hospital's "moms only" policy for contact with newborn babies, Gerry couldn't get enough of his son Blaze.

Rhonda, every inch a new mom, holding Blaze

Before leaving the hospital, Gerry stopped to pay the bill with a wad of rupees. Hiranandani, like most Indian hospitals, is a cash-only business. The NICU stay and circumcision totaled less than $800 U.S. dollars. As American parents know, you can barely buy three baby aspirins in a U.S. hospital for that amount of money.

**Back at the** VITS hotel, the Surrogacy India travel fixer Amit had surreptitiously upgraded the Wiles to a two-room suite—he knew they were watching their rupees and probably wouldn't spring for the larger quarters themselves. In the hotel bathroom, Rhonda gave Blaze his first bath on a blue and white, horseshoe-shaped inflatable plastic cushion they'd brought from Arizona. Rhonda's parents met their grandson via Skype. During one of many diaper changes, Blaze peed on Rhonda for the first—but surely not the last—time.

The Wiles documented every small milestone. Every moment felt like a miracle. Gerry used up two gigabits of camera memory recording Blaze's earliest days.

As if to make up for the grueling years of his creation, Blaze immediately proved a blissfully easy baby. He slept in the middle of Gerry and Rhonda's green and yellow hotel bedspread. Unlike many new parents petrified of germs and strangers, Gerry and Rhonda took Blaze everywhere; after such a long wait, they wanted him with them every second. Blaze fell asleep on every noisy, bumpy taxi and rickshaw ride during the next two weeks. Lying across Gerry's lap, he dozed during many meals out at Mumbai restaurants with the SI team. He stayed asleep as his parents held a tiny umbrella over him in India's monsoon rains. Even the fireworks from the Ganesh Chaturthi festival—booming throughout Mumbai— didn't wake him.

Blaze even slept throughout his elaborate, traditional Indian naming ceremony at the buttercup and creamsicle SI headquarters. The celebration included dozens of the Wiles' adopted friends and family. Of course, the doctors. But also a virtual life raft of fairy godparents—SI employees, their lawyer Amit, their travel fixer (also named Amit), their driver Agit, Dr. Sudhir's mother, several pregnant surrogates from next door, the various receptionists, relatives, intended parents and egg donors from Australia, the United States, and Europe who were also in India trying to make babies. All the people who had befriended Gerry and Rhonda, and helped make Blaze's conception and birth possible, crowded into Surrogacy India's pastel office to witness the miracle of his safe arrival into the world. Every person, including Blaze, received a blessing of a *tika*—a few grains of rice ceremoniously pressed into their forehead—as they walked through Surrogacy India's front door.

Shashi, who was still recovering from her emergency C-section, was unable to come.

Rhonda wore a red, orange, and blue Indian kurta top, a gift from the doctors. Gerry had on an oversized pale-gray, collarless linen shirt, also a gift, with a label that read XX XXXL—the largest size available in India. It just barely fit. Dr. Yashodhara looked beautiful in a full-length pink and yellow silk sari draped over her left shoulder. Over his blue jeans, Dr. Sudhir wore a sheer white sherwani top that fell below his knees, the silk embroidered with white sunbursts, stars, and curling vines. Blaze's colorful bassinet was draped in bright orange chrysanthemums. Blaze himself was tightly swaddled in a blue-and-white gingham blanket, reminiscent of the pinafore worn by Dorothy in *The Wizard of Oz*, the tight crisscross pattern in amusing contrast to the bright flowing silks and linens of India.

One of the SI employees, Mendhi, decorated the Wiles' forearms in reddish-brown henna: traditional, intricate flowers for Rhonda, a huge BLAZE tattoo for Gerry. An employee named Nagma, a former surrogate herself and Shashi's care-taker, unveiled an enormous clay pot of biryani, tender morsels of chicken simmered for hours in a creamy, spicy blend of onion, garlic, ginger, turmeric, cumin, tomatoes, yogurt, and mint. An opulent platter of fragrant basmati rice sat next to a tray of tandoori chicken. A steaming bowl of Punjabi *bhurtha* made with roasted eggplant and tomato was nestled next to stacks of freshly baked traditional flat roti bread. Dr. Yashodhara had prepared a small round chocolate cake. To wash everything down, there was a case of chilled Diet Coke.

Something for everyone.

During the traditional naming ceremony, while Blaze was being passed from—and individually blessed by—every woman in the room, Gerry and Rhonda named Dr. Yashodhara and Dr. Sudhir as Blaze's official Indian godparents. The doctors,

Rhonda and newborn Blaze at the traditional Indian naming ceremony held for him at Surrogacy India's headquarters in Mumbai

in turn, made Gerry and Rhonda honorary cofounders of Surrogacy India; they presented special SI business cards with the Wiles' names embossed on them in blue ink.

Two sets of dreams had come true the day Blaze was born. Surrogacy India had their first American parents. Gerry and Rhonda had their baby.

As for Blaze, he was renamed as well. Dr. Yashodhara's family religion is traditional Indian Buddhism; it seemed apt for Blaze to receive an honored Buddhist name. Blaze's Indian name is Buddha's original one, Siddhartha, which loosely translates into "one who has achieved all wishes."

Dr. Yashodhara and Dr. Sudhir just called him "Sid."

*Ananta Chaturdashi Day* is the last day of Mumbai's Ganesh Chaturthi festival. During the eleven-day extravaganza, local Maharashtras eat *modak,* a sweet dumpling made from sliced nuts, coconut powder, sugar, and cardamom, rumored to be the Hindu deity Ganesh's favorite treat. On the last day, millions parade through the winding city lanes, dressed head to toe in white linen—or bright yellow, orange, purple, or pink silks. They throw red rakta chandan powder into the air and on each other—and then dump 150,000 terra-cotta clay statues of the elephant-headed god of prosperity in the Arabian Sea. The idea is to give Lord Ganesh a grand send-off toward his ancient home on top of sacred Mount Kailash, while washing away with him all the misfortunes and sins of man.[1]

Amid the chanting, singing crowds, and chalky red dust coating the streets and sidewalks, Rhonda, Gerry, and Blaze arrived at the U.S. Consulate in the Breach Candy neighborhood in south Mumbai on time for a 9 A.M. appointment. Gerry had assembled a small stockpile of critical documents: both his and Rhonda's passports, their marriage certificate, Blaze's Hiranandani birth certificate, Blaze's passport application, two

2-inch-by-2-inch photos of Blaze. Plus all the paperwork from Surrogacy India, including records of Gerry's frozen sperm, Rhonda's ovarian stimulation, the egg donation, the embryo transfers and corresponding beta numbers, and the surrogate's medical tests.

After a brief interview and review of the Wiles' small pyramid of documents, plus the $150 passport fee, on September 3, 2009, Blaze Xennon Wile officially became a U.S. citizen. He was eight days old.

Another payment needed to be made before the Wiles left Mumbai with Blaze.

In total, Rhonda and Gerry paid Shashi about $5,000, per their contract with Surrogacy India. This is a lot of money for an Indian woman living in a Mumbai slum. It is also a lot of money for an American firefighter and nurse.

However, $5,000 is about one-fifth to one-tenth what the Wiles would have had to pay an American surrogate. So perhaps the critics concerned about exploitation of third-world women are right: foreigners are exploiting Indian women for cheap labor. Although, as Rhonda Wile points out, these critics "never saw the smiles on the faces of our surrogates."

Dr. Nayna Patel runs the esteemed Akanksha Infertility Clinic in northern India near the Pakistani border. She is an Indian woman herself, and a bit of a legend in the global surrogacy community. She has overseen over one thousand IVF babies and 150 surrogate births.[2]

Wearing her trademark double-strand pearl necklace, her long black hair pulled loosely back over her shoulders, Patel probes the ethics of Western women partnering with their Indian sisters. "At one end of the world, there is one woman who desperately needs a baby and cannot have her own child," Patel explains. "And at the other end, there is a woman who badly wants to help her own family. If these two women want to help each other, why not allow that?"[3]

Still, to be on the safe side, Dr. Patel opens a bank account for each surrogate she hires. She deposits all payments from clients in the surrogate's name—not her husband's. This way, the surrogate has a measure of financial independence and control of her earnings within India's patriarchal society, where so much of her life is governed by her father and her husband.

Dr. Anita Soni, who oversees the maternity ward at Hiranandani and has delivered hundreds of surrogate babies, believes that surrogates do face injustice.

As she sees it, though, it's not the medical clinics, or the intended parents, who do the exploiting.

To Dr. Soni, centuries of Indian culture are the culprit.

"The surrogates are pushed into a corner by Indian society," Soni explains. "They have no income source except to sell themselves. Surrogacy is superior to prostitution. It is fair, honest, legal income, and the women need it to provide for their children."

Surrogacy India surrogates earn over four times the average annual wages of an urban Indian woman.[4] In equivalent purchasing power, Indian surrogates are actually far *better* paid than U.S. surrogates. The Indian surrogacy payment buys more in India—a house, two decades of school tuition—than an American surrogate's payment in the United States. Indian surrogates, at least ones who work with reputable clinics, voluntarily agree to the surrogacy, and are well compensated for their work. Although India's surrogacy industry is still in its infancy, India's 2009 Assisted Reproductive Technology Regulation Bill and Rules has been sanctioned by the independent International Federation of Social Workers' policy on cross-border reproductive care.[5]

Sitting in his cheerful yellow office, Dr. Sudhir worries more about clinics that might not ask clients so many questions, risking babies brought into families without the time, resources, or psychological fortitude to raise them. Dr. Soni worries that laws do not protect the surrogates. Dr. Yashodhara hopes that one day, sound regulations will protect the intended parents and babies from unscrupulous clinics and surrogates. Dr. Sudhir wonders how many red lights will be run before India decides on, and enacts, punishments for surrogacy's vandals.

Rhonda and Gerry took matters into their own hands to make sure their surrogate did not feel exploited. They visited Shashi at the Surrogacy India clinic to say their final good-bye before heading home to Arizona. Shashi wore a dark red and gold sari, and seemed to be recovering well. Surrounded by her two young boys and her husband, she was quite eager to go home herself.

Rhonda and Gerry hugged her repeatedly and told her, again and again, that she had made their dreams come true. They showered her with small gifts. Gold earrings, makeup, a leopard-print throw, a new purse, candy, and Power Ranger toys for her sons.

Blaze did not join them for the farewell. Surrogacy India felt it was still too soon for Shashi to see him. Instead, as the two women hugged good-bye, Shashi whispered to Rhonda, "I hear he is beautiful."

Rhonda smiled and whispered back, "He is perfect."

Both women had tears in their eyes.

Then, with Surrogacy India's knowledge and blessing, the Wiles gave Shashi an unexpected $1,000 bonus. A huge smile broke across Shashi's face. The money made up the final payment on her family's new home.

It's not just foreign surrogacy, exploitation of women, and global assisted reproduction that trouble factions opposed to assisted reproductive technologies (ART) and surrogacy.

Critics of surrogacy and ART spotlight the rate of breast,

uterine, cervical, brain, and other cancers among women who have taken high levels of hormones as part of IVF and other fertility treatments.

High-profile cases include Elizabeth Edwards, wife of 2004 presidential hopeful and former North Carolina senator John Edwards. She died in 2010 at age sixty-one from metastasized breast cancer. In 1996, when she was forty-eight, Elizabeth Edwards's sixteen-year-old son Wade died in a car accident. In order to have more children following her son's wrenching death, Edwards underwent hormone treatments to conceive and carry two children. They were born when she was forty-nine and fifty-one, respectively. Elizabeth Edwards died a decade later, in the midst of a scandal involving yet *another* baby, this one fathered by her husband and his presidential campaign videographer Rielle Hunter.

New York playwright Wendy Wasserstein bore a daughter at age forty-eight after reportedly using hormones to become pregnant. Wasserstein died seven years later from lymphoma. In October 2011, *E! News* host and reality TV star Giuliana Rancic discovered she had breast cancer at age thirty-six, after two unsuccessful IVF attempts and one miscarriage.[6] Many of us have an aunt, a friend, a cousin who developed cancer after being treated for infertility; the connection between the two seems to make sense anecdotally.

However, as tragic as these cases are, there is no conclusive medical evidence that fertility drugs or ART treatments increase a woman's risk of cancer. These are the facts: fertility drugs stimulate the ovaries, causing estrogen levels in a woman's body to fluctuate. High estrogen levels have been linked to breast cancer, so it seems logical that the use of fertility drugs might also increase cancer risks. However, according to the Susan G. Komen Breast Cancer Foundation[7] and many other reputable nonprofit medical agencies, most investigations, including a meta-analysis of twelve studies on the fertility drug clomiphene (Clomid) and other types of fertility drugs, found no link to breast cancer, uterine cancer, or other cancers.[8]

The truth is that breast cancer and uterine cancer are common among women. Women run a one-in-eight (12 percent) chance of developing the most common cancer, invasive breast cancer, whether or not they have ever taken hormone supplements. It may be that women who experience infertility (whether or not they use hormone treatments) are inherently at greater risk for cancer, because infertile women usually experience fluctuating hormonal levels long before they even know they are infertile. Although the use of fertility drugs does not appear to increase breast cancer risk, studies with longer-term data are clearly needed to confirm these findings and to ease our society's collective worries about any possible causation.

A deeper, perhaps more disturbing question is whether, and why, a woman's desire to have a baby overshadows the potential health risks. Women like Wendy Wasserstein, Elizabeth Edwards, Giuliana Rancic, and Rhonda Wile all consciously decided to take hormones to have babies, even though they, too, had surely heard the rumors about the potential danger to their health.

What is the more powerful motive? The desire to create new life, or the need to protect your own? Should women be defended against our own biological urges? Should baby making come with a warning label?

On other fronts impacting surrogacy, legislative initiatives have been put forth in Colorado, Florida, Ohio, Mississippi, and ten other states to redefine a person as existing, legally and biologically, from the moment of fertilization. Under "personhood" logic, full legal and citizenship rights attach to embryos, no matter how they were created or who created them. The anti-abortion movement is behind these petitions, with more mobilized in all fifty states by the national Personhood USA organization in Colorado. The aim is to outlaw abortion, not assisted reproductive technologies.

However, the personhood movement has ramifications for surrogacy, because embryos play such a vital role in surrogacy and ART. Freezing embryos or discarding defective embryos could possibly become a crime: murder or manslaughter. Personhood opponents, including the American College of Obstetricians and Gynecologists (ACOG), ASRM, RESOLVE, and many medical associations, believe the movement is antifamily and unfair to infertile couples, and could have the unintended result of producing subpar pregnancies and forced gestation of unwanted babies.[9]

But the troubling question raised by the personhood movement remains: Is an embryo a person?

Tackling yet another ethical issue is Lindsey Kamakahi, a former egg donor, who is pursuing a civil legal case alleging anticompetitive price fixing by fertility doctors. Kamakahi claims that egg donors are paid too little by clinics, lawyers, and doctors, who together collude to reap huge profits while depriving egg donors of their just financial dues. The sale of embryos undeniably offers the largest single opportunity for price gouging in the infertility market. Eggs, unlike sperm, constitute a resource more scarce than red diamonds. Their number is fixed, and they are expensive, time-consuming, and invasive to extract from fertile women.

Nearly twenty thousand donor eggs are used to create IVF and surrogate babies in the United States every year. You've probably heard the radio ads, clearly targeting fertile college students and young women in their early twenties: "You can earn $5,000 and give the gift of life!"

But the upbeat ads do not capture the complex, invasive nature of the process. In order to harvest eggs, the donor must be injected with three different hormones over several weeks. First, shots to suppress her normal ovarian function. Second, more to stimulate multiple egg creation. Third, a last round to jump-start ovulation, which releases the eggs. A clinic technician then retrieves the mature eggs by inserting a needle into the ovaries and suctioning out the eggs. Donors are paid for going through the hormonal treatment and extraction—not for giving up their eggs. This explains why the term is "donating" one's eggs, even though donors are paid.

Free market forces are at work. Eggs do sell for the ASRM-recommended $5,000 per cycle. However, eugenically "ideal" eggs, harvested from tall, blond, athletic, Ivy League graduates, are rumored to command up to $100,000. If an infertile woman's eggs aren't viable, the cost and coordination of egg donation can be significant components of IVF and surrogacy expense. How much of the fees wind up in the pocket of the lawyer, the clinic, or the donor herself depends on each individual agreement between the parties involved. None of this is explained in the rah-rah radio ads.

Separately, the Center for Bioethics and Culture (CBC), a conservative evangelical group affiliated with Trinity International University, alleges that surrogacy, IVF, and other fertility treatments constitute "reckless endangerment" of women and babies. Jennifer Lahl, a pediatric nurse and the director of the CBC, has produced a movie titled *Eggsploitation*, in which she unveils what she calls fertility medicine's "dirty little secret." Lahl claims that women are pressured and coerced into donating their eggs to infertile couples and the clinics that serve them. Lahl is a frequent public speaker on the subject, and has testified before the U.S. Congress on the risks of fertility treatments.

In response to these and other allegations, many U.S. surrogacy clinics today have taken steps to prevent exploitation of women, embryos, sperm-donor children, and clients. Several offer "egg-sharing," where multiple couples split the cost of retrieving eggs from a donor who may produce dozens of eggs at once. It is also fairly common for couples who have conceived to offer their unused embryos for "adoption" by other couples. RESOLVE lists several scholarships to pay for infertility treatments, from nonprofit groups such as the Fertile Dreams organization and the Pay It Forward Fertility Foundation. Many clinics offer private insurance, guarantees, and financing options to cover the costs of eggs, IVF, and other treatments. Other groups argue for increased transparency and tracking of sperm and egg donors for the children's future sense of self and access to their ancestral medical history.

Perhaps there are ways to ensure that donors, clients, and babies are never exploited in the maze of ART. Perhaps, over time, the global surrogacy industry will develop and enforce practices and payments that are fair and just to all involved, under every imaginable circumstance. Until then, the niggling doubts remain—the grave questions underlying the personhood proponents, Kamakahi's lawsuit, the oversimplified egg donor ads, the anonymous sperm donors, and Lahl's "eggsploitation" charge. Underpinning the individual ethical questions lies a larger one: Is our society insane to rely on anonymous market forces to regulate buying and selling body pieces that are assembled into living, breathing babies?

The point being: much of surrogacy, egg donation, and other components of ART remain unmapped emotional, legal, and ethical terrain, cumbersome to regulate or control, messy and perplexing to everyone involved.

Much like parenthood itself.

The Wiles' final stop before leaving Mumbai with Blaze was the Foreigners Regional Registration Office (FRRO). A division of the India police system, the FRRO regulates the entry, movement, and departure of all foreign visitors to India who stay longer than two weeks. Blaze would be nineteen days old by the time the Wiles left the country. Even though their son was born in Mumbai, as a U.S. citizen, he was still technically a foreigner.

As such, Blaze Xennon Wile needed an exit visa to leave India.

So once again, Gerry, Rhonda, and Blaze were waiting in line in downtown Mumbai, along with a packet of official documents, including the Consular Report of Birth Abroad, a letter from Hiranandani confirming Blaze's birth, and their plane tickets home. This time, the wait was a long one.

Fortunately, the weather in Mumbai that September day was cool and dry, relatively speaking. The rectangular pinkish-white stucco building that houses the third-floor FRRO office is on Badruddin Tayabji Lane, behind St. Xavier's College, in yet another crowded Mumbai neighborhood. Several tall green trees, many covered in thick leafy vines, provided shade for the hundreds of foreigners queued to secure their exit visas.

Blaze, Rhonda, and Gerry got their stamps after only a day of drama and delays—helped by a last-minute infusion of several hundred rupees in baksheesh. Not all international surrogacy clients are so fortunate. In some parts of India, new parents spend weeks, or even months, securing the proper stamps and approvals to leave the country with their babies.

The Wiles left India the night of Monday, September 14, 2009. A family of three headed home for the first time.

If Gerry and Rhonda had been able to adopt, or had been candidates for IVF, or had hired an American surrogate, the process might have taken years in the United States and cost north of $100,000. Instead, in less than two years, for roughly

$35,000 for the three pregnancy attempts and four trips to India, they were going home with Blaze. Their baby. For good.

*For most American* parents, getting a newborn home safely from the hospital or birthing center is usually a short, terrifying journey marked by white knuckles gripping the steering wheel, two elevated heart rates, and several false shrieks of alarm. One parent peers through the windshield with an intense, spoon-bending gaze, while the other hunches over the tiny bundle strapped into the car seat in back. Every pothole is a land mine. Every oncoming driver is either a crazed lunatic or drunken teenaged neophyte.

Climbing Everest might be less stressful.

And usually, their infant sleeps beatifically through it all.

Rhonda and Gerry's trip home with newborn Blaze from Mumbai to Mesa required two airplanes, over twenty hours, three security checkpoints, and passage through twelve time zones. Flying northwest over Afghanistan, Turkey, Italy, and France, Rhonda held her son in her lap, his Kiddopotamus cotton swaddler wrapped tight as a sari. Blaze slept for the entire trip home from India to Phoenix, to the delight of Rhonda, Gerry, the flight attendants, and everyone else in their row.

Rhonda, however, did not fall asleep once during the drawn-out trip. Her number-one thought as she watched over her son and waited for the miles to fly by was simple: she couldn't wait to introduce Blaze and Frankie. Her beloved puppy was now thirteen. Frankie was frail and ailing, but still a beautiful snowy white with her black nose and one black-tipped ear.

The three members of the Wile family arrived in Phoenix on Tuesday, September 15, 2009. Despite the very long trip,

Rhonda and Gerry felt exhilarated to be coming home with the baby for whom they'd waited so long.

When Rhonda, Gerry, and Blaze stumbled through the front door of their stucco and tile Mesa home, tired and disheveled from the plane rides, but happy to be back, Frankie showed a demure inquisitiveness in Blaze. She sniffed his small head and then licked him a few times as he lay in his new car seat on the tile floor next to her. But then she lay down as if to say to Rhonda, "Nice, Mom, but during the last thirteen years I've gotten quite accustomed to being the baby myself." Rhonda took several pictures of her two babies, and spent hours sitting on the living room floor between Frankie and Blaze.

"I told them I loved them both," Rhonda explains now, smiling sadly.

On Monday, September 21, six days had passed since the Wiles had come home from India. Blaze was twenty-seven days old. Frankie was thirteen years and eight months.

Early that hot September morning, Rhonda was drying her hair in the bathroom, exhausted and bleary-eyed from the flights home, the twelve-hour time change, Blaze's midnight feedings, and the stream of friends and neighbors excited to see the baby. She looked outside her window and began screaming for Gerry.

Frankie lay motionless underneath the lone tree in the Wiles' small pebbled backyard.

Her old white friend had been declining for months, Rhonda knew.

"She had lost several pounds . . . muscle she really needed," Rhonda says now, describing the changes in Frankie during the Wiles' three-week absence in India to collect Blaze. "She seemed kind of frail, but I thought she just needed a few more days of TLC to rebuild her strength."

In all the exhilaration of Blaze's safe entrance into their lives, it had not occurred to Rhonda that Frankie's exit might be drawing near.

Gerry and Rhonda rushed outside together and bent down, cradling the old dog's head in their arms. After taking two quiet, deep breaths, Frankie died in the shade provided by the small tree and her owners' bodies. With a dog's uncanny wisdom, Frankie had held out for Rhonda and Gerry to return home safely before letting go.

Later that day, after caressing and brushing Frankie's dead body for nearly two hours, Rhonda tearfully sent out a blog post titled, "Today Dog Heaven Got Another Angel."

Frankie died knowing that Rhonda now had another baby to love.

*Despite grieving over* Frankie, Gerry and Rhonda were eager and especially proud the day they took Blaze to Dr. Mark Gentile, their new pediatrician in the nearby town of Gilbert. During the initial exam, Gentile remarked that Blaze seemed much older than three weeks, particularly given he'd been born almost one month before his due date. Gerry showed him the pile of records of thorough care and neonatal testing Blaze received at Hiranandani, documents Gerry had carefully shepherded home from Mumbai. Blaze was clearly thriving, eating well, gaining about half a pound a week, and sleeping easily.

Rhonda took a month off from work. She had stepped down from administrative director to regular floor nurse, and switched to a specialty hospital fewer than ten minutes from home, reducing her responsibilities to have more time at home with Blaze. She would still work exhausting twelve-hour shifts, but with less stress and responsibility, and a far shorter commute.

Gerry returned to his straight-on forty-eight-hour schedule at the firehouse forty-five minutes away.

Blaze managed to avoid colic, and ear infections, and the other common plagues of early childhood. His light brown skin, several shades darker than Rhonda's fair skin and even a shade darker than Gerry's, seemed immune to baby eczema and the itchy, flaky cradle cap so many babies develop. Within six weeks, he was sleeping six hours straight through the night. At two months old, he had doubled his birth weight.

Although both Gerry and Rhonda worked long, tiring shifts, the good news was that their exhausting workdays were followed by extended periods off. Their plan was to stagger their monthly schedules so that they could devote their non-working days to Blaze, and minimize hired day care. This meant less time for each other, but the sacrifice seemed right. They found a babysitter to come to their house for the few days a week that both Gerry and Rhonda had to be at work at the same time. By Halloween, Rhonda's parents had arrived for the winter in Mesa. The Reycrafts quickly became entrenched in their new grandson's daily life.

Blaze smiled early and often. As they had since his newborn days in Mumbai, Gerry and Rhonda continued to take him everywhere with them. He particularly loved meeting new women. Blaze smiled in infectious delight at females of all ages on outings to Guru Palace, the supermarket, gas stations, and the local parks of Mesa. Blaze and Gerry watched football together, sitting on the couch during the fall season—although Blaze could barely sit up.

The Wiles excitedly decorated their home for Christmas. It was their first Christmas without the beloved Frankie, but it was their first Christmas with a baby in the house. Unlike the despair of Christmas the year before, now the Wiles had someone to take to Santa at the mall.

And they did.

After years of childless holidays, the Wiles finally had someone to take to meet Santa at the mall.

*Of the many* fallacies about infertility, the biggest is why people cannot get pregnant or carry a pregnancy to term without a surrogate to help them. The primary culprit has nothing to do with eggs, sperm, the ethics of hiring a surrogate, or any of the complications reproductive endocrinologists look for.

The main reason people fail to have babies is far more basic: they give up trying.

Research shows that over 55 percent of people who do not conceive spontaneously *never even seek medical advice*. They remove themselves from the baby chase without ever asking for intervention or assistance; from the beginning, the pressure is too painful and intense to bear.

Many couples give up after only one round of IVF. A 2004 study conducted by Sahlgrenska Hospital in Sweden found that more than half (54 percent) of all infertile couples who failed to conceive after one attempt at IVF refused to try again, even though the Swedish health service would have covered two more IVF cycles for free. Thousands of women dropped out of treatment after one cycle, having found the psychological, emotional, and physical burdens of a failed IVF cycle too great.[10]

Another surprise is that many of these couples do not split up.

"Oddly, the divorce rate is much lower among couples whose fertility treatment failed than for the general population: 10 percent versus 50 percent," explains Jacky Boivin, a British researcher at the Cardiff University School of Psychology's Cardiff Fertility Studies Research Group.[11]

Of course, the other primary reason infertile couples stop trying to conceive is cost, particularly in the United States. The cost to fix a broken leg is about $16,000. To have your appendix removed can run $10,000 to $32,000. Both of these routine procedures cost more than one cycle of IVF treatment. But most people have no idea of the expense of routine medical procedures, because insurance normally picks up most of the bill.

When you are undergoing IVF or hiring a surrogate, however, you write every check, since having a baby continues to be classified as elective by U.S. insurance companies, government, and military administrators.[12] According to New Life Agency, standard ART treatment in the United States costs roughly $16,000 to $36,000, depending upon how many cycles of IVF you or your surrogate require to get pregnant, and whether you need an egg donor or can use your own eggs. You pay the cost whether you get pregnant or not.

Without insurance reimbursement, many couples simply cannot afford conception or surrogacy. Not to mention the $220,000 the U.S. government estimates it costs to actually raise a baby. But just because couples stop treatment does not mean they give up hope.

What would you do if money stood in the way of you and your baby? If your employer, your state, your insurance company said, *No—we won't cover what it costs for you to get pregnant or to hire a surrogate to carry your baby.* Would that stop you?

Those who keep trying find the money somehow. Researchers from the University of California San Francisco found that nearly 50 percent of couples seeking fertility treatment used savings or withdrew money from their retirement funds. Thirty-two percent financed ART through credit card debt. Seventeen percent refinanced their homes. Twelve percent sold investments and possessions. Four percent worked extra jobs.

How far would you go? Would you change jobs to find more comprehensive insurance coverage? Would you move to a state that mandated fertility coverage? Sell your car? Drain your retirement fund?

If you are infertile, hope that you will one day have a baby becomes nearly as priceless as the baby itself. The good news? Hope is one of the only ingredients in the baby chase that costs nothing. Hope is still free.

Hope may be free, but it can also be cruel.

Thursday, August 26, 2010, marked Blaze's first birthday.

At one year, Blaze had seven small white teeth. He could say "Hi" (and he did say it over and over, dozens of times a day). He occasionally coordinated a hand wave along with the greeting.

He was attempting to walk. Mostly, he fell down a lot.

Rhonda taught him to dance in his high chair. She gave him his first haircut. Gerry saved a curl of silky black hair. Rhonda became minorly obsessed with styling his hair into a spiky gelled mohawk. Blaze learned to put his toys back in the toy box during cleanup. He laughed a lot. He was thirty inches tall and weighed a mere twenty pounds—a long and lean little guy.

His first year had flown by astonishingly quickly. Rhonda

and Gerry took Blaze to Canada to celebrate. They spent a week at Niagara Falls with Rhonda's parents; Blaze got to meet his cousins, aunts, and uncles. Blaze also got acquainted with grass for the first time—the substance being scarce in the Sonoran Desert—by crawling on his grandparents' lawn. His squawks made clear he did not like it.

One morning back at home in Arizona, Blaze ate the dog food Rhonda put out for the new puppy. The Wiles had gotten another Catahoula, this one a gray, black, and white dog with light blue eyes. Neyla adored children, Blaze in particular. Blaze loved her—and her food—right back.

He was a perfectly normal, perfectly healthy little boy. He was the type of baby who can lull first-time parents, even Rhonda and Gerry, into thinking *Parenthood is so easy, we should have more kids right away!* Rhonda and Gerry, after everything they had been through, definitely wanted more babies. Plus, they wanted Blaze to have a sibling.

For Rhonda and Gerry, however, having another baby was obviously not going to be as easy as letting nature take its course, gradually adjusting to the coming baby over nine months of pregnancy.

In late November 2010, a few months after Blaze's first birthday, Rhonda picked up the home phone to hear the familiar voices of Dr. Yash and Dr. Sudhir. The docs had a pressing question. And they needed an answer within seventy-two hours.

Blaze's pretty young egg donor from northern India had been in touch with the clinic. She wanted to do one more egg donation—her last one. SI still had samples of Gerry's frozen sperm. The Wiles would not need to come to Mumbai for the fertilization or embryo transfer. Neither the doctors nor the Wiles paused to remark upon the astonishing fact that the Wiles could, in fact, be eight thousand miles away during their next baby's conception.

Any babies born would be full biological relations to Blaze, a gift most parents take for granted, but one that Rhonda and Gerry had long abandoned being able to give their family. A sibling would be a precious, lifelong treasure to a boy who, despite a loving extended family, was linked biologically only to his father and Gerry's twenty-four-year-old daughter. Blaze would have a companion who shared his genes, his biological mother, his unusual birth story, and his birth country.

With a younger brother or sister, Blaze would never be alone.

A fog of caution held Rhonda and Gerry back. They felt they'd rung the jackpot with Blaze. Could they handle another baby? Emotionally, psychologically, financially?

Rhonda and Gerry knew the ordeal they faced. The conscious debate and decisions. The tests. The money. The contract with another surrogate. The heartache of potential negatives. A trip two continents away to get their baby.

They discussed the pros and cons, again and again, unable to commit.

Rhonda and Gerry knew full well everything that could go wrong along the path from egg donation to sperm fertilization to embie implantation in a surrogate's uterus. They knew not to get excited. Statistically, they probably would not have any more babies, they told each other as they vacillated. They repeated these discussions, without reaching resolution, during Blaze's early-morning breakfasts, as they got ready for work, and in harried cell-phone calls during breaks in their shifts.

Finally, they told Dr. Yash and Dr. Sudhir they might as well try, since it probably wouldn't happen.

On Tuesday, November 30, 2010, their dark-eyed donor produced eighteen eggs. On December 2, Dr. Pai transferred three embryos to their new surrogate. Her name was Gauri. Gauri, whose husband still did not have regular paid work, had finally decided to try surrogacy as a way to feed her family. The Wiles were her first clients. On Tuesday, December 14, Gauri passed the pregnancy test with flying colors. The fertilization, transfer, and implantation all went flawlessly.

The Wiles were having another baby.

Make that babies. All three embryos had implanted successfully. Gauri was pregnant . . . with triplets.

Gerry and Rhonda were thrilled—and also sickened. After years of zero babies, suddenly they had too many. They would, under Indian law, have to selectively "reduce" one of the embryos. Any couple doing IVF knows they might have to confront this ugly decision. Rhonda and Gerry tried to focus on the captivating fact that more babies were coming their way, instead of the heartbreak of saying good-bye to one.

Fortuitously, nature took its course. One fetus spontaneously aborted at five weeks gestation.

Six and a half weeks into the pregnancy, Surrogacy India sent a sonogram across the ocean to the Wiles' living room in Mesa. There were two perfectly formed, crystal-clear egg sacs. Gauri was due to deliver the Wile twins in late August or early September, right around Blaze's second birthday.

It was time to return to India.

Most pregnant women carry a single baby at a time. Growing and delivering babies one by one is significantly safer and healthier, for both women and infants. However, in preparation for IVF, women like the Wiles' Muslim egg donor inject hormones that stimulate production of twenty to thirty eggs per monthly ovulation cycle, rather than the one or two that occur naturally.

As a result, multiple births in the United States and elsewhere have skyrocketed since surrogacy and IVF became mainstream infertility treatments. The twin birthrate in the

United States has jumped 70 percent since 1980, according to the Centers for Disease Control and Prevention. Every year there are over sixty thousand babies being pushed along our nation's sidewalks in twin strollers solely due to ART.[13]

It's hard to understand the logic from the outside. How can intended parents intentionally, consciously, even happily, risk the moms' and the babies' health?

ART doctors like Dr. Yashodhara and Dr. Sudhir, as well as patients like the Wiles and surrogates like Gauri, all want to maximize the chance of pregnancy. The goal of ART, after all, is pregnancy—not babies. Banking on a single embryo implantation has been considered far too chancy, given the cost and invasive nature of IVF, despite the risk of multiple fetuses and birth defects.

The true risk for people with impaired fertility? Attempting to have babies one by one. The strain on the gestational mother and the risks to the unborn are secondary when infertile couples, like Rhonda and Gerry, have been desperate for years—starving—for children. They live with the grim reality that they, or their surrogate, may never become pregnant, not even once. In IVF attempts with women thirty-five and older, the embryo fail-rate is nearly 70 percent, pressuring doctors and patients to improve their chances with multiple embryos.[14] Many couples feel their first pregnancy may be their last— their only chance to have children. Additionally, many do not have the money to try to conceive more than once. So some welcome news of a twin or triplet pregnancy with effusive joy despite the dangers and financial sacrifices.

Multiple births are, unfortunately, *far* riskier and more expensive. The hospital costs for the eight babies born to infamous Octomom Nadya Suleman were estimated at over $1 million.[15] Like Sulemon's babies, the majority of multiples are born before thirty-seven weeks of gestation, often requiring neonatal intensive care. Common multiple-pregnancy side effects are anemia, gestational diabetes, high blood pressure, and blood clots. Additionally, miscarriage rates are higher for multiple pregnancies; transfer of multiple embryos may in fact lead to *decreased* pregnancy rates for some women.[16] Premature birth, low birth weight, and birth defects are all more common in multiple births versus single births.

And death: twins are five times more likely than singletons to die within a month of birth.

Triplets are nearly fifteen times more likely to die within a month of birth.

As the field of surrogacy and ART has grown, some countries, including England and Italy, have established parameters for the maximum number of embryos that may be implanted during IVF. Dr. Maurizio Macaluso, former head of the U.S. Center for Disease Control's reproductive health branch, has called for intended parents, fertility doctors, surrogates, and insurance agencies to consider cost savings calculated in the hundreds of millions of dollars per year. The CDC now recommends—but does not have the authority to require—single embryo transfer as standard practice for couples and surrogates undergoing IVF.

And then there are the issues of what to do with "leftover" embryos that doctors can keep alive—or at least suspended indefinitely as potentially alive. There are more than half a million frozen embryos currently stored by fertility clinics throughout the United States.[17] Many have been abandoned by couples who no longer need them. Others are used for scientific research or offered to unrelated infertile couples for adoption.

Custody battles and inheritance fights over disputed embryo "ownership" are winding their way through the U.S. legal systems. Personhood USA continues to advocate for legal citizenship for embryos, largely as part of the anti-abortion movement, but with far-reaching impact on ART as well. Do these embryos have rights? Do we, as a nation, have an obligation to treat them as citizens? If you contributed the egg or the sperm, even as a paid, anonymous donor, do you have an obligation to decide what happens to "your" babies? If not, who shoulders this responsibility?

"It is strangely easy to freeze and thaw human embryos," writes *Washington Post* reporter Liza Mundy in *Everything Conceivable*.[18] "Embryos don't get freezer burn. Unlike, say, hamburgers, human embryos can be frozen, and thawed, and frozen, and thawed again, and used."

This is good news for infertile couples around the world. But as with nearly every aspect of fertility medicine, technological advances come with a high ethical, and financial, price tag.

There were, of course, many things about their new surrogate, Gauri, that Rhonda and Gerry did not know. Sure, they had the detailed questionnaire she completed before becoming their surrogate, and frequent medical updates about her pregnancy on the Wiles' Surrogacy India personal Web site. They could see her shy, pretty smile and brown eyes during their regular Skype viewings, which occurred about once a month when Gauri came to the clinic for prenatal care. But Gauri kept her inner turmoil to herself.

The Wiles couldn't know how disquieted Gauri felt at times about carrying their babies. She wasn't ashamed about becoming a surrogate; she did not regret her decision. But she encountered dilemmas that no woman can predict in advance of becoming pregnant with another couple's children.

It troubled Gauri to hear the babies' heartbeats. Although she had been raised by a culture that valued submissiveness in women, when she went for her monthly checkups, she always asked the doctors to turn down the ultrasound volume, so that she would not have to hear the *thump-whoosh-thump* that usually exhilarates pregnant women. Gauri also turned her head away when the ultrasound screen showed pictures of the two babies she carried. She hoped to have a Cesarean, so that giving birth would feel more like an operation than labor. She made a point of stressing to friends that she'd gotten pregnant through an operation—not through sex with a man.

Despite the fact that her children could see that her body had changed, she never found a way to tell them she was pregnant. She couldn't find words to explain that she was carrying Rhonda and Gerry's babies to earn money to feed and care for her own babies. In many respects, Gauri was trying to pretend, to her family and herself, that she was not actually pregnant.

Gauri knew she would not hold the twins after birth. She would not see them, feed them, or hear them cry beyond the inevitable noises in the delivery room. In all likelihood, she would never see the babies again. Her babies might never meet her, might never know who carried them for nine months, nurtured them, and made their faraway existence possible.

She would spend a week resting at the clinic, recovering physically and psychologically. As did Shashi after Blaze's birth, and all the other surrogates at SI—Surrogacy India's standard policy for surrogates' well-being. Even in the unusual cases when a surrogate insists she feels no mixed emotions about the task she has completed, giving birth to—and immediately giving away—a baby or babies you have carried in your uterus for nine months can feel like abandoning a piece of yourself.

Or being abandoned yourself.

It is your body. It is not your baby. But try telling that to a woman who has just given birth, flooded with maternal love, hormones, and the intense, overpowering biological instinct to nurture and protect her offspring.

Maybe your mind understands. But how can your body? A compassionately run clinic like Surrogacy India does everything it can to help surrogates detach and heal after pregnancy. But they are no match for human biology and millennia of maternal instinct.

Dr. Anita Soni at Hiranandani Hospital, however, dismisses this syrupy view. And it's not because she's incapable of sentimentality. Despite her regal authority, she has plenty of emotion herself. She has four recent wedding pictures in her office. A passionate Christian who married over twenty years ago in a customary Indian ceremony, she always longed for a traditional Christian wedding, complete with white wedding gown. After two decades of marriage and two children, she convinced her husband to grant her wish. The wedding photos picture the fifty-year-old Soni, in a white lace veil and elaborate white dress, remarrying her husband. Their grown daughter served as bridesmaid and their grown son served as ring bearer. The pictures are strategically positioned throughout her office so that they can be seen from every corner of the room, including from a prone position on the examining table.

Having delivered over one hundred babies born to Surrogacy India's gestational surrogates, Dr. Soni argues the most difficult aspect of paid pregnancy comes not when the babies disappear into the intended parents' care.

"The surrogates are emotionally well prepared for that reality," Soni explains in her lilting Indian accent. "Look, their lives are hard. They are tough women, even at eighteen or twenty. All slum women have already faced far greater disenchantments than giving up a baby they always knew they would give up."

The challenge comes when they receive their final payment, Soni believes, and it is less than they initially believed it would be. Sometimes there are deductions for housing, medical treatments, and vitamins. Because the surrogates have made such a physical and psychological sacrifice for money, any deduction of their earnings strikes a powerful blow, a feeling that they have sold their bodies and their babies short. And despite Indian laws and guidelines, the surrogates feel helpless to object if they disagree with the financial accounting.

"Also, who worries about long-term postnatal care?" Dr. Soni points out, shrugging her shoulders and looking around her empty office as if to show that no one does. "It is true, and right, that surrogates get world-class ob-gyn care while they are here, while they are pregnant and immediately after, when Western clients foot the bill. But what if complications arise four months later? Four years later? Who will take care of the surrogates when they are once again poor women thrust into India's health-care maze, rather than prized surrogates serving wealthy foreigners? No one."

To date, Surrogacy India has had only 20 percent of their surrogates express interest in repeating surrogacy.

The Wiles' first surrogate, Shashi, used the surrogacy payments to buy her family shelter, a basic human necessity. However, Gauri was even more vulnerable, because she needed the money for a far more primal survival requirement—to feed her children and herself on a daily basis. She depended on the surrogacy compensation for her family's very existence, since neither she nor her husband had consistent jobs.

"Gauri?" Dr. Soni asks rhetorically. "Yes, she is strong. But Gauri and her family, they need every single rupee promised them."

"Hello?"

Rhonda was lying on her bed, on the phone with her sister

in Canada, when the line beeped. It was a scorching Phoenix night, Thursday, July 14, 2011. Rhonda looked at the phone, which showed an Indian exchange. Rhonda told her sister she'd call her back and then clicked on the other line.

The Arizona summer had been spectacularly hot. One single 118-degree day shattered ten years of records. The nearby Monument wildfire raged through 478,000 acres of national forestland, requiring round-the-clock duty for 4,656 firefighters before it was extinguished.[19] Separately, the Bear Wallow Wilderness fire, started May 29 by two cousins on a camping trip, had burned 538,000 acres and cost $79 million to extinguish. There were also thunderstorms and dangerous flash flood warnings as the Sonoran Desert weathered its own monsoon season.

Ten days before, on July 4, 2011, less than five years after launching Surrogacy India in a Mumbai internet café, Dr. Yashodhara and Dr. Sudhir delivered Surrogacy India's one hundredth baby. Together, they had made one hundred dreams come true for infertile couples from America, Australia, Europe, and India. They celebrated with a modest office party, more of Nagma's delectable biryani, and coffee cups with the one hundred baby names etched into the ceramic. Rhonda had opened a brown package covered in Indian stamps with her and Gerry's two mugs the day before.

Thousands of miles away in Germany, the U.S. women's soccer team had pulled off a spectacular quarterfinal World Cup victory over Brazil. In France, citizens celebrated the storming of the Bastille prison in 1789, the beginning of the French Revolution over two hundred years before. Americans were still absorbing Osama bin Laden's execution in Pakistan two months before.

Around the world, television news programs were filled with more terrifying images from Mumbai: on July 13, downtown had experienced its second terrorist bombing in three years. Nineteen people had been killed as bombs exploded in three different crowded downtown neighborhoods, including Opera House, an area the Wiles knew well. The Wiles had received an e-mail that everyone at SI, including their surrogate Gauri, was fine.

Rhonda froze with the home phone tucked between her ear and shoulder. Gerry was working on his laptop in the kitchen one room over. Blaze slept a few feet away in his room, decorated to look like a small fire station complete with a fire-truck bed. Rhonda instinctively walked to Gerry, her eyes wide.

Gerry could hear what he thought sounded like Dr. Yashodhara's soft voice. Was Gauri all right? She had been scheduled for an ultrasound. Her due date was six weeks away. At first Gerry assumed the call was a routine report of the results, or further reassurance that despite the bombings, Mumbai overall was stable and secure.

Then Gerry heard Rhonda say, "Oh my God."

His heart pitched. He reached for the kitchen counter for support.

Everyone at Surrogacy India was fine. Including Gauri. But there was exciting news.

Well, kind of.

After eight months of a routine, healthy twins' pregnancy, Gauri had precipitously gone into labor at thirty-four weeks. Her cervix was four centimeters dilated and 70 percent effaced. If the doctors did not intervene, the twins would arrive within hours. Dr. Soni would administer a muscle relaxer, terbutaline, via IV drip to weaken Gauri's contractions and delay her labor.

How soon could the Wiles get to the hospital?

Of course, obstetrical doctors order many expectant parents to the delivery room without delay, especially when labor is imminent. But the Wiles' hospital was over eight thousand miles and half a day of time zones away.

Gerry and Rhonda barely slept for the next sixty hours. The first calls went to their employers. Could they get off work? Then they called the neighbors next door, a retired Maryland police major and his wife, who loved Blaze like their own grandson and often did small, vital favors for the Wiles. Could they take care of their new blue-eyed puppy, Neyla, weeks earlier than expected?

Gerry called their Indian travel agent, Amit Kulkarni, at his office in downtown Mumbai. Could he make hotel reservations? Meet them and their considerable luggage at Chhatrapati Shivaji International Airport in the middle of the night?

Then he searched the airlines. Gerry spent four hours online, trying to find affordable last-minute flights to Mumbai. It would cost over $1,000 above their airfare budget to leave within twenty-four hours. The financial blow would come on top of the lost wages both he and Rhonda would experience because of their sudden departure. Finally, he found flights that would get them to Mumbai. The Wiles would leave Phoenix on Sunday, July 17, at 7:15 A.M. on Delta Flight 1492. Three entire days after Gauri's labor began.

Hopefully they would arrive before the babies did.

Then they had to shop and pack. The Wiles needed to stockpile American infant supplies, impossible to come by in Mumbai. Five hundred diapers for preemie twins and larger ones for Blaze, who at twenty-three months was not yet fully toilet trained. Ten cans of Similac. Avent plastic baby bottles and rubberized nipples. Ten tubs of baby wipes. Two infant car seats. Thermometers. Mylicon and Motrin. Baby clothes. Gifts for Gauri and her family and the doctors, nurses, and staff at Surrogacy India—everyone's favorite treats were bags of miniature candy bars, the individually wrapped pieces of Hershey's, Kit Kat, and 3 Musketeers that American parents put out on Halloween. Plus clothes and toiletries and other supplies that Blaze, Rhonda, and Gerry needed for their monthlong stay in Mumbai during the end of another steamy monsoon season.

It was like mobilizing a small military campaign. They took turns going to Walmart and Target. Their baby necessities filled five extra large rollaboard suitcases.

This would be Rhonda and Gerry's fifth trip to India in four years. It would be Blaze's first trip back to the city of his birth. He would turn two on August 26 amid the doctors and women he could not remember, but who had made his life possible: the teams of sisters and boys working the maternity ward at Hiranandani; Dr. Hrishikesh Pai who transferred the fertilized donor eggs, carefully hatching them with his laser; Dr. Anita Soni, who cared so well for Shashi and made sure that all surrogates and babies at Hiranandani were treated with the finest medical care and pain alleviation possible; Doctors Yash and Sudhir, who created the clinic that created him.

The Wiles eagerly anticipated meeting Gauri, whom they had seen via Skype so often during the last nine months. However, they knew that many surrogates control the time spent with their baby's intended parents, trying to set an emotional boundary in a complex relationship. How often they saw each other would be up to Gauri. There were also plans to see Shashi, the surrogate who carried Blaze and bought her family a house with the money paid to her by Surrogacy India. Shashi, now twenty-six, had recently decided to become a gestational surrogate for Surrogacy India again, this time to pay for her two sons' education.

There were no plans to connect with the egg donor who had provided the oocytes for Blaze and his two siblings. The Wiles had never met the young Muslim woman who lived in northern India, despite her priceless contribution to their family. She lived several hours from Mumbai. She had never expressed a desire to meet the Wiles or the children she helped them create.

The three Wiles flew first to Minneapolis. A three-hour layover. A quick meal at Chili's. A change of planes. Then an eight-hour flight to Charles de Gaulle Airport outside Paris. A frantic change of terminals via a shuttle bus, another line for security, several escalators and winding corridors that were several inches too narrow to navigate with Blaze's heavily laden, supersized American baby jogger. Gerry pushed; Rhonda pushed. Surrounded by bags, Blaze gripped the sides of the orange stroller wide-eyed, like a tiny spooked passenger on an out-of-control Disney ride.

U.S. Secretary of State Hillary Clinton was also headed to India that day. She and a twenty-five-member delegation from the State Department were traveling to New Delhi for two days of negotiations regarding international air safety, terrorism, investment opportunities, cyber security, and women's empowerment. One assumes Clinton had an easier time getting to India than the Wiles. Although it is sticky to argue whose quest was more urgent.

After landing in Paris just before 8 A.M., the Wiles had a three-hour delay in France for the nine-hour-and-twenty-minute flight to Mumbai. Aeroports de Paris offered fifteen minutes of free Wi-Fi in Terminal C at Charles de Gaulle. In the crowded, boisterous waiting area for Gate 88, Rhonda found a spare plastic seat and checked her e-mail via her beaten-up purple covered iPad.

She clicked on a message from Dr. Yashodhara. Gauri's oxygen levels had dropped precipitously. Dr. Soni had to stop the terbutaline drip. She had given Gauri the drug Pitocin, a synthetic hormone that accelerates labor.

"The babies will probably be born before you get here," Dr. Yash warned.

The plane carrying Blaze, Rhonda, and Gerry was scheduled

to land at Chhatrapati at 11:45 P.M., Monday night, July 18, 2011. Four days after Gauri's labor started. Dr. Yash and Dr. Sudhir would meet the flight no matter what time it arrived. They would take the Wiles straight to the hospital, hoping the twins could wait to be born until their family got there to hold them.

Six hours into the nine-hour flight, the Boeing 777 hovered somewhere over Afghanistan. Blaze and Gerry were asleep. Rhonda was wide-awake in the middle row of seats, with Blaze's soft body across her lap. The family was surrounded mostly by Mumbai natives returning home after summer visits abroad—small children, old men, and lots of women who changed into brightly colored saris after the plane took off. Even one set of four-month-old twins from New Jersey coming home to meet their grandparents. The black-haired girls wore matching hot pink Nike soccer warm-ups.

Once again, Rhonda couldn't sleep. Would Gauri's body be able to wait? Thirty-four weeks was terribly young for twins to be born. The latest ultrasound had shown that each twin weighed less than four pounds. The nurse in Rhonda knew that babies born so early were at risk for lung problems, cerebral palsy, and other long-term health complications.

What if one twin died? Could both die? Rhonda remembered the British mother she'd met who had flown thousands of miles to cradle her dead son in the hospital morgue. She tried to focus on the fact that later the same mother had a healthy baby girl via surrogacy.

All that mattered was for the twins to be born healthy, for Gauri to have a safe delivery. The doubt that had gnawed at Rhonda throughout the past six years rose up again. Maybe she was not meant to be a mother. Maybe she was defying fate by orchestrating—forcing—this pregnancy.

Maybe fate was about to fight right back.

Five hours later, in the early minutes of Tuesday, July 19, 2011, the doctors spotted Rhonda, Gerry, and Blaze making their way through the crowded Mumbai airport. Two steel luggage carts and Blaze's bright orange baby jogger nearly obscured the small family from view. Only three years before, during the Wiles' first visit to India, this same floor had been dirt. Now it was sturdy, albeit grubby, standard-issue airport linoleum.

India, such an ancient country, was growing up.

Dr. Sudhir began jumping up and down behind the security cordon. He wanted Gerry to spot him amid the crowds of friends and relatives, thronging the international terminal at 1 A.M. despite the late hour and humid rain of the monsoon season. Dr. Sudhir's dark face was split open by a huge white grin.

A few minutes later, overcome by enthusiasm, the doctors broke through the crimson airport security rope. Gerry engulfed Dr. Sudhir in a bear hug as Rhonda wrapped her arms around Dr. Yashodhara. As soon as the two women separated, Blaze held up his arms to his Indian godmother. Holding Blaze in her arms, Dr. Yash smiled prettily for a second.

She took a deep breath before she shared the news.

As the plane had flown through the night skies toward Pakistan, Gauri could wait no longer. Nearly two thousand miles away, and thirty-three thousand feet below the plane carrying Rhonda, Gerry, and Blaze through the night, the Wile twins were born at 9:09 P.M. and 9:25 P.M. on July 18, 2011, at Hiranandani Hospital via natural delivery.

Dr. Yashodhara and Dr. Sudhir were both in the delivery room. Gerry and Rhonda had already designated the doctors as the twins' Indian godparents, as they had with Blaze. As the Wiles had instructed, since the twins couldn't see their own faces at birth, they were greeted by their Indian godparents' smiles. The docs welcomed the Wile babies to the world, documenting every second with pictures and videos for Rhonda and Gerry. The doctors had promised each other to wait until they saw the Wiles at the airport to tell them the babies' gender.

The first Wile family photo taken after the safe arrival of their premature twins via surrogate in July 2011 at Hiranandani Hospital.

A boy and a girl. Four pounds each. Small, but perfectly healthy.

The Wiles were now a family of five.

Although at this point, Rhonda and Gerry could not have cared less about money, it is worth noting that almost none of the medical expenses the Wiles' three babies incurred were covered by their health insurance policy.

Not the hormone shots Rhonda took in 2008. Not the payments to Surrogacy India for Rhonda's treatments, the surrogates' medical procedures or prenatal care, or the NICU expenses. None of the $4,000 they spent on Gonal-f.

Not the plane tickets to India in 2008, or 2009, or 2011.

Not the money paid to the U.S. government for visas or passports.

Gerry tried submitting the receipts from Hiranandani and Lilavati hospitals to the Wiles' U.S. health insurance company. The insurance company replied with a letter reiterating their standard policies: the fertility treatments, surrogacy payments, and maternal and neonatal care expenses were incurred out of the country, and they were not for an emergency or a medical necessity.

Every single expense was rejected.

Hiranandani Hospital prohibits 2 A.M. visits, even from delirious new parents who've traveled across two continents. Instead, the doctors drove Rhonda, Gerry, and Blaze and their five suitcases from the airport to the Lakeside Chalet, a Marriott residence hotel in the parklike neighborhood of Powai, a quick ten-minute rickshaw ride away from Hiranandani Hospital. The modern skyscraper featured in the movie *Slumdog Millionaire* towered over the nearby placid lake that justifies the hotel's Swiss moniker.

The doctors stayed with the Wiles until 6 A.M., sharing minute details of the twins' birth, recreating every moment Rhonda and Gerry had missed so it would seem they hadn't missed anything. While the four adults talked, trying to keep their voices at whisper levels, Blaze slept on a nubby beige couch in their small suite—slumbering as perhaps only toddlers can, as inert and unmoving as if lacking bones.

Early Tuesday morning, the Wiles learned that the dirt floor at Chhatrapati Airport was not the only thing that had been updated since their last visit. They were stopped in the lobby of Hiranandani Hospital, their newborns a few floors above them in the nursery. The Indian government had established a new requirement for surrogate births: before intended parents could meet their babies, a government advocate had to interview the parents and the surrogate, ascertain that the surrogate had not been coerced into the pregnancy, and confirm that she had been paid the correct amount in full.

The Wiles would not be able to leave India without an official document, covered in bureaucratic ink stamps, confirming that they had taken care of their surrogate per the contract.

A receipt, if you will. For their babies.

The measures had been established for wise and obvious reasons—not to use newborn babies as ransom, but to ensure that Indian women, already made vulnerable by illiteracy and lack of economic options, were not forced into carrying babies by their families, by wealthy, powerful foreigners, or by deceitful fertility clinics. However, to jump through another bureaucratic hoop—and risk another potential bribe—when you've traveled twenty-seven hours to see your newbies is a bit of a buzzkill. As well, the officious meeting is no cakewalk for a surrogate who has just given birth and is grappling with saying farewell to vulnerable infants her body has nurtured and protected for nine months.

Still, one brief meeting with the surrogacy advocate in the marble-floored lobby at Hiranandani Hospital was a sand dam in comparison with the months adoptive parents obsess about an American birth mother changing her mind, or the years and dollars a court custody battle could consume disputing a surrogacy or adoption agreement, or the lifetime of childlessness infertile couples once had to endure.

The Wiles counted themselves lucky.

Autumn in the metro Washington, D.C., region usually leans toward idyllic blue skies, low humidity, and crisp breezes. Romantic fall wedding weather torn straight out of *Brides* magazine. But the first week of September 2011 brought four consecutive days of heavy monsoon rains, as unremitting as anything the Mumbai skies dish out. The Potomac River swelled above its low-slung banks with muddy, churning, red-brown water. Maryland, Virginia, and DC government agencies handed out free sandbags to residents. Traffic, routinely awful during the initial Congress-back-in-session rush, crippled DC drivers for four straight days. Roads flooded and stoplights stopped working.

On the second day of the monsoon rains, a three-story crane used to repair the forty-five-foot-tall pinnacles crowning the National Cathedral—damaged during a rare 5.8 magnitude earthquake in August—tipped over backward in the slippery mud. No one was injured, but the drama made for striking evening news clips.

On the fourth day of the nonstop rains, President Obama gave a thirty-two-minute speech imploring Congress to pass his $447-billion jobs bill to defibrillate the flailing U.S. economy. The nation prepared to observe the ten-year anniversary of the September 11, 2001, terrorist attacks on New York City's Twin Towers and the Pentagon across the Potomac River from DC. Radio and television stations ran 9/11 memorial tributes. Local yoga studios chanted one hundred continuous "ohms" to cleanse the city's spirit. A *Washington Post* columnist opined that it was time to move on.

Friday, September 9 brought a return to normalcy, climatewise. The heavy rains broke that morning at 11 A.M. The sky resumed shining its bright September blue. The stoplights started blinking red, yellow, and green once again.

At Shady Grove Fertility Center just off the DC Beltway in Rockville, Maryland, the odd monsoon deluge had not stopped the 420 doctors, nurses, and staff from their baby-making routines: meeting with patients, harvesting eggs from fertile young donors, finalizing contracts with lawyers, clients, labs, and medical clinics. A unique, orchestrated medical response to the heartbreak of infertility, a collective human tragedy vastly removed from terrorist attacks, 9.1 percent national unemployment, earthquakes, and construction accidents.

The new normal in the world of fertility medicine.

If you take back roads instead of the crowded, anonymous

Beltway to the office complex that houses Shady Grove Fertility Center, you pass through some of Maryland's prettiest, most fertile woodlands, originally the Tehogee Indian Trail, a Native American trade route built by the Canaze nation in the 1600s and early 1700s. These days, South Glen Road winds through dozens of small grassy knolls and deep glens shaded by one-hundred-year-old oaks, past streets with quaint, evocative names like Red Barn Lane and Shepherd's Creek Road. Most homes are single-family ranches or larger, freshly painted two-story wooden homes recently built to look like old farmhouses. You even pass by the large homes of the senior partners at Shady Grove Fertility, most of whom live in Potomac, Maryland, one of *Forbes* magazine's most expensive zip codes in the United States. There are still a few old general stores in operation along the curving back roads, and a smattering of struggling horse farms underneath the massive power lines bringing electricity to DC's five million metro residents. Country clubs and private-school campuses sprawl across the sleek emerald glens at regular intervals. Slim white-tailed deer graze on the roadsides in the afternoon sun.

The neighborhood immediately approaching Shady Grove becomes more congested and noticeably less charming, with a redbrick Hilton Garden Inn, concrete office buildings, and acres of shiny new clapboard semidetached houses. An empty field—surely soon to be filled with townhomes or a shopping mall—is temporarily dotted with weeping willow trees and dozens of migrating black and gray Canadian geese.

Huge blue-glass windows wrap around the four floors of Shady Grove Fertility's boxlike, 32,000-square-foot headquarters at 15001 Shady Grove Road. Late on a Friday afternoon, long after most area employees had headed home to beat weekend traffic, the parking lot was crowded with minivans and SUVs. There wasn't space to park a bicycle. In the lobby, a female doctor in navy scrubs, white hairnet, and booties greeted

262

an Asian couple in their thirties with a friendly wave and a smile of recognition. "I'll be right with you," she called out with cheerful authority as the couple got into the elevator and headed up to the bustling fourth-floor reception area.

The beige waiting room looked like any crowded suburban American doctor's office, with cloth-covered straight-back chairs and a large split-screen TV on mute showing Nascar racing and a countdown to the fall NFL season. The first hints that this doctor's office went beyond traditional medicine were the dozens of brochures in Plexiglas wall cases with indecipherable titles: "The Andrology Center." "Pulling Down the Moon Integrative Care." "Shared Risk 100% Refund Guarantee for IVF." And "Donor Egg: Making Fertility Treatments More Affordable for You!"

The couple from the elevator sat talking softly, holding hands, not meeting anyone's gaze. A grandmotherly woman in her late fifties joked with her thirtyish daughter. In the unisex bathroom, a handwritten sign read: ATTENTION LADIES! IF YOU ARE HERE FOR AN *EMBRYO TRANSFER* PLEASE DO *NOT* EMPTY YOUR BLADDER!

Shady Grove Fertility Center, still private after two decades of astounding growth, today is indisputably the United States' market leader in treating infertility. According to the CDC, Shady Grove alone performs nearly 4 percent of the nation's IVF cycles, many of them for surrogates. Their mission is clear: to help couples have babies. Lots of babies. A baby born every three hours, at least at the latest tally. Dr. Patrick Steptoe and Professor Bob Edwards would have been very proud.

Although truth be told, Shady Grove in many ways mirrors every other large fertility practice today. The focus is on pregnancy, the Big Fat Positive. And its offices, like so much of ART, are completely devoid of actual children.

A large laminated sign in one corner of the waiting room politely explains the puzzling absence of children: OUR POLICY

263

AS AN INFERTILITY PRACTICE IS NOT TO HAVE CHILDREN IN ANY OF OUR OFFICES. Children—the prized goal of every client in the reception area—are relegated to a first-floor lobby waiting area, similar to an airport's cell-phone parking lot, to separate them from couples desperate for a child of their own. The patients' waiting room, where emotions are raw, is meant to be a small oasis in a world where others' children are constant salt-in-the-wound reminders of life's lack of fairness when it comes to fertility.

Shady Grove Fertility Center is one of the largest, most comprehensive fertility treatment centers on the planet. Over four hundred people work at Shady Grove, including twenty-four doctors, Ph.D. scientists, and geneticists. Patients from all fifty states and over thirty-five countries around the world have chosen to receive infertility care through one of Shady Grove Fertility's seventeen locations.

Over the twenty years from its founding in 1991 until 2011, the center fostered the births of an astounding 27,000 babies. During Shady Grove's first year, one ART baby was born every twenty days. Now a Shady Grove baby is born roughly every 180 minutes.

Annually, Shady Grove physicians perform over 5,500 IVF cycles, including over eight hundred egg donation cycles, and an equal number of ovulation inductions and IUI cycles. The clinic also provides donor egg retrieval, laser-hatching, freezing and thawing of egg and sperm, embryo transfers, gestational surrogacy, and preimplantation genetic diagnosis for couples at risk of passing along genetic diseases. The center offers resources to address all patient needs, including financial aid and payment plans. For so many infertility patients, after the physical and emotional challenges, money remains the largest obstacle to a baby.

In 2010, Shady Grove Fertility's positive pregnancy rate was 42 percent.[20] The pregnancy rate using donor eggs averages 56 percent. Shady Grove conducted 3,328 fresh egg retrievals. Their scientists thawed 784 frozen embryos. They successfully transferred 3,123 embryos. Their "high-order multiple rates" (more than two fetuses per pregnancy) clocked in as one of the lowest in the nation at less than 1 percent. The center has helped nearly two hundred gestational surrogates carry babies for couples, like Gerry and Rhonda Wile, for whom IVF and other conventional fertility treatments have failed.

Shady Grove—and other large fertility centers such as the Cornell–New York Presbyterian Weill Center for Reproductive Medicine, and the University of California San Francisco's fertility center—is modern medicine's equivalent of the U.S. Marine Corps attacking infertility like the enemy many find it to be, a cruel, crippling, lifelong killer that strikes its victims randomly and uncaringly.

Yet, like many other grand-scale fertility treatment clinics, despite its size and impressive statistics in a booming, evolving industry, Shady Grove cultivates a holistic humanity. It isn't the McDonald's of infertility treatments. It's a medical practice that treats patients with all the gravitas of the Hippocratic oath. Its founders and partners adamantly resist turning Shady Grove into a shopping mall for consumers desperate for the best baby possible or horrified by the messy inconveniences of pregnancy and birth.

There is a formal ethics board run by a group of fertility experts. Over the years, this board has made many difficult decisions to avoid ethically questionable fertility procedures that are nonetheless currently perfectly legal in the United States. Shady Grove offers surrogacy services only in the case of proven medical need (that is, not to avoid stretch marks or a work interruption). The doctors regularly decline to conduct embryo and fetus sex selection. They also will not conduct cross-generational egg donation (from daughter to mother, for instance). They refuse to assist in "family balancing," where a family with boys might want to orchestrate a daughter.

The center runs free monthly support groups. The Andrology Center specializes in testing and treating male infertility. Pulling Down the Moon, the center's proprietary holistic treatment program, offers yoga, massage, acupuncture, nutrition, and "sanctuary" services for sufferers. There are programs for alternate family building, which includes adoption, gestational surrogacy, and deciding to remain child-free. Shady Grove was the first program to include a full-time psychologist, Sharon Covington, who has been an important part of the partnership since 1991. Not surprisingly, Shady Grove physicians and employees, ranging from social workers to the CEO, are regularly invited to share their institutional best practices at the most prestigious fertility conferences around the world.

One of the Shady Grove partners, Dr. Robert J. Stillman, is a handsome, sixty-four-year-old reproductive endocrinologist from Queens, New York, who conducted his medical training at Duke University, Harvard, and Georgetown. Dr. Stillman spent eighteen years in medical academia at George Washington University before joining Shady Grove in 1997. Twenty years before, he lived in the United Kingdom on a research fellowship at Hammersmith Imperial College, in close proximity to Professor Robert Edwards and Dr. Patrick Steptoe's miraculous 1978 IVF triumph of Louise Joy Brown's birth.

"It was undeniably exciting," Dr. Stillman says of the first IVF baby. "It was unbelievable. A miracle. We all knew how long and hard Steptoe and Edwards had worked. We thought IVF might have an application to a few cases of women with blocked ovarian tubes. We had no idea the revolution it would bring about. I never thought it would one day lead to 27,000 babies right here."

Dr. Stillman and the thousands of other ob-gyn doctors around the globe in 1978 had no inkling how quickly in vitro technology would be replicated around the globe, how many critical fertility innovations such as gestational surrogacy

would follow, and how many people's heartbreak would be re-
placed by joy. No one predicted ART and surrogacy would
grow into a $10 billion global industry. No one grasped that by
2010, there would be nearly 150,000 IVF cycles performed in
one year in the United States alone.[21] No one imagined that
one day, it would be common practice to hire another woman
to carry a baby for you.

Back in India, the day after her twins were born, Rhonda
felt a flood of joy—and relief. She and Gerry and Blaze had
made it to India. The babies had completed their journey, too.
She was now the mother of three. Blaze had his precious
brother and sister.

Rhonda and Gerry's hard work and faith, plus the endless
determination of the doctors, surrogates, and technicians at
Surrogacy India, had overcome nature's obstacles to her becoming the mother she always dreamed of being.

Two days after the twins' birth, *The Times of India* reported
that the twentieth victim of the July 13 Opera House triple
bombings had died at J.J Hospital; his wife had given birth to
their third child just six weeks before. As if in response, Hillary Clinton declared, "We cannot tolerate a safe haven for terrorists anywhere," an attempt to ease tensions between India,
Pakistan, and the United States. The results of the prestigious
national chartered accountancy exam were announced. For
the first time in Indian history, girls took the top three places.
Additionally, girls' collective pass rate of 21.9 percent for the
first time exceeded boys' pass rate of 19.8 percent.

Progress indeed.

After less than twenty-four hours in the NICU, the twins'
pediatrician released them to Gerry and Rhonda's care in the
hospital room they had rented. The twins would stay for another few days' observation at Hiranandani. Now at least

everyone could be in the same room together. The tiny babies were remarkably healthy for preemies. The Wiles already had several dozen photos of each baby, of the babies with Blaze, of the entire family smiling together, of the doctors holding the babies, of Dr. Soni holding the babies . . . You get the picture.

The Wiles named their tall, skinny daughter with exquisitely fine features—like her mother and her surrogate—Dylan. Dr Yashodhara picked her middle name, choosing Tara, which means "star." The stockier boy with big feet they named Jett Ajja. Ajja is Dr. Sudhir's family name. In addition to their first and middle names, within a week everyone at Surrogacy India planned to celebrate the twins' safe arrival by giving them Indian names, complete with an in-office ceremony, gifts, and traditional Indian refreshments, as they had with Blaze two years before.

That first night, her back spasming from five days of stress, lack of sleep, carrying Blaze and the heavy luggage, plus two long international flights, convinced both Wiles that Rhonda should be the parent sleeping in a regular bed at the hotel with Blaze. So Gerry signed into Room 17 on the eleventh floor of Hiranandani Hospital and settled in for a night of feedings and double diaper changes every three hours.

Early the next morning, after a long night alone in the hospital with Dylan and Jett, Gerry prepped the babies for a trip down two flights for their daily weigh-in at the newborn ward. Rhonda and Blaze would arrive in a few minutes via auto-rickshaw. The family planned to spend the day feeding the babies, changing their American Girl–sized diapers, taking several dozen more pictures, and updating their Facebook pages and the blog so their family and friends could all share the wonderful news.

Gerry wanted to accomplish the daily mandatory hospital weigh-in before Rhonda and Blaze arrived. He swaddled each baby carefully. He then tucked Dylan and Jett into the crook of his right arm.

Twins! Five-month-old Dylan Tara Wile (with hair) next to her brother Jett Ajja Wile, at home in Mesa, Arizona.

Rhonda quickly mastered the art of feeding two babies simultaneously.

One of the maternity ward sisters, dressed in a blue uniform, offered to carry Jett.

Gerry smiled. "I pull 300-pound people out of burning buildings," he explained, laughing. "I can handle two four-pound babies."

In the elevator a few minutes later, a diminutive, elderly Indian man with white hair and smooth mahogany skin reached up to tap Gerry's shoulder. He wore crisp tan pants and a dark, tailored Indian dhoti. He held up one palm, open in the universal question gesture.

"Twins?" he asked in accented English.

Gerry nodded.

Then the older man held up both hands and incanted a silent blessing over Dylan and Jett, asleep in tiny white hospital blankets the size of napkins. Together, the babies took up less than a third of Gerry's forearm.

"May your family be blessed," the Indian gentleman said solemnly to Gerry in the crowded elevator.

Gerry bowed back to him and said, *"Namaste,"* the traditional Indian greeting that bestows respect, gratitude, and recognition onto another human being.

"We are already blessed," Gerry whispered to himself, as he walked off the elevator, cradling the youngest two members of his exceptional family.

*Surrogacy is built* upon medical, legal, and financial transactions, inextricably mixed with tsunamis of dreams and disappointments. Behind each embryo transfer lies a real live family with real live hope for a baby. This hope, quite often, turns into a pregnancy, and subsequently into an actual baby or babies. All born to people who, as recently as 1978, would otherwise never have become parents. Millions of babies like Blaze, Dylan, and Jett, who, without ART and gestational surrogacy, would not exist.

Plus over 500,000 fertilized embryos that no one is quite sure what to do about.

None of the doctors or earliest patients could have predicted that surrogacy's innovations would be so expensive and psychologically stressful that many infertile patients would be unable to seek or complete treatment. Or how many ethical, legal, and societal complications would arise. No one had the audacity to grasp that infertility, as the human race had understood it for thousands of years, could be eradicated for the vast majority of sufferers.

No one could have imagined that on October 25, 2011, eight thousand miles away from their babies' birthplace, the five members of the Wile family, who had flown, relatively uneventfully, back from India in late August, would start another day dominated by the absurd joy of life with a rambunctious two-year-old and healthy twin infants. Back in Mumbai, the doctors, nurses, and staff at Surrogacy India focused on creating the clinic's second one hundred babies.

That day, an exhausted mother named Rhonda Wile posted the following words for 800 million potential readers on an Internet communication powerhouse called Facebook:

"Holding your sweet child as they fall asleep in your arms. The very best feeling in the world. This is how I was meant to be a Mommy, and I wouldn't change it for the world."

Infertility remains a cruel and unfair affliction. Today's surrogacy solutions are imperfect, slapping several ugly warning labels onto your rosy dreams of parenthood. Your child may not be biologically related to you. You may not have as many children as you once dreamed of. You may get three children when you wanted one. Lifelong medical and psychological challenges, for both you and your spawn, may linger. You may bite your pillow many nights, wondering whether you were meant to be a parent, or have tantrum-plagued doubts that you are a less patient, nurturing parent than you might have been. And for shizzle, the whole shebang is going to cost way more than anyone should ever have to pay to have a baby.

In other words, parenthood for people forced to turn to gestational surrogates has become just as messy, unpredictable, chaotic, crazy-making, expensive, and long-lasting as it is for those folks who got pregnant on the first try.

But the awe-inspiring news remains awe-inspiring: Even the infertile can have babies today.

To parents and babies, it didn't and doesn't matter that no one foresaw or comprehended the enormous depth and scale of problems commercial surrogacy would one day solve. Or the complications successfully treating an age-old curse would raise for many individuals, religions, governments, and societies. Ironically, since infertility has never threatened the human species' survival, in many respects the radical advances in fertility medicine are irrelevant to the human race overall.

The heartbreak of being infertile is individualized and lonely. So too are the joys of a healthy pregnancy, via your own body or a surrogate, and the bliss of a newborn baby, of finding your own path to parenthood or accepting that you will remain child-free. Each case of infertility, and its resolution, represents a unique personal apogee. But the individuality of the misery, and the ecstasy, do not make creating a baby, or letting one go, any less transformational.

Thus ends this tale of one vasectomy, two vaginas, two continents, and two very, very hot cities.

One mother, Rhonda Wile. One father, Gerry Wile.

One egg donor. Two gestational surrogates. Hundreds of dedicated doctors working across continents and over the course of decades.

Three healthy babies. Blaze. Dylan. Jett.

One (very) happy ending.

Or more accurately, a very happy beginning. The beginning

of parenthood and family life for one small family of five. And the dawn of gestational surrogacy as a solution for millions of people who could not have families without the miracles of assisted reproductive technologies, and the men and women who make surrogacy today's most radical infertility solution.

Dylan Wile, 2013

Jett Wile, 2013

The three Wile children are full biological siblings despite being born via two different India women. Gerry and Rhonda plan to keep the family's connection to India alive through exposure to Indian culture and frequent trips to their unique birthplace.

Rhonda Wile always knew children would bring her priceless joy—and she was right.

The Wile family, June 2013

# Acknowledgments

Thank you to Jennifer Weis at St. Martin's Press. This book is as much yours as mine.

Thank you to Alice Martell for helping deliver this book, as well as *Crazy Love* and *Mommy Wars*, alive and kicking.

Most especially, thank you to Gerry and Rhonda Wile, for opening these personal, at times painful, chapters of your lives to me and to so many others. Any mistakes in the retelling of this story are mine alone, not theirs.

Thank you to so many dedicated St. Martin's collaborators: Dori Weintraub, Steve Snider, Sally Richardson, John Sargent, Danielle Fiorella, Mollie Traver, Helen Chin, Jessica Preeg, Lisa Senz, Sarah Goldstein, and Elizabeth Catalano.

Thank you to my early, honest readers: Dr. Elin Cohen, Heath Kern Gibson, Michele Dreyfuss Ph.D., Gene Legg, Bradford Richardson, Dr. Yashodhara Mhatre, Dr. Sudhir Ajja, Jamie Williams, Sherrie Smith, Barbara Collura, Dr. Robert Stillman, and Karen Lieberman Troccoli.

Thank you to the various kind friends who always asked how it was going and never looked bored as I blabbed away with my endless answers: Pat Laing, Jeri Curry Thorne, Phil Klein, Gail Davis, Julie O'Keefe, Lindsey Rosenfeld, Lauren Synar, Sarah Leverett, Kim Yancy, Ashley Schreder, Regina Malveaux, Chris Caiola Appleby, Michel Martin, Bruce

*Acknowledgments*

Vinokour, Kathy Richardson, Robert Haft, David Bradley, Judy Schlosser, Steve Hills, Julie Gunderson, Susan Riker, Michele Norris, Erna Steiner, Ampy Vasquez, Donna Farnandez, JP Dowd, Jolene Ivey, Pat Davidson, Soraya Chemali, Carrington Tarr, Jimbo the Southern Gentleman with the Northern Address, Julia Knight, Jodi Dehli, Burt Davidson, Linda Coe, Eduardo Gerlein, Dani Tucker, Joanne Pinaire, Kevin Hortens, Shelly Hall, Christie Rentzel, Theresa Goodwin, Leonard and Betty King, Christine Courtois, Carlotta Hester, Bob Caiola, Sally Collier, Lila Leff, Sennait Blackman, Alison Kenworthy, Angel Nash, Tim Morgan, Page Evans, Vivian Brown, Hermine Dreyfuss, Patrick M. Connelly, Matt Smith, Kara Dowd, Marc Dannenberg, Sarah Nixon, Brandye James, John Cameron, Bruce Depuyt, Mary Haft, Katherine Bradley, Rebecca Cooper, Ania Sender, Adam Mansky, Ann McDaniel, Roger Smith, Joe Steiner, Judy Taub, Hillary Howard, Matt Appleby, Dale Overmyer, Rebecca Roberts, Kathy Rahbaran, Susan Barreca, Perri Morgan, Ken Troccoli, Sally Dunkelberger, Leslie Lehr, Sarah Tompkins, Tania and Walter Sechriest, Ian Hoorneman, Harry and Laura Lerner, Debbie Brenneman, Charlie Esposito, Monica Holloway, Leslie McGuirk, Melissa Boasberg, April Delaney, John Delaney, Amy Anderson, Robin Caiola, Kelli Austin, Marilyn Potts, Laura Cole, Sunita Leeds, Aru Kulkarni, Kay Kendall, Susan Smith, Sarah Woolworth, Sherry Benson, David Stang, Ken Wolf, Kennett Marshall, Jennifer Brown, and John and Rachel King. A shout-out to all my beloved Harmon relatives, my Newfound neighbors Carmel Sauvageau, Bob Wickham, Michael and Nancy Lincoln, and Bud and Jan Connor, and all my pals at TED, *The Washington Post*, Longacre Farm, Gail Davis Speakers, One Love, DC Volunteer Lawyers Project, the National Domestic Violence Hotline, Little Folks, Johnson & Johnson, Casa San Mateo in Positano, Down Dog Yoga, Fuel Pilates, KamaDeva East Hampton, Trustees Council of Penn

278

## Acknowledgments

Women, Minot-Sleeper Library, Gilly's of Bristol, The Maret School, Harvard College, and Wharton business school.

Thank you to my very own family of five—Perry, Max, Morgan, and Tallie. Special appreciation to Max for his sense of humor, Morgan for her hugs and cooking skills, and Tallie for her inventive grading system and occasionally constructive criticism. My inspiration for this book sprang from a belief that everyone who wants a baby deserves a baby; I count myself lucky for getting three of my own.

# Notes

## Part 1: What's the Big Deal About Not Having Babies, Anyway?

1. http://www.fertilitysourcecompanies.com/blog/?p=368.
2. http://www.cnn.com/2013/03/04/health/surrogacy-kelley
-legal-battle/index.html.
3. Edward Luce, *In Spite of the Gods: The Rise of Modern India*
(New York: Anchor, 2008), 277.
4. Luce, 145.
5. http://www.nytimes.com/2013/01/12/world/asia/for-india
-rape-victims-family-layers-of-loss.html?_r=0.
6. Luce, 333.
7. Luce, 330.
8. Luce, 153.
9. Luce, 122.
10. http://news.bbc.co.uk/2/hi/business/3487110.stm.
11. Luce, 126.
12. *The Times of India*, "Child Sex Ratio Worse in Rural
Maha," July 10, 2011.
13. http://english.aljazeera.net/indepth/features/2011/10
/2011104153855524923.html.

14. Luce, 149.
15. http://www.ahrq.gov/news/nn/nn051911.htm.
16. State-by-state legal data from www.creatingfamilies.com.
17. *The New York Times*, "A Life Affirming Female Force, Ready to Rumble," July 8, 2011.
18. http://www.alexiafoundation.org.
19. Elisabeth Bumiller, *May You Be the Mother of a Hundred Sons* (New York: Random House, 1990).
20. http://www.nytimes.com/2011/05/26/opinion/26kristof.
21. http://chnm.gmu.edu/wwh/modules/lesson5/lesson5.php ?s=0.
22. http://abcnews.go.com/Health/story?id=2728976&page=1# .TsGBVM016eY.
23. http://en.wikipedia.org/wiki/In_vitro_fertilisation.
24. http://www.nobelprize.org/nobel_prizes/medicine/laure ates/2010/.
25. Luce, 142.

## Part 2: Baby Making Becomes Big Business

1. http://www.people.com/people/archive/article/0,,20078051 ,00.html.
2. http://www.nytimes.com/1988/06/23/books/surrogate -mother-s-story.html.
3. All fertility clinic statistics are from Centers for Disease Control and Prevention annual Fertility Clinic Success Rates Report data.
4. Liza Mundy, *Everything Conceivable: How the Science of Assisted Reproductions Is Changing Our World* (New York: Anchor, 2008), 12, 38.
5. *The Collection*, June 2011 issue, "The Global Baby."
6. The USDA's most recent estimated cumulative expense of raising a child to age seventeen is $220,000.

7. Jancee Dunn, "Melissa's Secret," *Rolling Stone,* Issue 833, January 2000.

8. http://www.rollingstone.com/music/news/melissa-ether idge-in-child-custody-battle-20110923.

9. http://www.nytimes.com/2007/07/16/opinion/16marquardt .html.

10. http://www.highbeam.com/doc/1G1-163494326.html.

11. http://www.infoplease.com/askeds/us-home-size.html.

12. http://www.thesurrogacysource.com.

13. Mundy, 30.

14. http://www.huffingtonpost.com/2012/05/15/elizabeth -banks-surrogacy-son-allure_n_1518108.html.

**Part 3: One Vasectomy, Two Vaginas**

1. Encyclopaedia Brittanica. http://www.britannica.com /EBchecked/topic/557970/Lazzaro-Spallanzani.

2. http://www.nytimes.com/2012/08/27/opinion/fertility -services-for-veterans.html?_r=1.

3. http://www.dadsagain.com/about-dadsagain/dr-sheldon -marks/.

4. Liza Mundy, *Everything Conceivable: How the Science of Assisted Reproductions Is Changing Our World* (New York: Anchor, 2008), 12.

5. RESOLVE Web site http://www.resolve.org; Holly Finn, "My Fertility Crisis," *Wall Street Journal,* July 23–24, 2011.

6. http://www.cdc.gov/nchs/fastats/fertile.htm.

7. Centers for Disease Control and Prevention, Division of Reproductive Health, Assisted Reproductive Technology, Fertility Clinic Success Rates Report. http://www.cdc.gov /art/ARTReports.htm.

8. Some form of male sterility causes half of all infertility, Mundy, 10.

9. http://ww2. protectyourfertility.com.

10. http://history.nih.gov/exhibits/thinblueline/timeline.html.

11. http://www.webmd.com/baby/ss/slideshow-fetal-develop ment.

12. http://www.vivo.colostate.edu/hbooks/pathphys/reprod /fert/fert.html.

13. Dr. Allen J. Wilcox of the National Institute of Environ-mental Health Sciences.

14. http://www.cdc.gov/art/ARTReports.htm.

15. Mundy, 40.

16. Mundy, 39.

17. http://www.npr.org/assets/news/2011/11/FertilityWhite Paper_Final.pdf.

18. Anecdotal: Dr. Yashodhara at Surrogacy India, July 2011.

19. http://my.clevelandclinic.org/disorders/miscarriage/hic _miscarriage.aspx.

20. http://www.nytimes.com/2012/02/27/health/research /scientists-use-stem-cells-to-generate-human-eggs.html.

21. Finn, "My Fertility Crisis."

22. http://www.today.com/id/45262603/ns/today-today_health /t/fertility-math-most-women-flunk-survey-finds/#.Uazd 7M3Yj8U.

23. Finn, "My Fertility Crisis"; http://www.redbookmag.com /health-wellness/advice/infertility-treatments.

24. http://www/dailymail.co.uk/tvshowbiz/article-2317205 /Sofia-Vergara-confirms-use-surrogate-starts-Modern -Family-fianc-Nick-Loeb.html.

25. http://www.plosone.org/article/info:doi%2F10.1371 %2Fjournal.pone.0008772.

26. Mundy, 40.

27. Finn, "My Fertility Crisis."

28. The miscarriage rates in this paragraph refer to a woman using her own, fresh (not frozen) eggs. For infertile

women of all ages, donor eggs from a young, healthy woman have a greater chance of successful birth than their own eggs. http://www.cdc.gov/ART/ART2009/index .htm.

29. http://www.npr.org/assets/news/2011/11/FertilityWhite Paper_Final.pdf.

30. United States Department of Agriculture, "Cost of Raising a Child Calculator." http://www.cnpp.usda.gov /calculatorintro.htm.

31. http://www.nydailynews.com/news/crime/noted-surro gacy-lawyer-theresa-erickson-sentenced-role-baby-selling -scheme-article-1.1028320#ixzz2SVy2h6rR.

32. http://abcnews.go.com/US/attorney-pleads-guilty-baby -selling-ring/story?id=14274193#.TylcOM12mPW.

33. U.S. Attorney's Office, Southern District of California, August 9, 2011, "Baby-Selling Ring Busted" press release. http://www.fbi.gov/sandiego/press-releases/2011/baby -selling-ring-busted.

34. http://www.lifesitenews.com/news/baby-trafficking -scandal-just-the-tip-of-the-ivf-surrogacy-iceberg-expert/.

35. http://www.creatingfamilies.com/default.aspx.

36. http://www.nydailynews.com/news/crime/noted-surrogacy -lawyer-theresa-erickson-sentenced-role-baby-selling -scheme-article-1.1028320#ixzz1ndh8Dq8C; http://www .utsandiego.com/news/2012/feb/24/two-sentenced-baby -selling-case/.

37. http://www.nypost.com/p/news/local/how_socialite_ brought_down_black_XKvByEEFRTpSMaYuRYmcXJ/1.

**Part 4: Heartbreak, Miracles, and Money**

1. www.payscale.com.
2. http://www.indianmedguru.com/gynecology-dr-yashod hara-mhatre-india.html.

3. http://quickfacts.census.gov/qfd/states/00000.html.

4. http://www.scribd.com/doc/16389906/The-Indian-Surro gate-Purchase-the-entire-ebook-at-httptheindiansurrogate com-for-just-USD999.

5. http://www.fda.gov/BiologicsBloodVaccines/Tissue TissueProducts/QuestionsaboutTissues/ucm102842.htm.

6. Kimberly Leighton, assistant professor of philosophy, American University, on *The Diane Rehm Show*, January 26, 2012. http://thedianerehmshow.org/shows/2012-01-26 /adoptees-using-dna-find-family.

7. *People*, "Are Sperm Donors' Kids at Risk?" March 19, 2012; www.donorsiblingregistry.com.

8. http://www.nytimes.com/2011/09/06/health/06donor.html ?pagewanted=all; www.donorsiblingregistry.com.

9. http://www.newlifeagency.com/surrogate_maternity /surrogate_advocacy.cfm.

10. "Services and supplies associated with maternity care, including antepartum care, childbirth, postpartum care, and complications of pregnancy, may be covered when the surrogate mother is a TRICARE beneficiary and has entered into a contractual agreement with the adoptive parents.

    "The contractual agreement will be considered primary coverage. Any undesignated amount, or amount designated for medical expenses under the contract, must be exhausted before TRICARE will cover otherwise covered benefits for the TRICARE beneficiary.

    "Maternity services provided to a TRICARE beneficiary acting as a surrogate without a contractual agreement are not a covered benefit." http://www.tricare.mil/CoveredServices /SeeWhatsCovered/Surrogacy.aspx?sc_database=web.

11. http://www.lightplanet.com/mormons/daily/policies_eom .htm.

12. http://www.csmonitor.com/The-Culture/Family/2012/0507

/Mitt-Romney-brood-grows-twin-grandchildren-born
-using-surrogate.

13. http://www.religion-online.org/showarticle.asp?title=807;
http://www.ivf-worldwide.com/Education/christianity
.html.

14. http://www.ivf-worldwide.com/Education/judaism.html.

15. http://old.usccb.org/prolife/tdocs/donumvitae.shtml.

16. http://www.usatoday.com/news/religion/story/2012-02-25
/pope-conception/53241696/1.

17. http://www.ehow.com/about_6313132_surrogate-vs
_-concubine.html.

18. http://www.irishtimes.com/news/genetic-mother-wins
-surrogacy-case-1.1318340.

19. Holly Finn, "My Fertility Crisis," *Wall Street Journal,* July
23–24, 2011; the CDC 2009 data shows 50 percent as a
more realistic figure. http://www.cdc.gov/art/ART2009
/PDF/01_ARTSuccessRates09-FM.pdf.

20. http://www.dailymail.co.uk/news/article-447423/Adopt
-baby-girls-India-begs-Britons.html#ixzz1RlNyLnmj.

21. www.adoption.state.gov.

22. www.IndiaAdoption.com; www.adoption.state.gov.

23. http://www.washingtonpost.com/national/david-headley
-witness-in-terror-trial-ties-pakistani-spy-agency-to
-militant-group/2011/05/23/AFEEb99G_story.html.

24. http://www.mayoclinic.com/health/prenatal-care/PR00112.

25. http://pewresearch.org/pubs/1802/decline-marriage-rise
-new-families.

26. http://pewresearch.org/databank/dailynumber/?
NumberID=1410.

27. http://pewresearch.org/pubs/2147/marriage-newly-weds
-record-low.

28. www.cdc.gov/nchs/fastats/adoption.htm.

29. U.S. Department of Health and Human Services, www
.childwelfare.gov.

30. www.adoption.state.gov.
31. http://www.adoptionservices.org/index.htm.


**Part 5: Operation Birth in India**

1. http://hinduism.about.com/od/festivalsholidays/a
   /ganeshchaturthi.htm.
2. www.ivfcharotar.com.
3. Adrienne Arieff, *The Sacred Thread: A True Story of Becoming
   a Mother and Finding a Family—Half a World Away* (New
   York: Crown, 2012).
4. http://articles.timesofindia.indiatimes.com/2011-07-26
   /india/29815683_1_capita-income-average-income
   -household-income.
5. http://isw.sagepub.com/content/53/5/686.abstract.
6. http://www.foxnews.com/entertainment/2011/10/17/e-news
   -host-giuliana-rancic-diagnosed-with-breast-cancer
   /#ixzz1bkMi9B70.
7. http://ww5.komen.org/BreastCancer/FactorsThatDo-
   NotIncreaseRisk.html.
8. http://www.ocrf.org/index.php?view=article&id=751
   %3Astudy-confirms-no-link-between-fertility-drugs-and
   -cancer&option=com_content&Itemid=241.
9. www.RESOLVE.org/advocacyblog.
10. http://www.timesonline.co.uk/tol/news/uk/health
    /article1038160.ece.
11. Stats on 55 percent not seeking medical advice and di-
    vorce rates both from Boivin's research, http://women
    .timesonline.co.uk/tol/life_and_style/women/families
    /article4356115.ece.
12. Department of Defense TRICARE Health Care Pro-
    gram. http://www.tricare.mil/CoveredServices
    /SeeWhatsCovered/Surrogacy.aspx?sc_database=web.

13. http://www.cdc.gov/nchs/births.htm; http://www
    .washingtonpost.com/national/health-science/older
    -mothers-fertility-treatments-driving-a-big-increase-in
    -twin-births-new-cdc-report-says/2012/01/04/gIQAfc1caP
    _story.html.

14. Centers for Disease Control and Prevention, Division of
    Reproductive Health, Assisted Reproductive Technology,
    Fertility Clinic Success Rates Report. http://www.cdc.gov
    /art/ARTReports.htm.

15. http://www.youtube.com/watch?v=FD2qMf-eVaw.

16. Center for American Progress, "Future Choices: Assisted
    Reproductive Technologies and the Law," Jessica Arons,
    December 17, 2007, 7. http://www.americanprogress.org
    /wp-content/uploads/issues/2007/12/pdf/arons_art.pdf.

17. "Future Choices," 14. http://www.americanprogress.org
    /wp-content/uploads/issues/2007/12/pdf/arons_art.pdf.

18. Elizabeth Mundy, *Everything Conceivable: How the Science of
    Assisted Reproductions Is Changing Our World* (New York:
    Anchor, 2008), 7.

19. http://www.usatoday.com/weather/wildfires/2011-06-16
    -arizona-wallow wildfire_n.htm.

20. http://www.sart.org.

21. http://www.sart.org.